I Did Not Know

Brian Keith

outskirts
press

I Did Not Know
All Rights Reserved.
Copyright © 2025 Brian Keith
v1.0

The opinions expressed in this manuscript are solely the opinions of the author and do not represent the opinions or thoughts of the publisher. The author has represented and warranted full ownership and/or legal right to publish all the materials in this book.

This book may not be reproduced, transmitted, or stored in whole or in part by any means, including graphic, electronic, or mechanical without the express written consent of the publisher except in the case of brief quotations embodied in critical articles and reviews.

Outskirts Press, Inc.
http://www.outskirtspress.com

ISBN: 978-1-9772-8177-7

Cover Photo © 2025 www.gettyimages.com. All rights reserved - used with permission.

Outskirts Press and the "OP" logo are trademarks belonging to Outskirts Press, Inc.

PRINTED IN THE UNITED STATES OF AMERICA

Table of Contents

Special Thanks i
Introduction.. iii
1. The Power of Violence and Wickedness is in The City 1
2. Parents Raising Children in Drug Free Homes 16
3. My Sports Position 24
4. The Intelligent Human Brain 43
5. Drugs Controlling the Intelligent Human Brain........................56
6. Staying in School, and My Brain's First Drug Experience 75
7. Searching for Employment and Still Addicted To Drugs............88
8. More Addictions with Drugs and the Consequences 117
9. Drugs Finally Damaged My Brain Functions 150
10. Physical Rehab and Other Patients Injuries 173
11. Signs from God and My Heart Is In Pain 189
12. Opening Doors And God's Word (bible) Concerning Sin 207
13. Come To Jesus...243
14. God Making Your Name Great Through A Relationship.........260
15. Just A Few Personal Words to Share..269

Special Thanks

First, I give praise, honor, and thanks to the Lord Jesus for giving me a second chance at life. This second chance came about because of the obedience Jesus presented unto His Father. Due to Jesus obedience and surrendering unto His Father (The God of Heaven), His "Way Of Life" has been passed on to those who are willing to receive it. Those who have received Jesus, and confess their sins, and is forgiven are given a second chance at life.

Jesus was sent to the earth for the purpose to teach the Word of God and forgive (rebuke all unrighteousness) sin. Due to that purpose, Jesus came with the authority to turn wicked people into children/sons of God. As this story narrates, and exposes my living, you will read how Jesus turned wicked Brian Keith into a "Child Of God.

My old man, which was a body under the influence of sin, ignorance, and chemical controlled substance had me on an evil mission. However, through repentance and forgiveness that old man was destroyed at the cross with Jesus. Yeah, through the sacrifice and bloodshed of Jesus, that sinful creature (my old man) had been destroyed.

However, even while claiming to be Holy Ghost filled, and a Sanctified Christian, I kept ON awakening that old creature, and walking in my former ways. Oh my goodness, I backslid from the church time after time. The reason for the backslidings is because I did my testimony the wrong way. "I was not supposed to sit back and wait for someone to open doors. I was supposed to tell the people they are not on a land healing mission. But God, who sent Jesus to forgive, kept renewing and cleansing me. It is so great to experience the times of refreshing (forgiveness). If an act of forgiveness had not taken place, my living today, would be an unrighteous living. I truly thank the Lord Jesus for his forgiving power. I give thanks to none other, but the precious blood of Jesus, who is actually called, "The Word Of God".

To my precious family, I love you all dearly. Gloria, David, Neco, and Tiffany, you all have done more than enough for me. While things were kind a tough, you all have provided somehow someway. If it had not been for the four of you, I do not know where I would be today. I also cannot forget what the power of God's mercy has done. To my entire family, you were there for me as well.

Introduction:

This manuscript will explain why I claim to be **one** of the greatest athletes in the world. It's not so much that I talked it. My athletic talents and skills proved a "greatest" athlete point. Not too many athletes in the past or in the present are able to match my athletic ability. Most people are good at playing 1 or 2 sports, but I dominated in multiple sports. If you are a person who saw me perform, you are a visual witness. If you have never seen me in action; it will be revealed unto you in this book.

My life experiences are equivalent to many people on earth. As a person strolls down the road, and unexpectedly stumbles and fall, my hectic experiences came in like manner. The drill sergeant yells to his troops; hut 2, 3, 4- hut, 2, 3, 4. Yeah, in the same like manner, my experiences came in the exact same order. One event happened first, then the second, and then the third. You can most definitely expect, in alphabetical order, many unexpected experiences will march into your living.

What you are experiencing and going through today, someone else already came out of it. Whatever your life is going through, even if it is not desiring, you still have the power and ability to turn that thing into good. By-Brian K.

All experiences have appointments and schedules. Since that is so, every experience is achieved in time. Not only that, but also, every experience is associated with the "Will of God". It is even the Will of God for every man to experience both the good and the bad. Just as God programmed birds to chirp early in the morning, evil experiences are programmed to soar into people's unrighteous living. By divine appointment, Brian Keith experienced death. When Brian died for 11 minutes, it was appointed and scheduled for that to happen. Yes, truly, all of my harsh experiences came into my living, because the divine "Will of God" required it to be so.

Before proceeding farther into the story, I need to share something with you; this entire book was written and edited by me, the writer. *Hebrews 11:6- But without faith it is impossible to please him: for he that cometh to God must believe that he is, and that he is a rewarder of them that diligently seek him*. By faith, this book was written. By hope, this book was edited. It was very easy writing the book. However, the editing was the mountain I had to climb. While editing this book, I wanted to give up time after time. However, I was on a mission, and giving up was not the plan.

While reading this book, many mysteries concerning life will be revealed. This book will persuade people to obey the law, and worship God at the same time. This book is similar to a sketched drawing, because it will reveal the lines of life. Whether the subject is about prosperity or failure, this book will illustrate those facts. You will not be left clueless, because this book will explain every detail told. Providing thorough explanations, as well as teaching about life, is the main purpose for writing this book.

Wow! Who would have ever thought that God would choose **Brian Keith** to teach a world of people a thing or two. I never thought I would ever be the person to write a book. Not only that, but also, I am actually about to a teach country of people about life. To every individual reader of this book, you all have become my students, and class is about to begin.

Chapter 1

The Power of Violence and Wickedness is in The City

We have in this world many different types of cities and neighborhoods. Some neighborhoods are filled with danger and violence, while others are pleasant and peaceful. But do not get it twisted, anything can burst out at any given moment. Since technology has come into play, we are able to determine which city seems to be most unsafe. But do not be deceived, every neighborhood has its goods and its bads. Every neighborhood has it's up and it's downs.

But why are neighborhoods dangerous and violent? Or shall I ask, "Why are neighborhoods overwhelmed with violence"? It is because someone in the neighborhood with an unmerciful heart brought this violence. Whether it was a man or woman, violence came by one of them. Since that is so, then the people are the ones who causes neighborhoods to be filled with violence. By their actions, cities and neighborhoods become rated.

When negativity is in the people's minds, their hearts will soon tune in. Once hearts and minds conjure up a plan to do evil, violence is the next step to take. In your neighborhood, if peace and quietness have been stripped from it, the movement of violence performed that work.

Peace and violence will never have communion. Peace operates in quietness, softness, and humbleness. However, violence operates loudly, harshly, and will always break the law. Peace and violence will never abide in the same place, nor will they operate at the same time. Every time violence approaches, if your mind and heart is set, peace will vanish. After peace leave the premises, violence then plagues the entire region and or environment. Basically, it's a mind thing.

Most cities are divided into 4 parts; A North, a South, an East, and a Westside. Wow, in my city, all four sides have been given over the violence. In my city, on the North, a murder was committed. Just the other day, on the Southside, a rape was committed. Just last week, on the Eastside, a "gang" of young men had beaten a man unconscious. On the Westside, a man was stabbed with a knife. Therefore, in most cities, it is possible that all 4 sides have harsh actions.

The bible gives us another word for violence. This other word is "wickedness". Wickedness, just like violence is a horrible activity performed before the eyes of God. Wickedness occurs when people break God's commandment and the laws. Wickedness is so cunning; it causes people to harm one another through violence.

Wickedness and violence are like twin babies born on the same day. When twins are born, there is always one baby born before the other. Each infant has a set time to be born. Wickedness and violence operates just like twins born.

I have cousins who are twins. The boy was born before the girl. Of course, the boy and girl were born on the exact same day, but the timing of birth differs. The boy could have been born at 9:30 am, while the girl could have been born at 10:00 am.

It is the same birth timing effect with violence and wickedness. Wicked intensions can be in a person's thoughts at 9:30 a.m., and at 9:45 a.m., a violent act might be performed. Therefore, just as my twin cousins were born on the same day, violence and wickedness operates on the same day, too.

In my neighborhood, on a daily basis, a wicked deed had been performed. Somewhere in my neighborhood, either an act of violence was performed, or just a breaking of the law was in action. In the atmosphere of my neighborhood is nothing but the furious Power of Violence and Wickedness.

Other people from different locations would be in drastic fear, when taking a quick stroll through my neighborhood. People would be in fear because of the violent ratings this neighborhood earned. Unexpectedly, and unrehearsed, an evil episode is brought to a visitor's attention. It would be a person's bad luck to walk through the projects, and suddenly come face to face with an unexpected tragedy.

One of the evil activities I remember seeing in my neighborhood were brutal fistfights. These one-on-one brawls were harsh; they were cruel, and somewhat horrible to the human eyesight. Either my ears heard about these uproars, or my eyes watched these physical battles take place.

One day, with my own two eyes, I stood and watched a man bleed badly as he fought against another man. Due to all the violence and wickedness occurring in the neighborhood, the community seemed to be possessed with the force and strength of evil. From all of the mental anger, fussing, and verbal cursing, wickedness through violence filled the neighborhood with horrible reaction. The people's mental tempers and evil thoughts were quick to lean toward negativity, rather than striving to be problem solvers.

The word quarrel means to have a dispute or disagreement with someone. Continually having disagreements creates quarrels. Quarrel also means to find a way to prove that your complaint is right, and nothing else seems to matter. When people attempt to find fault in one another, a quarreling event soon occurs. Everyone loves finding fault in others; just satisfy his or her own personal emotions. Another word for quarrel is altercation.

I've heard them say, "Sticks and stones might break my bones but words will never hurt". A bunch of liars quote that. All I got to do is say something behind your back and that will get the party going.

Oscar Wilde, of the 1800's quoted; "*arguments are to be avoided; they are always vulgar and often unconvincing*". In other words, Oscar Wilde is saying, "refrain yourselves from quarrels; don't even waste your time, because the dispute will never end. One argument brings up another situation, and the same argument elevates to something that happened 3 years ago. Avoid, avoid avoid arguments!

Disagreements are never solved by arguments. Most arguments can go on and on and never come to a position of halt. An argument can jump off in the noonday, or even before bedtime. However, after arising from sleep, the disagreement might still be there. You opened your eyes to another day, but you woke up with the same disagreement.

Everything has a starting point, or shall I say, "Everything starts at the seed". An argument is much so a seed. Once an argument has occurred, a seed is suddenly planted. Then, from out of nowhere, the brain begins to operate in anger. The longer two people argue, the more the argument is being watered. Then, once anger has craftily slid its way in, then suddenly, physical brutality takes over from there. And it all started from a seed of anger.

One day, as I slept, I heard a man yelling as if he was being beaten. A loud scream, pitched with pain, is what I heard. When I had gained enough boldness to get up out of the bed, and take a sneak peek out the window, I saw a man lying across the concrete. I suppose, this man was a victim of being shot. I actually woke up from sleep and saw a man who had been shot.

When someone has been shot, the city help (police or ambulance) is called to the scene. When police cars and emergency health vans arrive, from their presence, the neighborhood is filled with "protection and care". When this gun-shooting performance brought the police and ambulance to my neighborhood, it was because of the "Power of Wickedness". For the present moment, let us not lean on the fact that gunshots were fired; let us draw our minds on the fact that wickedness empowered a man to shoot a gun.

It is against the law for anyone to carry a concealed weapon, which is for the gun carrier's personal use. The second law broken is called, "assault and battery" or "unlawful use of a weapon". It is against the law for any man or woman to seek personal judgment by a bullet. No matter how angry you become, you are never supposed to pull out a gun and shoot a living man. Anytime a person pulls out a gun, and shoots bullets at another human being as pay back, God does not find pleasure in such an activity. Besides, guns and violence operate from The Power of Wickedness and God never hire people to work actions of evil.

(From the bible) _Romans 12:17 recompense no man evil for evil._ In other words, the bible is saying, "do not perform evil on a person as a work of compensation" (payback). Although, altercations will surprisingly pop up, you are commanded not to use evil as reimbursement. Never use evil to applaud or render payback. When people use guns, they try to solve disputes through the works of evil. God is the one who knows how to recompense every person. Therefore, let God do his work, and you do yours by stepping back.

Therefore, put far away from among you all lethal weapons (guns and bullets). Putting weapons away from among you is the same as putting away from among your personal ways to condemn (judge). Not only that, but also, self-judgment is cast away, too. Let God be the judge. God is the one who holds the authority to judge all actions done. Let each individual stop pursuing after personal satisfaction. Self-satisfaction only leads to self-judgments. Put away the weapons; put away the bullets, lest you find yourself reaping from that very same performed act.

Also, it says in the book _of Romans 12:19 "vengeance is mine, I will repay, saith the Lord"._ God is the judge of all the earth. People need to step out of the way, and let God do what he does best. When it is time for someone to be judged, let God fulfill that task. But how can people let God do his job (judge), when people get themselves caught up in mess every single day.

Time after time, we all have heard the saying, "Only God can judge me". Not only have we heard it, but we all have said it times before too. Most people say that quote, when trying to justify their wrong doings. Many people live their entire lives saying, "**Only God can judge me**". I suppose it brings comfort to the table of their hearts. No one desires to be judged, and no one wants to admit being wrong.

Only God knows how to provide a person with a precise judgment. Earlier in this story, concerning the young man who had been shot, his situation probably went beyond means. It probably did not have to go as far as bullets being presented in the scene. Although, a disagreement and an argument transpired between two people, the gunslinger had no rights to insult a person's body with bullets. Only law enforcers (police officers) have rights to insult the body with bullets. When people try recompensing, they go beyond the point of making it a fair and equal judgment. The world is filled with The Power of Wickedness, and from it, people are led to recompense one another from their own personal evil tactics.

James 1:20 says, for the wrath of man, worketh not the righteousness of God. In other words, human wrath (anger) will never be equal to the righteousness of God. Human anger will do something to a person, that not even the New Testament God would do. Human wrath always takes situation to far.

Humankind does not know how to recompense anyone. Harming someone is the only action humankind will do. God wants to help and forgive, but humans seek to beat and kill. There is a big different between God and man, when it comes to recompensing.

When a person loads bullets in a gun's clip, each bullet is counted as an item of wickedness. If nine bullets are loaded in the clip, that is nine times the item of wickedness is set for use. If the first bullet hits not your desired target, you will keep shooting the murder weapon until a bullet thrash through the enemies flesh. Every time a person pulls the trigger of a gun, he or she has just sent off an item of wickedness. As I said before, God's plan is to help and forgive, but human's passion is to beat and kill.

Movies, TV shows, and live scenes in the projects taught me about guns and violence. From the five senses located within my body, two of them became active learning tools. My hearing and my sight learned about guns and violence.

The same actions of violence I saw at movie theatres, and on the television screen, are the same motions of violence displayed in my neighborhood. I thought only certain actions of violence were only performed on TV and at movie theatres. However, the violence I saw performed in my neighborhood enlightened my understanding. I soon realized if I saw a violent scene on television, that it would be possible to witness the same violent activity in the projects. In other words, I saw wickedness and violence being performed everywhere. Wickedness, wickedness, wickedness, is there a solution to stop wickedness from being seen and performed.

Take heed to this mathematical equation; it will teach you that guns and violence will never solve problems in life; violence + guns = unresolved problems. Also, violence + guns = continued problems. Whatever relates to a continuation of wickedness does not have the ability to solve problems. Wickedness only begets more wickedness. Its intention is to add more problems into a person's life. Wickedness wants to kill you or empower you to kill someone. Wickedness has great power!

If people focus on activating their skills and talents, their mission in life will be more peaceful. If people persuade themselves to active their skills and talents, a brighter earth will be created by God. When skills and talents are being used, violence will soon flee from the land. Not only will violence flee, but also, human recompensing will face a closed door. Just as a man in the military is placed on active duty, in the same sense, people need to put their talents and skills on active duty as well.

Once people allow their minds to focus on their talents and skills, they will continually seek ways to display them. Your skills and talents have the ability and power to bring about peace. They only need to be used by its maker (God}in order to bring about the peace. If any man/woman is seeking better in life, it is necessary to activate those skills and talents. If people seek to exercise their skills and talents, then wickedness, violence, and weapons of war will lose their high ratings. Then the world would not be so polluted with ongoing mental hatred.

Do not get the wrong idea here. Human skills will not change the earth. It is the Word of God which gets in your brain and used your talents and skills. If God is in your brain, then surely everything involving the mind will be used, even talents and skills. It's not human using the skills when God puts you to work.

Take a moment and think about the many horrible valleys wickedness has taken you through. Whether it was mental or physical, examine the experience. Then envision within your mind what wickedness is doing to every community in the land. When you do that, you have just seen a mental picture of what wickedness is doing and can do to you.

Your community is like the shadow of your body. If actions of wickedness can destroy communities, it can destroy your body as well. If wickedness is killing nations, then it can surely kill you too. Whatever wickedness does to your city or community, the same type of experience can be displayed upon your body. Just as violence and wickedness takes peace out of communities, it will take peace out of your living. Whether big or small, wickedness can do a body just as it does to a community.

Although, the police might not see you performing bad deeds, GOD is most definitely viewing every action done. People really need to stop worrying about hiding from the police. People need to worry about what God is watching them do. There is nothing kept, held, or done in secret Almighty God cannot see. It should be somewhat scary to us, that God sees every act done under the sun.

An active blizzard, hurricane, tornado, or a big bright star cannot hinder God from seeing what humanity is doing. Therefore, if handling concealed weapons is active in your life, the police might not see it, but God sees the object as if you are totally naked.

God has been watching evil and wickedness operate for a very long time. Evil and wickedness has been mobile through human bodies ever since Cain killed Abel. Even after Noah built the ark, and then entered therein, the people on the outside were living wicked lives. From the days of Adam and Eve, up until the birth of **Brian K. Irons**, God has been viewing actions of wickedness. For more than 2,000 years, God's eyes have watched people do deeds that bring heaven's judgment.

<u>Genesis chapter 6:5 And God saw that the wickedness of man was great in the earth, and that every imagination of the thoughts of his heart was only evil continually.</u>

Although, the scripture was originally spoken and recorded more than 2000 years ago, the same performances of "wickedness" is still active in our world today. Yep, wickedness is still being performed on the earth. The true reason why wickedness is mobile in our land is that it lives inside of the people. Once wickedness lives inside a person, it soon operates through the entire body. What God has been viewing thousands of years ago; he is still viewing the same executed works today.

Imagine God watching performances of wickedness for hundreds and thousands of years. Do you think God has had it up to the neck with watching this stuff? For more than 2,000 years, this stupidity has been in session, and that's a very long time. To put a scare in you; we are living in the last and evil days, and God is soon to do something drastic. When God does something drastic, you had better be counted out. Once God thinks to do something drastic, if your life is entangled in wickedness, you will also the feel the drastic effects.

In the sight of God, wickedness is wickedness, nothing more and nothing less. The day, or the time of the year does not make wickedness any different from what it is. There is only one type of wickedness, and only one type of evil. Therefore, if people today are living wicked lives, and more than 2,000 years ago lives were wicked, then law-breaking activity has been in motion for a very long time. People were murdering back then, and in today's society, murder is still in the court system. Nevertheless, God's mercy has been operating on the earth for more than 2,000 years. Does God have a plan to stop evil in its tracks? Is there an answer to cease wickedness, or bring it to a state of halt?

Genesis 6:7 And the LORD said, I will destroy man whom I have created from the face of the earth; both man, and beast, and the creeping thing, and the fowls of the air; for it repented me that I have made them.

God spoke those words during the days of Noah. Why did God plan to destroy all the living? All because of the people's wickedness, God planned to destroy everything. Actions of continual disobedience angered God's emotional side, and the wrath God is soon to be displayed.

Oh, my goodness, you mean to tell me God became so angry, that it repented him that he ever made humankind. God became so sorrowful and grieved in heart to have ever made a person similar to you and me.

Wow, back in Noah's day, the people must have really been wicked. Better yet, the people engaged their bodies in so much disobedience, that it opened God's mouth to say, "*I will destroy man whom I have created.* Need me to remind you, that this comment was spoken from the mouth of God himself. Nevertheless, the thing (wickedness), which caused God to destroy the earth many centuries ago, is the same thing in our land today…The Power of Wickedness!

When God said, "*I will destroy man whom I have created*", he did just that. When God says he is going to do something, he must carry out the plan. *I will destroy man whom I have created* was not so much as a prophesy; it was a promise. God sent rained from heaven and caused it grow into a flood. The one-year-old grows into a two-year-old. The 6-year-old grows into 7 years old. Therefore, sooner or later, small drops of rain have the ability to grow into a flood.

Every human and animal on earth drowned in the flood. The earth became a pool filled with unusable flesh. Just like people get angry and seek to harm the life of a living being, well, God got angry and destroyed every living species.

Before God destroyed those people, he showered them with ongoing drops of mercy. God gave them so many chances to stop the nonsense. They never took heed to Noah's message. They kept on living selfish lives and relying on the desires of their heart. Their imaginations were only evil continually. Hey, hey, hey, God's mercy ran out, and the flood ran in.

Well, I thank God for a new plan to destroy wickedness. Instead of God destroying wickedness and humankind both together, he supplied the earth with his traveling mercy, and a plan that will bless the earth. His divine plan is to destroy the works of wickedness, not humanity. In a later chapter, I will expose and explain the new plan of God, which will destroy wickedness alone, and not humankind with it. Do not worry; I will remind you when I am about to reveal God's new plan to destroy. God's new plan will creatively cause safety and peace to become available unto us all. Well, thank heaven that the bible says, <u>God is plenteous in mercy, and slow to anger.</u> HALLELUJAH!

Mercy is exactly what God has been displaying in my neighborhood and even throughout the world today. God has plenty of mercy stored, and he never runs out of it. People file bankruptcy all the time, but never will God go broke in mercy. There is not a man on earth who has more money than God has with mercy. You can add up all the money in the world, new and old, it will never count higher than the spending of God's mercy.

As I went outdoors to play, I saw a tiny object idled on the ground. The way the object looked, it could have passed for being a half-smoked cigarette. I knew it was not a cigarette because it was extremely thin and kind of rough looking. Cigarettes are smooth and perfectly round in shape. Besides, I have seen dozens of people smoke cigarettes right before my very eyes. Therefore, I already knew what a cigarette looked like. However, this lumpy round shaped object on the ground, <u>I Did Not Know</u> its actual name.

Often times, as I saw this thin lumpy shaped object, I became suspicious about it. I knew it was something smoked, because the tip of it was burnt. Concerning the looks of it, I was still puzzled, because <u>I Did Not Know</u> its name.

As I grew older, I found out the name of that funny looking object. It is called, "a joint", which is a chemical controlled substance or mind-alternating drug. Therefore, while being outdoors in my neighborhood, I saw marijuana for the very first time. Well, when I was young, I might have seen someone smoking weed, but I probably paid not too much attention.

In my outdoor playing area, I saw another object lying on the ground. This second object was in the form of a capsule or tablet. There the other object lay on the ground idled. The capsule was opened and empty. Was a person in that much pain that pouring the insides out of the capsule necessary? Whoever did this must have been in serious pain.

I had no understanding why the capsules were opened in the first place. I thought capsules were to be swallowed whole and never pulled apart. Another thing that amazed me was the fact that the capsules were outdoors, open, and empty. Well, nevertheless, the capsules on the ground were for more than what I thought they were for.

The reason why I thought those capsules were for healing purposes is because; those capsules looked similar to the ones I have seen in my parent's medicine cabinet (bathroom). The capsules or medicine my parents kept in the medicine cabinet had names printed on them and were kept in boxes or containers. These capsules were for bringing healing to the body.

I never touched any of those capsules on the ground. I only looked at them. Well, later on in life, as I grew older, I found out that the capsule was from a drug called, "Heroin".

I physically ran through this neighborhood as if peace and harmony were abiding in it. I was a kid; so therefore, <u>I Did Not Know</u> that drugs were the main reason for the neighborhood's terror.

Sometimes, while playing my rock throwing game, I would hear gunshots. Then, I would see people running. After the gunshots were fired, my mother would hear the uproar from the apartment building. She immediately came searching for me. However, little did my mother know, as soon as I heard gunshots fired, I would immediately run to the stairs that lead to our apartment.

When drugs are active in people's brain, the dope itself empowers people into doing horrible deeds. Yeah, people were pulling the trigger because drugs and quarrels filled their minds. No matter who is in the area, when drugs are controlling a brain, it will cause harsh things to appear in the view of anyone. Here I am in the neighborhood entertaining and having fun all by myself. Then, suddenly, human bodies brought violence into my view. The drug's powerful force was sending people throughout the neighborhood in strict motions of rage. Not only is the neighborhood controlled by The Power of Wickedness, but human bodies were controlled by it too.

Now that I am a lot older, the two items I saw in the projects (marijuana & heroin) are street drugs. I now understand why I heard gunshots and saw so much violence. I now understand why police officers were chasing people on foot throughout the neighborhood; I now see why murdering and law-breaking actions were at its fullest. It was all because of drugs have activated its power in people's lives (brain & body).

Drugs have become "big timers" in this evil world. Drugs have become very popular throughout its history. It is possible that, in every home in the United States, someone in a household knows personally about drugs.

Let me give you one or two examples about activation. Example 1- When you are about to iron your clothes, you normally plug an iron into an electric outlet. Once the iron has been plugged into an outlet, the power for it to receive heat is soon activated. After heat has surged into the iron, you may then iron your clothes. In other words, if there is no current flow of electricity surging into the iron, it will not perform.

Example 2- at some point, every car must be refilled with gasoline. Gasoline has power, and it gives the car the ability to roll. Although, the vehicle has a motor built within, it still needs gas to keep its system continually operating. Gas is the engine's activator. Without gasoline, the engine will only choke. The car will not take you to your destination, if gasoline is not in it.

Gasoline, electric, and drugs all have the power to bring about activation. Without a brain, drugs cannot generate its seducing power. The car, the iron, and the brain can all be activated by what humankind puts in it.

While I was living in the projects, a relative of mine had been gunned down and murdered. My immediate family never found out the ultimate reason why he was murdered. However, since drug usage promotes wickedness and unmerciful reactions, substance abuse is probably the reason for my family member's death. Nevertheless, the man who killed my cousin was filled with the unmerciful ways of wickedness. Yeah, wickedness slaughtered my cousin's life many years ago. Yeah, The Power of Wickedness killed my cousin.

My heavenly warning and suggestion to the world is this; do not allow drugs to make a direct contact with your anatomy (brain and body). Do not allow the arrow, dart, or missile of drugs to hit your life. Run, run, run for your life because drugs desire to strike you and seriously cause ruin in your life. ***STAY AWAY FROM DRUGS, I SAY, STAY AWAY!***

Speaking of bullets! I remember when a bullet came into the apartment where my family and I lived. As my parents and I were living in the projects, someone shot a bullet through the front door of our apartment. This gun shooting incident happened by "chance" from ignorant people. When the bullet went through the front door, wickedness and stupidity was the reason why such an event took place. When the bullet went through our front door, my little sister was playing in her baby walker. She was walking around the house in her "baby walker" having kiddy kid fun. Then, suddenly, a person whose living is filled with The Power to do Wickedness sent a killer (bullet) into her play area. Just that fast, and just that quick, an innocent child could have been severely injured or even murdered. Now that I am thinking about this situation, I thank God for his mercy in our home at that particular time.

God, please expose the plan that will creatively bring harmony and peace into the land. God, please destroy The Power of Wickedness.

Chapter 2

Parents Raising Children in Drug Free Homes

Usually, when raising drug free homes, there are certain activities that should not happen. A lane for human drug trafficking will not be made at the front, the back, nor the side door. Not only will raising kids in a drug free home stop excessive drug trafficking, but also, it will prevent evil from spreading throughout the residence. What I mean by the phrase "drug trafficking"; is when people invite themselves to your home on a regular basis, just to use drugs. A drug free home automatically stops drug abusers from continually approaching it. When a residence becomes a "drug tracking" home, that house becomes unstable in all its ways.

Not only does the home become unstable, but also, in due time, it will lose its peace. Your home is like your community (neighborhood). Whatever drugs does to your community, the same event can happen to your home. Everyone goes to the neighborhood to intake drugs, and people will congregate in your house to do drugs, too. If drug usage is active in your home, your house will soon become the neighborhood drug parlor. Soon and very soon, the house will lose its peace and warmth. I now see why Joshua was glad to have a house serving the Lord.

A dope-craving individual will disrespect your home one way or another. No matter how many times you command a drug user not to visit your residence after midnight, he or she will disobey your commands. The dope head will visit your house again and again, as if you gave not a command. Your words mean nothing. More also, you mean nothing. The only thing that matters is, the person's brain is yearning or feigning to be filled with illegal intoxicants.

A drug seller or dope user's characteristic is a mental trait the children should not witness. When kids frequently perceive dope characteristics in the home, they soon become rebellious. The children "gradually develop" what is called a "rebellious spirit or a "stubborn attitude". In so many ways, the child's rebellion came, after seeing so much drug trafficking. This is not always true for the rebellion part, but in so many ways, it is. Therefore, keep drug characteristic out of the home. It is time for the loving parents to be identified as true Joshua leaders.

A leader often directs, guides, and becomes a role model to the child. A leader should be seen as an upright individual. Leaders normally led his or her followers (children) down the "right path". The leader must do everything from a sincere heart of love.

Another bad characteristic that should not be displayed in the home is this; parents should not escort or command their company (drug using friends) to go to another room just to get high. That procedure usually does not work. Unfortunately, people and parents assume that commanding their children to another area of the house, before getting high is a good tactic. Well, actually, going to a different area in the home does hide the physical activity of drug usage from the children's sight. However, there is another "mental sense" in the child's brain that will become nosey.

Although, the children might not see drug use in action, the aroma from marijuana will cause the kids to sense wrong is in the house.

When children smell the scent of marijuana, they immediately become suspicious. They became suspicious because, first of all, you invited your company to another area of the home. Secondly, the smell of dope alerted your child's intellect, and now your sibling knows mommy or daddy is doing something abnormal. Children will begin to wonder why mother or fathers always take the company to a particular area in the house.

The eyes and ears on all children are their main tools for learning. Those two bodily functions (eyes and ears) are vital participants when being taught. When your children watch you do unrighteous or righteous deeds, it is like viewing an event on the TV screen. Children continuously learn how to count numbers, or the official order of the ABC's from watching video tapes or TV. When a television show has taught your child a thing or two, that child has intelligently learned from what was seen and heard. Parents, remember this, every action or episode performed, either by mouth or by physical movement, your children are observing, listening, hearing, and more also, learning.

So loving parents, tell me, where is your influential leadership? Where is your performance of unconditional love and cherishing affection? Do you as a father or mother feel as if you are a leader in your home? Whether you feel as if you are a leader or not, when your adorable baby was born, you automatically became the ultimate leader. You took the time to have sexual relation, which produce the infant, now you have to take the time to direct the child's life. Telling your children not to do drugs is showing true leadership. However, if chemical usage is active in the home, then you are not being a Joshua leader. Stop allowing wickedness to come into your home in the form of chemical control substances.

The bible says, *1st Corinthians 13:13 and now abideth faith, hope, and charity; but the greatest of the three is charity* (love). That scripture means more of what I am about to explain. I wanted to use this scripture as a love token for your parental understanding. Parents can have faith for their child's success; parents can have hope for their kids to have a decent living, however, if the parents aren't teaching and expressing love in the home, then nothing else truly matters. From the mouth, parents always tell their children, "I love you". Nevertheless, actions speak louder than words.

Have you ever heard the phrase; "actions speak louder than words"? If you have not told your kids that you love them, then your performed actions will speak for you. People say, "I love you" all the time, but if they are not showing love in the physical form, then true love is not at work. When trying to prove your love, it must be demonstrated and expressed in action form. When you speak from the mouth that you love your kids, then outwardly it must be proven. Speaking love, and showing love, both must be at work. 1 plus 1 is 2, and speaking love plus showing love is the greatest addition of all. Therefore, let the house abide in love, by keeping chemical controlled substances out of it.

There are two types of love, which need to be demonstrated toward your children. There is a time for tough love to be demonstrated, and there is a precious moment for soft love to be displayed. Every mother and every father must have an understanding heart on which type of love to express. Every situation requires a certain type of love. When tough love is to be expressed, charge in with tough love. When soft love is to be performed, hold on to that. Showing tough love or soft love is part of the deal.

If parents do not show, and exalt love among their children, many times the children will venture out into the world searching for "love". When your children seek or search for true love, it is greatly possible for them to find love the "wrong way" or in all the "wrong places". Not only must parents display acts of continual love, but also, a high level of care must be connected. Without true care, there is no true love. The type of love you plant inside your children's mind is the same performance of love the kids are going to display in public areas.

Children should always remember the counseling their natural parents or any guardian has given them. Therefore, when desiring to do anything, you will do things the parent or parents will approve. Anytime a child does a particular deed taught by the parents, it will put a beautiful smile on mommy and daddy's face. However, if mother or father sees or hears about a bad deed performed by their sibling, parents think back, did the child view it being done by you? If so, then the parents cannot be upset at the child. If any parent is using drugs in the home, and later on in life, mom or dad witnessed or found out their child is in-taking drugs, the parent should not be disappointed. The child is only repeating the activity seen by one or both parents. Therefore, not only does counseling with words teaches the children, but also, as I said before, whatever the parents do in the view of their children, will educate them too. Therefore, in your home, let the Spirit of Joshua abide in it.

I wonder how many front and or back doors have been kicked in by the police force (the law). I wonder how many times a door has unexpectedly been knocked off its hinges, while infants were inside? When the police force has been commanded to tear into your home for a drug bust, they come without warning. The same entrance drug users use to enter into your home is the same pathway the local police force will barge into your home.

If any chemical control substance (drug) is hidden in your home, your house is plagued and affected by wickedness. Just by bringing drugs into your home, the dope itself brings The Power of Wickedness along with it. Drugs and wickedness are attached one to the other. Just as an unborn infant is attached to the belly of the mother, drugs are attached to the associations of wickedness. You will never find any street drug that does not carry wickedness along with it. They stay connected for life. Therefore, if you are hiding drugs in your home or hiding them in your possession, wickedness is being hidden as well. In fact, drugs give birth to wickedness.

Since it is against the law to have drugs in your possession (home), whenever the police busts in it, it is not the physical men (police) breaking in. It is the law boldly proceeding into your home to righteously condemn and judge you. If drugs (wickedness) are found in your residence, the law then comes alive seeking to convict and complete its work. Since the law clearly speaks against having drugs in your home, the law must do its job through righteousness and find what it is looking for (drugs).

Actually, since God is the one who has ordained the laws, when the law comes to judge, it is by the law's power such an event is taking place. When the law (police) boldly rushes into your home, it comes to imprison, and make your life miserable. Therefore, purposely keep drugs out of your brain, and deliberately keep them out of your home.

Not only will the local police break into a "drug trafficking" home, but also, drug addicts will break into your residence as well. Drug users and dealers will break into your residence and rob you at gunpoint. Either drug users will rob you, or friends will prepare the moment to break into your home, and steal. You can be at home, or away from home, however, the law, or drug-filled brains (evil men) will attempt to barge in. If the law is not after you, drug users will be after you. Either the police or drug heads will be planning for the right moment to come into your place of dwelling. Therefore, neither can you dodge the law, nor can you hide from drug users. Everyone, as well as the police knows that drugs are in your home. The law's job is catch you with drugs, then judge you; and the dope head job is to rob you of your possessions.

Hey parents, never think you have the house under control when drugs are stashed in it. Having drugs in your home will cause you to lose control over it. A package of drugs might only cover about 3 to 4 inches of space throughout the entire home, but from their explosive and evil power, the entire residence will be under dope's authority. Any form of evil can break loose in your home when drugs share a couple of inches of space within it. Drugs might be hidden in the attic, but they are powerful enough to cause ignorance throughout the entire building.

Parents, give your kids ongoing personal counseling as much as you can. Regardless of how hard the struggle seems to be, never give up on your child. As long as your child is living under your roof, eating food you have purchased, you have official rights to call for a moment of counseling. Send your child away with lively counseling. When the child packs up and move out of your home, and begin to live on his or her own, you are "righteously" free from any of the child's worldly experiences.

If your child has done something that made his or her life bitter, did you, the parent ever warn your child about it. Many actions and performances us kids have done, our parents never would thought their child would do something like that. Many parents never thought in a million years that their child would walk down a certain road in life. Although, our parents have explained unto us the firsthand consequences for doing certain things, however, we did them anyway.

Every child will receive a reward for his or her own personal actions and mistakes. No one is permitted to suffer for someone else's mistakes. If you have willingly committed the act, then you must take the full blame. If any child is caught breaking the law, he or she must bear the full blame.

When kids or people do unlawful actions and a judgment comes upon them, that is called, "reap what you sow". However, I call it "The Judgment's Day". That rule (reap what you sow) most definitely implies to the entire world of people. Every human being will reap whatever he or she has sown in life. The "reap what you sow" law does not care about age. If a person sows it, then guess what, there must be a season to reap it. God provided the world with that law; therefore, it shall and will be active on earth until the end.

The "reap what you sow law" has not a mind to express kindness. If the reap what you sow law did have a mind, it will still think about rendering payback. Can you imagine the number of people who did an evil work, and from it, they reaped death. On earth, I am sure there were many people who reaped death as their actual judgment. The reaping what you sow law exposes itself on many different levels. Whether the judgment is heavy or light, it will perform its divine duty.

Whatever level or measurement of judgment a person reaps; it will not minimize its authority to please anyone.

Little children, in order to be successful, you must be obedient. You need to be obedient to your parents, as well as being obedient unto God's laws. It is an honorable thing to be obedient unto your parents, but it is a greater honor to obey to God. Therefore, not only should kids obey their parents, which are the leaders that control the earthly home, but also, children should obey God, who has the power and control over the entire universe.

Obedience is the master key that opens doors to prosperity. In this life, no one will see full future prosperity unless a form of obedience is active. For example, let us say that you applied for a particular job, and the job requires for your body (system) to be free of drugs. In order to earn this job, you must obey the rules by having a drug-free system (body). Therefore, you cannot intake dope into your body. Once you pass the drug test, and have been given the position, you have just walked into the ways of prosperity. Regardless of the amount of money the occupation pays, prosperity is not based on financial gross. Prosperity comes after being obedient to rules and regulations set before you. Joshua was prosperous, because of obeying God's laws.

My 3rd book, which is titled, "*Keep Your Vision*", is a good book concerning being obedient in order to inherit what your heart desires (prosperity). This book shall be published soon.

Chapter 3

My Sports Position

From all the wickedness, drug trafficking, and human violence in my neighborhood, evil incidents always came about. Because of The Power of Wickedness, human bodies were empowered to activate works of unrighteousness continually. All day long, and all through the night, wickedness prevailed in my neighborhood. Nevertheless, God's mercy allowed my family and I to depart from the projects alive.

It is possible my parents used sports as a substitution for my rock throwing habits. Whatever the reason was, here I am at the boys club about to sign up to play sports.

As my mother and I entered the boys club, I was very nervous. This boys club was packed with a great number of little league athletes. I soon realized these young men were here for the same purpose I am here for. It was probably more than 20 to 30 or more young athletes in this club.

At this boys club, I became a member of the football and baseball team. For many years, I played those two sports for this boy's club. Therefore, the name **Brian Irons** became a familiar name at this boys club.

As I played sports year after year, my talents and skills became better and better. My talents and skills made me feel as if I was the man in charge. The athletic talents and skills I utilize in game situations made me feel as if there was none like me. My recorded statistics proved unto me that I was an awesome athlete. In playing sports, the phrase, "actions speak louder than words" is a great factor. Well, in a minute, I am about to explain my sport skills unto you in wordbook form.

As my parents and I stood in line, the club organizer came and greeted us. The club organizer called out a few team names that were in my age league bracket. The A's, the Astor's, the Cardinals, the Eagles, and a few other team names he called out.

I signed my name on the Cardinals roster. After signing my name on the tryout roster, my mom and I were told to return to the boy's club on a certain day, so that we could meet the baseball coach face to face.

A day or two later, my parents and I drove back to the boys club to meet the Cardinal's Coach. When my mother and I met the coach face to face, we introduced ourselves, and shook hands. I told the coach my name is **Brian Irons**, and he said; call me "Coach" or "Mr. Younger". Mr. Younger gave us a short speech concerning the rules about becoming an athlete on his team.

An athlete might be good in sports, but there are rules he or she must still abide by. Every parent was present with their child, so we all heard the coach's speech and rules, at the same time. (Good Lord, my parents have rules, my baseball coach has rules, and God has rules (his laws). It seems like everybody in the world has rules.

The coach told the players and parents, "I will not tolerate foolishness on the field". The coach said, "If an athlete does not obey his rules, he is going to ask the player to sit on the bench, and wait for his parent to arrive. The coach also said, "The player's name just might be deleted from the try-out list, if disobedience is in action".

Well, here I am on the baseball field to show my skills. I ran to the outfield, because there is where I wanted to play. I did not care if it was left field, right field, or center field.

As I positioned myself in the outfield, I saw numerous rocks and clods of dirt in the area. While looking at the rocks, my mind became intrigued. It was almost as if the rocks had a mouth, and were saying, "pick me up, pick me up".

Temptation kicked in, and there I was in a battle with what to do. It was very hard looking at those pretty rocks, and not having one in my hand. Suddenly, temptation won, and I began to pick up rocks and stash them in a pile on the baseball field.

So, I picked up a rock, and began launching them at the athletes on the baseball field. After I threw the rock, I then acted as if I was in my baseball pose waiting for the ball to be hit towards my way. <u>I Did Not Know</u> any of these players, but here I am launching rocks at them. Just about every practice session, I threw a rock at one of the athletes.

Soon, the players realized I was the person who through the rocks. After the players realized it was me, they went and told the coach.

So, the coach yelled out saying, "Irons, come here". His voice traveled through the air loudly, and my ears heard the pitch thereof. I trembled inside. It seemed like his voice had a physical movement, because when I heard it, my body shook, as it does when a person sneaks up from behind. Suddenly, I became frightened, because it sounded like the coach was quite angry. Besides, I did not want my name to be deleted from the try-out list.

With a belt, or with whatever was in my mother's hand, she would have spank my young tender bottom. If throwing rocks was the reason for being "cut" from the team, I do not know what my mother would have done. I have gotten in trouble so many times for throwing rocks while living in the projects. But this rock-throwing incident would have been the icing the cake.

As I began jogging toward the coach, the closer I got to him, the more I trembled inside. In my mind, I am saying, "please do not cut me from the tryout list".

Well, here I am, face to face with this angry coach. He looked straight into my eyes and said, "Irons", since you like to throw rocks so much, take this baseball and "pitch". Then he took off his baseball glove, and tossed me the ball. From that day forward, and throughout my little league baseball career, I became the first-string pitcher for the little league Cardinals.

I was the starting pitcher for the little league Cardinals baseball team for the next 7 years. After a while, I emotionally fell in love with the pitcher's position. The pitching position did fit me, since I did like to throw objects. I joined the team hoping to play as an outfielder, however, <u>I Did Not Know</u> I would be the Cardinals star pitcher.

After completing my first season as a pitcher, my record was very successful. My first year's pitching record, not counting playoff games, had a 90% winning record. My second season as a baseball pitcher also had a 90% winning record. As you have just read, my first 2 years in pitching were successful seasons. All my 7 years of pitching, my team's record stayed highly above the average of .500.

My pitching skills were voiced all over Boys Club. It was said that I was one of the best pitchers in my league and age bracket. Of course, there were other great pitchers in the league, and I was considered one of them. I believe I became a tough and dominant pitcher because of all those rocks I had thrown in the projects, while playing my "rock and bottle" game. Although, I was throwing curves and sinkers with rocks, however, I was still able to shift that same throwing talent to a baseball.

The same way I threw a sinker or a curve with a rock, is the same skill I utilized when throwing a baseball. Of course, I had to grasp each object (rock or ball) differently, but the flick of the wrist was still the same. To me, it was very easy; I had a special throwing sophistication, and it was not a problem throwing like that. I know it sounds untrue or unrealistic to throw sinkers and curves with rocks, but I had a skill and a talent, and throwing anything like that was a "piece of cake". I can also throw curves and sinkers with pennies, nickels, and quarters. Yeah, I even put money in the game, so I know my skills are awesome (talented).

There was this one team called, "Eagles". The Eagles were the talented squad that caused flaws to be collected upon my record. The Eagles had some very tough hitters on their team. Almost every year, my team (Cardinals) had to play against the Eagles in play-off competition. This team, the Eagles would make it to the playoffs because of their hitting ability. The Eagles did have a tough hard throwing pitcher, too. (Joe-Joe). However, my team would make it to the playoffs because of my pitching skills. My team was filled great hitters as well.

Loyal fans I had, and they traveled with the team to watch me pitch. Many of my fans asked my coach, "when is the next scheduled game" so we can come watch **Brian Irons** pitch. My fans wanted to be eyewitnesses in each game. They wanted to sit on the sidelines, and watch me do what I do best…. pitch. My fans knew they were going to see a great game pitched by me. They carried lawn chairs with them, and even blankets to lie on. All through the game, my fans yelled, "strike him out too, and get this game over with". I heard my mother on the sidelines saying those words, too.

My fans, my team players, and my family members gave me a pitcher's nickname. "The junk pitcher" is the name they called me. They called me the "junk pitcher" because the pitches I threw in game situation had great air movement. I was 7 years of age throwing pitches that lead people to give me a meaningful name, such as, "The junk pitcher".

I believe the talent and skill my brain has is far advanced for my age bracket. Although, I was 7 years old, I pitched as if I was a teenager. I did not have the teenage throwing power (velocity), but making the ball do tricks was a skill and talent I obtained. I had about six different pitches that I learned to throw at the age of 7. Three to four of my pitches were different types of curves. Having many levels of pitches that I could throw, is what made me an awesome pitcher. My pitching skills were totally unique, and truly "one" of kind.

My team had an important game to play. As this game was in progress, my team's score was trailing our opponent. Although, my team was trailing in points, the score was still close. This game was filled with a high level of intensity. My team was nervous, the other team was nervous, but there will only be one winner. Even though the other team was leading in points, my team was still putting up a good fight. This game was very important to my team, just as it is for our opponents.

While this game was in progress, I was sitting on the bench watching. I was actually a spectator. One of our other pitchers was on the mound pitching. He was displaying his best performance. He was doing his very best to prevent us from losing this game. While I was sitting on the bench, this game was not looking too good to my sight. When a team is trailing their opponent's score the entire game, it makes the loosing athletes worry. There is nothing like celebrating a win in the last game of the season. No one enjoys losing; everyone only enjoys winning.

Somehow, my team scrambled back, and tied up the score. When my team had finally tied the score, of course we began rejoicing. A championship game cannot end with a tie; therefore, we had to keep playing until a team player scored. This game is now going to extra innings.

A very scarce situation came about. The other team was at bat, with the bases loaded. Not only were the bases loaded, but also there was no outs. If one of the players on the opposing team hit the ball, it is very possible a player will score, and my team will be the losers. An important game like this, my team wanted me to be the pitcher on the mound. In fact, I was scheduled to pitch this game.

Before this game took place, my mother and I went to visit my uncle. While mother was inside the house, I was outside having fun. While having fun, I injured myself. This injury happened about 3 or 4 hours before game time.

There was an old skateboard lying in my uncle's front yard. The skateboard was very old looking. The skateboard looked like it had been rained on for a while because of the rust on it. It had rust spots all over it.

I picked the skateboard up, placed it in the streets, and started riding it. This street was very steep. The street looked like a roller coaster. It had sharp turns, and it kept going down. The hill was so steep that after riding the skateboard down it, I had to walk back up.

As I was rolling down this steep hill, I was probably rolling about 5 to 10 mph. That is a fast speed on a skateboard, and going downhill. Then, all of a sudden, a car came rolling up the hill, coming straight towards my way. It seemed like the moving automobile came swiftly from out of nowhere. I had to make a quick mind alternating decision. Either jump off the skateboard, and land on the hood of the rolling car, or leap off the skateboard, and land in the dirt and grass. I did not have much time to decide on which decision to make. It was like; wham bam and then the car came. So, less than two seconds, a choice had to be made. So, I made a quick decision, and decided to dive in the dirt and grass.

When I had landed in the grass, I began sliding on my chest with hands and arms stretched out. I slid about 3 to 5 yards in the grass. One of the first defensive reactions people do when falling or sliding forward is to stretch out their hands and arms. Well, as I dove in mid-air, I stretched out my hands and arms, and quickly became superman. For about a second or two, my body was airborne. When I finally landed in the grass, I began sliding. Then, the flesh of my right hand (pitching hand) encountered a piece of glass that had a sharp edge.

The sharp piece of glass thrashed through the palm of my right hand. To my hand, the glass did a work of flesh separation. When the glass split the flesh of my pitching hand, blood began gushing out. As I was watching blood gush out, I ran into my uncle's house crying. I went to show my mother, and what a surprise it was. Then, mother wrapped my hand with a towel. She drove me to the hospital, so that the professionals of healing wounds could take over.

When my mother and I arrived at the hospital, I was handled and treated immediately. My injury needed attention right away. Then a doctor came and got me, took me to a patient room, and sowed the open wound with a stitch. After the doctor stitched up my wounded hand, I then left the hospital. The doctor said unto my mother, "for a couple of weeks, your son need to be careful when using his right hand. Doc also said, "Be careful how you grasp objects, because the stitch might stretch and break, and the wound would re-open and start bleeding again.

When my coach heard what had happened, he became very frustrated and worried. He was probably wondering why my mother allowed me to ride a skateboard on game day. I was not thinking about a baseball game. I only wanted to have a little fun while visiting my uncle's house. Besides, <u>I Did Not Know</u> that riding a skateboard was going to cause an injury to my pitching hand.

As this playoff game was in its first extra inning, the other team was at bat, with the bases loaded. It was either win or lose. The team that scores first will win the championship game. So, there I was, on the bench, about to watch my team lose, because the bases were loaded and there were no outs.

Well, the coach turned his head and looked at me. As the coach fastened his eyes upon me, he then said, **"Brian Irons** how is your hand? Is there any pain in it? Can you pitch? We need you! I replied and said, "No", my hand does not have pain in it, and yes, I can pitch".

Now that I think about what I just did, I have great courage, and a strong heart. I mean really, this is a very important game, and if the team hits the ball and score, it would be as if my team lost because of me. I could have lied and said, "My hand is in pain". The coach had no other choice but to believe my words. But my heart and courage spoke up and said, "Yes, I can pitch".

Although, I did not pitch in the beginning of the game, I was put in a position to either come thru or chump out. I entered the game when the heat was on. If the team hit the ball and score, my team has lost the game. I will probably cry, and my teammates will too.

After the opposing team saw me take the gauge off my hand, they immediately realized I was a wounded pitcher. Even before the game started, when the other team's coach found out I was not going to pitch, they began rejoicing even then. They felt like they had a 90% chance of winning. This coach, along with his team players knew I was the little league Cardinals star pitcher. Nevertheless, they still had to get past the champion of throwing (Brian Irons) in order to be crowned as champions. Therefore, they had to face me anyway. Yeah, they had to see **Brian Keith**, who is the "grand wizard" of throwing.

I then picked up the baseball. I squeezed it with the injured hand a couple of times. Then I began to play catch with the catcher on my team. As I was loosening up my throwing arm, slight throbbing pains my hand felt. Nevertheless, I did not mention the pain to my coach because I wanted to rescue my team from nerve wrecking hour.

As I was warming up, the entire team gathered around me. The team players began whispering in my ears saying, "Irons" strike these dudes out. They also said, "We know your hand is messed up, but we need you to come through for us.

After I finished loosening up my pitching arm, it was time to get the game started again. During this particular time of the game, the infielders and outfielders came closer to home plate. They knew that, if our opponent's bat connects with the ball in any kind of way, the other team's coach is going to direct the 3rd base runner to head for home plate. Even if a ball is hit to the outfield, the 3rd base runner can tag up and head for home plate to score. Therefore, if a batter hits the ball on the field, that hit will probably cause my team to lose the game. Then my team will not be leaving the baseball field with a winning status.

Well, here I am, about to pitch with a sore and bruised hand with a stitch. This was the biggest test I had to take throughout my entire season of pitching. Not only were the bases loaded, but also, there were no outs. On top of that, I came into the game and had to face the top of the line-up.

The top of the line-up, which is the first three batters, are usually the best hitter's on the team. My, my, my, I must face the best hitters on the team, in a situation like this.

The first batter walks up to the plate hoping to hit a base hit, to be the winner of the game. He looked me in the eye, and I looked him in the eye too. I went into the pitchers wind up, and threw the ball. My first pitch was a curve ball. The batter swings and miss…strike one. The next two pitches were also curve balls: the batter swings at them both and misses…strike three, 1 out! The second batter walks up to the plate seeking to be the champion of the game. I threw three curveballs and struck him out too. The third batter comes to the plate; I threw three curveballs at him, and struck him out too. I struck the first batter out, the second batter, the third batter, and the inning was over. I came into the game, and pitched three straight outs just that fast. I am the best, I am the greatest, and there is none like me.

Hey, my reader, you would truly be amazed at how accurate my throwing really is. My mental will power is high tech as well, because I was not worried. Although, I was a little nervous, I did not fret. I went into the game, and threw only nine pitches, which turn out to be three outs. I am skillful, I am talented, I am the best in business, and I was born with this amazing ability.

After the three strikeouts were executed, it was then my team's turn to bat. To make a long story short, my team scored, and we earned game winning status. This competitive game goes down on record as my best baseball pitching performance ever. My one-inning game performance became a splendid lifetime memorial experience. Everything I do goes down as a memorial.

As little league athletes, after winning games, we would gather around one another, sing victory songs, eat chips, eat home cooked brownies, and drink soda pop.

Throughout my career of pitching, I earned a couple of MVP trophies. Yeah, a couple of trophies had the name **Brian Keith** printed on them. Throughout the years of pitching, it was said; Brian Irons is going to be the next best professional baseball pitcher.

If I make it to Major League Baseball, I am confident that I will have the most strikeouts in baseball's history. There is none like me.

Well, not too many athletes are as skillful as I am. I hope one day to say what heavy weight boxer of the world said, "I shook up the world; I'm a bad man".

Well, baseball season has now ended. It is now time for me to participate in another sport. Football is the next sport I am going to play.

My mother took me back to the Boys Club, so I could sign up for football. As I was signing up, my mother and I met the coach. Once we met the coach, he gave us the dirty lowdown. Yeah, the coach has rules just like God and my baseball coach does.

My very first year of playing football, I was a starting safety. I was 7 years old at the time. I was a tough safety. I was a hard-hitting tackler, too. I injured many young athletes.

The next football season came. I was 8 years old at the time; I signed my name on the football's try-out roster sheet. I jotted down that I wanted to play the wide receiver's position.

I knew I could catch a football with ease. If I can throw a football with either hand, then both of my hands are incredibly talented for grasping and catching. In addition, I had great visual judgment of the ball while it travels through the air.

The football try-out list is filled with a substantial number of little league players. Therefore, the coach had to focus closely to see who would earn a spot on the team. In other words, the team roster sheet needed signatures on it.

While the coach was watching and observing, the players were performing the best they could. Every athlete was giving his best performance. If any player wants his name added to the roster, he must perform at his highest ability. Therefore, every athlete must expose his best skillful performance unto the coach. An impression must be done. Every player's skill must win the coach's decision.

Another day of football practice had come. The coach was observing and watching the players display their talents and skills on the football field. This particular day, the coach gave the athletes a specific task to perform. The athletes were told to line up, and run out for a pass.

The coach physically drew a mark on the football field so that the players would see how far to run. The coach was looking to see who had the talent to play as a wide receiver. I patiently waited for this day to arrive, because my heart was set on playing the wide receiver's position.

Here I am sprinting on the football field to show my catching skill ability. Every time a pass was thrown to me, the ball never touched the ground. I caught every pass. There were no juggling catches; nor were there almost misses. I caught every pass with skillful grabs. I caught every pass with my hands, and no catches were caught with the help of my chest area. This particular day I was perfect at catching the ball. I even caught a few passes by diving for the ball. I really did not have to dive at times, but I did it just too to make it look good. I also caught a couple of passes with one hand, which was also on purpose too. I am talented, and yes, I am the best in business. I am what I am, and I only play the way I can.

The other players were having difficulties catching the ball. After I repeatedly watched these players have trouble catching the ball, I decided to show off a little. I ran out for a pass farther than what was required. Instead of running out 10 to 15 yards, I ran about 30. When I ran out for the pass, the coach hurled the ball to me with no hesitation. Yes, I caught that long pass as well.

After catching that particular pass, a big mistake I had made. The mistake was when I hurled the ball back to the coach from that length of distance. I threw the football back to him 10 times better than he had been throwing the ball to us. The ball was thrown unto him in a perfect spiral.

As I was jogging back to line up for another pass, the coach said, "Young man"! I looked, and he tossed me the football. After he tossed me the ball, he replied, "Try this position". That position was quarterback. From that day forward, I became the starting quarterback for the boy's club. I was the starting quarterback for the next 5 years. I wanted to play at the wide receiver position; however, <u>I Did Not Know</u> that I would be the star quarterback for the team.

In my little league years of playing football as quarterback, I earned two trophies labeled MVP (Most Valuable Player). In my youth days of quarterbacking, I have been compared to many NFL quarterbacks, even at this youthful age. I am the best; I am the greatest, and there is none like me.

Playing sports taught my mind how to be useful in two different ways. When I was a pitcher, my mental status knew how to be tough on the defensive side. When I was a quarterback, my mind learned how to be tough on the offensive side. Therefore, in my life, just by playing sports, my brain already knows how to be defensive, and it knows how to be offensive. Whether offensive or defensive, my brain already knows how to perform them both.

When I became older in life, high school sports became my next activity. I played football when I was a freshman in high school. I played baseball as a freshman and junior. After football and baseball seasons were over during high school, I quit playing those two sports for teams forever. Although, those two sports I played in the days of my youth, I soon fell out of love with playing them both. I fell completely in love with another sport called, "Basketball".

All four years of playing high school basketball was at Lindbergh Sr. High. I had a greater love for basketball than any other sport. Football and baseball were okay, but basketball became my new future athletic dream. The sport of basketball took over my athletic life, and yes, my desire is to display my skills and talents in the N.B.A, so that I can play against the professionals.

In my sophomore year, I started as a shooting guard the entire season. I also started as a shooting guard my senior year, too.

While playing basketball during high school, I have had many great experiences. Some experiences were emotionally pleasing, while others were very heart hurting. Each experience was a lesson learned.

One day, my school, Lindbergh, was playing against "Oakville Sr. High School". Oakville and Lindbergh were sort of like two schools at war. Just as the Cowboys and Redskins are competitive rivalries, well,

Lindbergh and Oakville are rivalries too.

Let me tell you about a basketball experience I encountered during high school. My team was playing against Oakville Sr. High. All during the game, I was envisioning myself stealing the ball from Oakville, and then running to the basket to dunk the ball for the very first time. I have dreamed of dunking the ball in game situation for a long time.

At this particular time, my team had a ten-point lead, going into the fourth quarter. Well, it happened, I stole the ball from Oakville's possession. After stealing the ball, I had a fast break all by myself. While I was dribbling the ball down the court, I began talking to myself, saying, "This is your time to get that dunk you've always dreamed of".

When I leaped in the air to dunk the ball, I missed it; the ball hit the back of the rim and flew high into the air. After missing that dunk, the coach became mentally heated. He got angry and snatched me out the game. Then he commanded me to sit on the bench. While I was sitting on the bench, Oakville scrambled back, and took the lead. After a while, I guess the coach figured he should put me back into the game, and forget the fact I missed a dunk.

Then the coach looked at me, and said, "Irons go back into the game". Well, to make a long story short, I stole the ball twice from Oakville, scored twice, and led my team to victory. Yeah, my mind is already defensive because I stole the ball twice from Oakville's possession. I am the best, I am the greatest, I shook up the world, and there is none like me. I am skillful and talented to the fullest. If you come up against me, I guaranteed you, you are going down for the count.

There was nothing in the world with strength to hinder or stop me from playing the game of basketball. I gave basketball my all in all. When I played street basketball in many neighborhoods and gyms, different people always said exalting words about my basketball performance. Many said I had too many "tricks" under my sleeves. In other words, I did the unbelievable thing just to score a point. Actually, it was hard for an entire team to contain me. People also said, "Bro you got too many moves", which is a true statement, because I can do everything with my left hand and my right hand. They said I was too quick. They said, they said, they said it all, and everything that was said was geared towards me.

As I played the game of basketball, people have compared me to many N.B.A. players. As people compared me to these N.B.A. stars, they even called me by their names. I have been compared to more than ten different N.B.A. players.

My basketball talents and skills are awesome. I am a right-handed b-ball player, but my left-hand ability confuses everyone. Sometimes, I will take a shot with my right hand, and the next shot might be taken with my left. It all depends where the defender takes me on the court.

With talents and skills such as mine, the people could not help but notice the skills which my body attained. I can purposely shoot a basketball from the old N.B.A. 3-point arc with either arm.

My arm talent or skill is different from 80% of the athletic world. The evenhanded talent I possessed is the reason why I dominated the b-ball court. There is not too many weaknesses in my skills, when it comes to playing basketball. My opponents never knew which hand was going to take the next shot. No matter how far I was from goal, the defenders never knew which hand would take the next shot.

Many times, I went to play on different basketball courts. Sometimes, I had to sit on the sidelines and hope to be picked to play on a team. As I stood, hoping to be picked to play, I was sometimes overlooked. I would not be picked because; the person who is picking his team does not know how good of a basketball player I really am.

When looking at me, you will see a long lanky bony man who looks like he is probably not worth taking a chance at being picked. When people do not know you, they pick teammates according to appearance. However, personally speaking, I love it when I am overlooked.

One day, I remember going to play basketball with one my friends. Even then, I would dominate the basketball court with finesse. No matter where I played basketball, talking trash to competitors was one of my greatest deeds.

While I was on the court skillfully punishing my opponents, I overheard some dudes on the sideline talking about hurting me. I heard them say, "He think he better than everyone, we going to see how good he is after the game is over. I kept on playing the game as if I heard them not. Then I began missing shots on purpose. I was in their neighborhood, and it was only me and one of my friends. Therefore, I was a bit scared. To make a long story short, I took a long and deep shot, and while the ball was traveling in the air, I dashed to my car for an escape.

Whether those dudes were serious or not, they did not know me to be speaking words like that. Comments like that should not come out of people's mouths, if they do not know you, and not be serious. These people probably never saw me before, and I have never seen them either; therefore, I took their words serious. To me, I ran for my life. People have been jealous of me all my athletic life for a very long time.

I went to Vashon Center one day, and skillfully demolished the teams I played against. I became so great in this gym; other athletes were signing their name on the player's list after mine. In order to play in this gym, every person had to sign his or her name on a sheet of paper. The next five names on the paper plays the winning team. Many people rushed to the paper, just to sign their names after mine. The next four names after mine will be the guys who play on a team with me. I suppose they felt they had a chance of winning, if I was on a team with them. Well, it was true, because my talents and skills would keep my team on the court for about 2-3 games before losing.

After the games were over, many athletes approached me and shook my hand. Some embraced me with exalting words before I left the gym. This gym of athletes compared me too many N.B.A stars.

I went and played basketball at Gamble Center, and my talents and skills trampled over all opposing athletes. I went and played at Cherokee Center, and demonstrated dynamically. While showing off my skills at Cherokee Center, a guy asked me to play on his team, in a basketball league. I replied, "Yes". Before I even met the other players on the team, the coach immediately added me to the roster.

The first game played was at Tandy Gym. I scored 26 points. Each period was 10 minutes. I could not play for long periods, because the athletes, who were on the team before me, were getting jealous. The people in the stands watched me run up and down the basketball court, as if they were watching a superstar from the N.B.A. Do you know how it feels to be a basketball player, and you can't be stopped?

In Buder gym, four high school students watched me play a few games of basketball, and asked me to sign my name on their books and papers. I grabbed a pen, and signed my name on their books. When the people in the gym saw me signing my signature on those student's books, they all looked at me with amazement. People usually never ask an athlete for his signature when playing street basketball, unless that individual is already famous, or well known. I may not have been famous at the time, but since I actually signed my name on those students' books and papers, my skills must be professional level rated. Have you ever been asked to sign your name on anything after displaying your skills and talents? Probably not!

I went to every Y.M.C.A. gym in city of St. Louis, and wrecked the court. One day, while playing at the Y.M.C.A., I hit the first 8 points. Every score is worth 1 point; therefore, my first eight shots were successful results. Just thinking about hitting 8 straight points in a roll; I have to get this off my chest; I am the greatest, I am the best, and there is none like me. Yeah, you heard me!

I went and played at Marquette Gym and skillfully smashed the competitors who were in there too. This gym of athletes set a 6'6 guy on me, thinking he would intimidate. Man please, my skills crushed him.

Competing against athletes taller than me only pumps me up. It is like Showtime at Rutger St. It roughly ignites my skills to show the people that; it makes no difference if a man is 7'6; he is not going to stop me.

My coordination, skills, and talents were tremendously great skills within my body. My talents and skills caused me to realize I could challenge or play against any number of basketball athletes at the same time. Playing against more than one athlete in a basketball game had advanced my techniques and skills. The talents, skills, and techniques my body possessed have made entire teams look horribly bad.

I have challenge 3 to 4 different athletes in a straight game of basketball. To me, playing against multiple athletes was normal. I never saw myself out being outnumbered. I only saw that, a basketball game is about to be played, and I truly want to be the winner. These games were half-court events, not full court.

Thinking about my basketball skills and talents, I really wonder, "how my skills and talents" would improve, once I begin training with professional basketball fitness instructors. With great shooting skills such as mine, once I get pro training in sharp shooting, I will probably break many high scoring records. Training with professionals will enhance my defensive skills, too. Once these pro trainers provide me with a routine exercising program, which is to strengthen my legs, I will be leaping out the gym like never before.

In fact, personally speaking, I have not seen my skills and talents perform at its maximum ability. Playing basketball in high school, or in recreational centers, is completely different from playing in a N. B. A. gym. Once a person makes it to the league of professionals, his talents and skills are automatically taken to another level. Just by playing before the N.B.C. cameras will hype up any basketball player, and he will play ball at unbelievable levels.

This is something for you to meditate on; sport skills are enhanced through experiences, and talents are given to the holder at the day of birth. Only God gives the talents, but we are supposed to practice and practice to better the skills, which operates from the talent. Although, I am a two-handed player, I still had to practice to better the skills that were connected to my talent. God is the one who supplied my brain with the talent and free skill to be highly favored in sports.

This particular talent (2-hand ability) or skill was given to me before I was born. When I was in the stomach or belly of my mother, my skills and talents were there as well. As I grew older, the talent was unwrapped, and there I was realizing I could play sports with either hand. I will never know why this talent and skill was given unto me and not unto you. But still in all, I have not seen a man or woman possess the talent I now have. Actually, I saw a man whose talents might be close to mine, but I'm not sure, if he is still on my level.

Chapter 4

THE INTELLIGENT HUMAN BRAIN

This chapter was the hardest to put together. I studied many books and website that taught on the human brain. As I studied different materials, one said a certain brain part does this, and another said it did that. So, I relied on the 3 out of five mode. If three books said the same thing, I went with that. Although, I went with the three out of five, that does not mean the other writings or explanations were wrong. No matter what is being studied on the brain, it is hard to pinpoint its exact every move and meaning. The brain has more than 1000 operating components.

I give all neurologists thumbs up for studying, and giving people a better understanding of how the brain works.

But let me give you some facts on who created the brain. The hands of God fashioned and made the first human brain. What did God use to make man? God picked up chunks of dirt, then mashed on it, and formed it into a man. Just like a potter makes products out of clay, God used dirt and made a man from it.

Only God has the power to make living beings. Humans only have the power or ability to make things. You need to remember the difference between the two, when it comes to the art of making.

God's hands are very skillful. Skills are always utilized through and by the working of hands. When God used his hands to make Adam, it took skills to do that. I used my hand skills to sports, but God used his hand skills to make a man. My hand skills and God's hand skills can never be in comparison. My skills are limited, but God's skills are miraculously unlimited. When it comes to skills, God has it greater than any.

On earth, Adam was the first person a brain was made into. That same brainwork God made in the brain of Adam is the same type of power Brian Irons brain possesses, too. My brain and Adam's brain both operates the same way. We are equal in mental comparison. Yeah, Adam's brain, **Brian Irons** brain, and every human being on earth have a brain that functions and operates the same way.

The hands of God formed the entire body itself, but a miraculous work was done when causing the inner body (brain) to operate. God breathed into the nostrils of Adam, and Adam's brain came alive. When the brain came alive, the body received the strength to move. The body of Adam was similar to a corpse, until God breathed the breath of life into it. This inner being or inner body is called, "**The Intelligent Human Brain**".

When God created "The Intelligent Human Brain", he gave it the ability to seek after life's necessities. Life necessities are things that are vital and important to a person's everyday living. While the brain seeks necessities in life, it automatically knows how to discern right from wrong. The brain knows what is good for it, and what is not so good. This is done by the brain's intelligence.

The word intelligence means: to obtain the ability to learn how to deal or adapt to living situations as they arrive. When quarrels or disputes arise in people's lives, they should allow intelligence to operate, rather than the character of ignorance.

The people in the projects did not allow intelligence to be in command; they allowed their brains to operate under the influence of self-judgment, which was from the decision of ignorance. Intelligence will provide you with a number of ways to fight and defeat your own trials in life. Whether a situation is harsh or easy going, the intelligence in the human brain will always search out the matter, and seek the best way to resolve issues. That's only if you are looking for an intelligent way to resolve matters.

When God made the brain, he also made for it a covering. This covering sits on top of the brain like a helmet. The helmet is a round-shaped hard bone. Its color is off white. This helmet is called, "Skull".

Before a "chick" is born, it sits and lives in an eggshell folded up. While the unborn chick is living in the eggshell, it has two coverings for protection. The eggshell itself is the first protection, and the chic, which sits on the egg, is the other protection. Well, in the same sense, The Intelligent Human Brain sits under the protective care of the hard bone skull folded up as well. The mother of the unborn chick shield's her eggs so that predators will not have the opportunity to touch and destroy the unborn chicks. Well, in the same sense, the skull clamps on the entire human brain and seals it from the outer predators. The eggshell is primarily a protective shield for the unborn chick, and the skull is the master "shield" for the meaty brain. Everything in life has a darling need for protection.

The skull is the brain's knight and shiny armor. The brain loves the skull, because it protects and sticks close to it. It is sort of like a marriage has taken place, because the skull and brain are united. The skull and brain have become one in unity, and nothing can separate them but death.

When the brain dies, it slowly disintegrates. Once the brain has experienced death, the skull is left behind. After so many years have passed by, only the skull remains in the casket. Therefore, as I said, "nothing can separate the brain from the skull but death."

A man thoughtfully made a helmet to protect the head of football players, and God thoughtfully made a skull to protect his creation (the brain). The human brain is filled with precious treasure, which is worth more than the amount of millions. The human brain is so relied upon, that is why God made for it a protector.

Every brain has only one operation, and that is to lead your life, in the direction you have chosen it to go. Whether a person is Black, Caucasian, Chinese, Asia or of any other race, God creatively designs each brain to operate the exact same way. Yet and still, every individual brain have different thoughts flowing through them on a continual basis.

It is said and recorded if blood ceases from circulating through a person's brain, physical death has come. Whether the blood ceases circulation from a stroke, or from a drowning in the water, once the intelligent human brain has experienced a halt movement of blood, physical death has come. If blood ceases from flowing through a person's brain for 4 to 8 minutes, physical death is experienced, or the individual's brain will be sent into a vegetated state.

As a judgment, God sent rain upon the earth, and destroyed it along with the people. While the rain was continually dropping from heaven, small puddles began to form. Then the puddles of water began connecting one to the other. From the connection of puddles, a flood had been formed. This flood, which God made with rain, became taller than any substance on earth. While the final judgment was being pronounced upon the people, they tried using physical strength to escape the flood's judgment. The earth became a pool of water, and all living species were forced to show their swimming skills. Mankind cannot tread nor swim in water for an entire day, let alone for more than 5 months. A moment for resting is required when any man is swimming.

Once a person's head is under the judgment of God, a sentence will always be pronounced upon it. Although, the brain is very energetic, it cannot perform continual living (breathing) while underwater. The judgment of God will rain on a person's life, until it kills that man.

Oh my, do you know what? When God destroyed those people in the days of Noah, he pronounced the death penalty upon them all.

Physical strength will never be able to stand up against the judgment of God. The flood came as a judgment unto the people, because of their wicked deeds done. God, through his flood's judgment, had sentenced all those brains to serve the death penalty.

The intelligent human brain is the master of the body because of its authorized power. The brain is the body's master. The body will do whatever the brain commands. In a sense, the body is a slave to the intelligent human brain.

Slaves must do whatever their master instructs them. Just as slaves are obedient unto their masters, the body is obedient unto "The Intelligent Human Brain". The word "master" means, to be lord over. The word master also mean- to control by the commanding of words, or by physical force.

Slaves are normally used for their master's purpose. A master has high rankings over all slaves. The master (the brain) gives orders and assignments to its pupils (bodily limbs) so that they will know what to do next. However, whatever commands the master has commanded the slaves to do; they must and will perform the task. Yes, the body is the brain's slave for all the days on earth.

I am about to tell and explain unto you a few slaves the brain has. If they are slaves, then they must be workers. The intelligent human brain has many workers (slaves) that perform different operations within the body. These workers, which are in the intelligent human brain, guides the body and keeps it active while performing many duties. Here are some official names of these workers that are crammed inside the brain.

In the brain, there are cells, neurons, cerebellum, cerebrum, hemispheres (left and right), frontal lobes, parietal lobes, temporal lobes, occipital lobes, brainstem, memory, and dozens more. Those components (workers) in the intelligent human brain operate mechanically, and they all ignite the body to perform different tasks on a daily basis. Meaning, each component in the brain has a particular task to instruct the body, for physical movement to be successful.

Also, when moving the body, the spinal cord is the brain's greatest help. In every person's body, the spinal cord is the backbone.

Many workers, which are in "the intelligent human brain", most people in the world have no knowledge of their historical facts. Probably, 85% of people in the world do not consider the knowledge and strength The Intelligent Human Brain truly has. Nor does anyone realize how important The Intelligent Human Brain really is. Therefore, I am going to supply you with a brief handwritten summary about the brain and its workers. I feel the need to inform you about the human brain, along with its exalted power.

Memory is the first worker in the brain I am going to teach. Memory maintains past and present commercial and non-commercial events. Memory is very vital when it comes to learning. Everything we learned in the past shall be remembered.

Without memory, people would forget where the toothbrush has been placed. Not only that, but also forget where the bathroom is. Every living species has some sort of memory operating in the brain.

The God created memory in the intelligent human brain is similar to the memory installed into a personal computer. A person downloaded memory into a computer, which gives it the ability to operate. On the other hand, God placed a memory system in the intelligent human brain, so that information can be downloaded into its operating system (declarative and or procedure memory). From a compact disc, memory is downloaded into a computer. But the intelligent human brain's memory is downloaded with amazing functions by the hand of God. Information and memory is added to a computer by a compact disc, and information and memory is added to the intelligent human brain from people's living experiences.

Another worker in the intelligent human brain is called, "Brainstem". The brainstem is said to be a person's survival kit. The brainstem's primary work is to control your breathing, heart rate, blood pressure, digestive system, and mental arousal. After God breathed into the nostrils of Adam, all the above-mentioned activities became a head motion. Nevertheless, the brainstem is the worker that helps keeps you alive, through the breathing.

Let me provide you with more performances that the brainstem does. When food has been swallowed into the belly, the brainstem is the active worker that has geared you into performing that act. Sneezing is also accessed by the brainstem. Sneezing is an act that happens unexpectedly, not on purpose. No one motivates the breathing or sneezing to take place, it happens on it's on. God gave the brainstem the charge to breath, and it took over from there. Through the lungs, the brainstem does the inhaling and exhaling for each living man. The only time people consider inhaling and exhaling is at the doctor's office when asked to do so. Other than that, the brainstem automatically performs the breathing. Just as a person pumps air into a tire, the brainstem pumps air into the body. Just as a man cannot control his wife, a person cannot control his or her breathing. If a person could control the breathing, that individual has the power to keep himself alive on earth forever.

Since heart rate and breathing (inhaling and exhaling) are controlled by this particular part of the brain, when this component has ceased from its natural use of performance, death and a burial place for the individual will take place.

Earlier, I said, "Whatever God makes (the brain)" it lives and operates forever. Although, the body will die one day, the brain (brainstem) (spirit) that's in a person never deceases. The brainstem is your arousal or awareness observer; therefore, after death takes place, your breathing will still be active. Whether you are commanded to enter into heaven, or sent to hell, your breathing will be active in one of those places.

Later in this interesting story, I will give you an example in full details where your mental status and spirit will live throughout eternity (forever). You need to know this, because I am sure everyone desires to see the windows of heaven opening up, and be welcomed. No man with good mental sense desires to live in the intensity of heat, which will be felt in "Hell". Again, the body might die, but long lives the brain.

Another worker in the intelligent human brain is called, the **"Cerebellum"**. The cerebellum controls every person's physical movement. Unlike the brainstem, which controls our involuntary movements, the cerebellum controls voluntary movements. Every limb you desire to move is done so by the cerebellum. To make a long story short, the cerebellum is your physical movement activator.

Here are some examples of my brain's cerebellum in action. When I rode my first bicycle, the cerebellum is the worker that controlled my legs to pedal it. While riding the bicycle, the cerebellum was graciously empowering my arms to guide it. Also, when I was riding that skateboard down the hill on the day of my baseball game, my cerebellum controlled my leg and ankle movement, so I could guide the skateboard.

When eating a bowl of cereal, the cerebellum guides the hand with the spoon, and then raises the utensil to the mouth. Wow, the cerebellum helps me to do many things, and <u>I Did Not Know it.</u>

Injury done to the cerebellum will cause a person's physical movement to be shaky and or unsteady. When injury is done to this organ in the brain, physical movement and coordination becomes a problem. Today, your body (limbs) moves at a normal pace, but if the cerebellum has suffered an injury, your movement will be thrown off track.

Another worker in the brain is called, the **Cerebrum**, not cerebellum. Do not get these two, the cerebrum and the cerebellum confused with one another. The cerebrum is the brain's performer that gives every person the ability to "think". This component (cerebrum) is our greatest head worker in life. Before a person decides to do anything, the thinking applicator reacts first. For the rest of your life, thinking will always be a necessity. Nothing can be done without a moment of thinking. We never realize a thought took place before we did what we did.

You thought about what you wanted to eat, before opening the refrigerator. Therefore, every person needs to protect his or her thought applicator. When doing so, you are literally protecting the performer that arouses or awakens your ability to think. As you protect your cerebrum, which is your critical thinking tool, you are guarding your ability to think accurately. Yeah, guard your thinking administrator.

Also, in the brain there are four other particular workers. These workers are located in the cerebral cortex of the brain. These four workers are called, "**Lobes**". Each lobe in the cerebral cortex consists of pairs. Each set of lobes has a specific name, and they perform different functions.

The first sets of lobes are called, "**Frontal Lobes**". The frontal lobes, along with the cerebellum, both play a role in controlling a person's physical movements. But let's not forget about the spinal cord, because without it, the body would not stand upright.

The frontal lobes help us utilize mental judgment. Mental judgments will be used every single day. In everything you do, mental judgment will be assessed one way or another.

When driving a car down the road, an act of judgment will be done. As the cerebellum controls a person's hands while driving a car, mental judgment is needed to keep the car rolling between the painted yellow lines in the streets. Mental judgment helps a person decides when to emerge into traffic.

The frontal lobes also activate emotions. The emotions that the frontal lobe displays are the type of emotions connected to sensitivity, caring, and loving. When you express love and care at a funeral, you are doing that by the frontal lobes power. When you cry because of losing a game, your frontal lobes gave you the ability to show that expression.

When you fall in love with someone, and your heart becomes broken, your frontal lobes gave you the emotional power to feel the pain. I have fallen in love before, and I have been hurt before, too. Since I felt the emotional pain of being hurt, my frontal lobes were active at that particular time. Emotions aren't just active in pain; they operate in good times as well. When I finally received my high school diploma, my emotion rejoiced during that particular moment and time.

If injury is done to the frontal lobes, a number of mental abilities will become bothered or damaged. For most people, they will lose their ability to sort out simple problems. They will lose the ability to use accurate judgments. When your emotions once did operate during sentimental moments, however, if your frontal lobes become damaged, you can lose that mental kindness. Anytime a person becomes angry, his or her frontal lobes are going through some serious emotional pain.

The second sets of lobes in the brain are called, "Parietal Lobes". The parietal lobes deal with bodily pressure and sensations. Once my hands felt hot water, the parietal lobes in my brain caused me to realize the water was hot.

It is also said, if injury takes place in the right parietal lobe, it may cause a person to have difficulty finding his or her way back to once known places and areas. For example, I know exactly where certain stores are located. But, if my right parietal lobe becomes injured, I will have difficulty finding where that same store is located. The parietal lobes helps a person find his or her way back home. Although, you remember where your home is, however, if the right-side parietal lobe becomes injured, you might forget where the home is located. You could be living in the same home for more than 40 years, but if injury is done to the parietal lobes, you might forget its location. Since animals recognize their surroundings, they have parietal lobes too, because they know their way back home.

The third set of lobes is called, "**Occipital Lobes**". These lobes are associated with sight. They give a person the ability to see. Sight is needed in mostly everything you do. These lobes, which activate sight, are highly recommended while driving a motorized vehicle. Although, good judgment is required while driving, nevertheless, sight is most important, too.

The fourth sets of lobes are called, "**Temporal Lobe**". The temporal lobes deal with the auditory system. When hearing is active in a person's life, the temporal lobes are yet working.

The four lobes mentioned in this chapter, of course, all do more than what I have explained. I just wanted to give a brief portion of information concerning them all.

Finally, yet importantly, the intelligent human brain has a worker in it called, Limbic System or Limbic Lobe. The limbic system gives us the emotional strength to show a little fear in our lives. When a person shows fear in his or her life, the limbic system is yet working. I know my limbic system works, because when a dog came towards me at a crazy speed, I jumped on top of a car. I think everyone's limbic system awakens, when a pit bull is approaching.

Emotions are a part of our feelings, and showing fear is a part of our being. Somewhere in life, fear will need to be displayed. In order to save your own life, fear must be activated. Therefore, the limbic system in our brain gives us the adequate strength to express a certain level of emotional fear. If you want to see another day in life, a little fear must be activated.

The limbic system is one of the most powerful tools that operate in our brains. Since the limbic system is our emotion and feeling center, our sensation to feel pleasure is connected here as well. At the same time, the limbic system activates feelings, emotions, sensations, and pleasures. When something causes you to feel good, the limbic system is the brain tool providing you with that reaction. The frontal lobes emotions deal with our temper and compassion, and the limbic system's emotions deal with feeling, pleasure, and sensation.

In the limbic system, there is a worker in it called, "Hypothalamus". The hypothalamus creates and regulates hunger, thirst, sex drive, and a few other functions within the body. This part of the brain will create daily the need to have food. When you became hungry, your limbic system alerted you of that. The limbic system will not delete the motion of hunger, until food has been eaten. Once food has been eaten, the limbic system becomes satisfied.

Before eating, the cerebrum (the thinker) becomes active first. You'll begin thinking of what food products desiring to eat. Once you've thought of what you want to eat, the cerebellum (limb mover) will then guide the hands to pick up the food of your choice. After you have eaten your food, the limbic system becomes pleased, and the sensation of hunger suddenly departs.

Drug usage and sex brings about a mental pleasure. Sex and drugs both operates through mental pleasure, emotion, and sensations, which are activated by the limbic system.

The body's pleasure performer, which is the "limbic system", is where all addictions are held captive. For most of us, once our limbic system has been introduced to sex and or drugs, the gate of addiction opens up. Once becoming addicted to sex or drugs, the limbic system become subjects unto their authority. The more sex a person has, the greater the limbic system becomes dependent upon it. The more drugs a person intake; the limbic system will become highly dependent upon it (drugs). Once the addiction of sex or drugs has kicked in the limbic system (brain), that person will become a slave unto either or. After the addiction of sex and or drugs charges in, that person can soon be controlled by its deadly pleasure. Nevertheless, the limbic system is a part of a person's lust and desire.

Since the brain has hundredths and thousandths of subjects that can be taught, if I decide to teach about the brain in its entirety, I will have to write the information in another book. I can go on and on teaching you about the working performance of the brain; however, I have provided you with enough information for you to consider the brain's creative power, which God made and created the brain to do.

After reading this chapter, you have just been informed how the brain's system works. You have read the many of activities the brain does. Not one component in the brain works or operates alone. The entire system of the brain works on one accord. Although, it is said that the brain has thousandths of workers within it, the brain is so awesome that it never becomes confused. Every brain part knows its job. Do you know yours?

From what you have just read in this chapter concerning The Intelligent Human Brain, I think you and I both need to always guard our brains. There are many predators in the land, and they all want to destroy all living brains. Those predators want to rip life up and out of our brains. Remember this; Life itself is in the blood, which circulates through the gifted power in the brain. Therefore, if any predator has your life captured, then surely, your blood is captured, too. Keeping your brain out of the reach of predators is the same as keeping your blood and life out of their reach of danger.

Chapter 5

DRUGS CONTROLLING THE INTELLIGENT HUMAN BRAIN

In the earlier chapter (chapter 4), I wrote facts concerning the brain's performance and intelligence. In addition, chapter 4 spoke about which brain component controls physical movement and inner activity. However, in this chapter (chapter 5), I am going to write about which sections of the brain drugs will forcefully tamper with and slowly destroy over a period of time.

Ecstasy- During the 19th century, ecstasy came with its damaging strength. The strength was powerful. The strength was so powerful that it tossed many people to and fro upon the earth.

In the 1980's, ecstasy became a popular drug. Ecstasy became so popular; it was found in more cities than there are countries. Ever since people have welcomed ecstasy into this country, many lives have been snatched by its seductive power. This drug does not have hands, but it snatches people lives, and tours them to unexpected places (territories). It drags people along the way, and leaves them clueless of how they got there. Ecstasy is most definitely a mind-alternating drug.

Ecstasy is a drug that first comes in powdered form. Normally, these days, the powder is compressed, and is then transformed into a pill.

In order to receive its negative and persuasive effects, a person has to agree on swallowing the pill. After ecstasy has been swallowed, it then sits in the stomach whole. No matter what else is inside the stomach, whether it is food or soda pop, ecstasy will relax in the stomach with those products. Just as sugar dissolves in water, in the same sense, the pill ecstasy dissolves into the blood, settling in the digestive system. This drug sits in the stomach for about 15 to 30 minutes, before its horrific activation begins.

The brainstem is the ultimate motivator to get this drug active within the anatomy. The brainstem deals with swallowing. Once ecstasy has been place into the mouth, the brainstem, which is the swallowing performer, gulps this drug into the belly. As this pill sits in the stomach whole, it soon becomes attached to the person's digestive system. The brainstem is our swallowing performer, and for years; people have been using it to gulp this illegal control substance. The brain stem enables the ability to breathe and live. Therefore, say no to ecstasy, and say yes to the living of your brain. The Intelligent Human Brain is a terrible body part to waste!

As the intoxicant's from ecstasy connects with the blood, it becomes attached to the user's life. When people insert ecstasy into the body, very swiftly, the ingredients in it take a cruise to the brain. Just as ecstasy, when transformed from powder to pill, once it becomes fastened to the blood; a mental change will soon take place.

Have you ever seen a change take place? Have you ever dropped dye in water before? Have you ever dyed eggs on Easter before? If so, then you have witnessed a change taking place right before your eyes. When dye is dropped into water, it begins dissolving right away. As the dye is dissolving, it began changing clear water to its color. If you drop blue dye in a bowl of water, the once clear liquid changes into the color blue.

The same type of change dye does to water, the same type of change ecstasy does to The Intelligent Human Brian. After ecstasy has been put into the body, it disintegrates and changes the entire inner being. After the change has taken place, the person's mental body is under this chemical's authority for the next several hours.

It is said that ecstasy will cause a person to have problems knowing reality and fantasy. Reality operates in truth, while fantasy operates in fiction. In the mind (brain), ecstasy will empower a person into believing beyond reason of facts, and then propel fantasy to prevail. Since this drug, when used, will cause a person to misunderstand fantasy and reality, it sounds like the brain is in a state of confusion. When a person becomes confused about reality and fantasy, his or her thinking ability has truly been altered.

Many times, after a person has put ecstasy in the brain, that individual can experience not knowing where he or she is. The ecstasy user can be posted at his place of home, and still appear to be lost. That sounds like a state of confusion. When an ecstasy user does not know where he is, the parietal lobes in the brain have been distracted. Remember, knowing your surrounding is a work done by the parietal lobes.

After ecstasy has set up shop in the brain, the organs in it become a marketplace. Ecstasy will begin to purchase several organs in the brain. Once ecstasy purchases any of the brain's organs, for the next several hours, it then becomes the owner of the head's components. Once a drug, such as ecstasy has been put into the brain, it will purchase your realistic thoughts, and sell back to you fantasy. Then, from out of nowhere, the thoughts in your brain will be taken on an evil tour. Strong mental and cognitive illusions will be imputed in the mind after ecstasy's powerful strength has met it. A state of becoming deceived will become a prime task, once ecstasy has taken over the thoughts of a person's mind. Nevertheless, our thinking performer (cerebrum) will be overpowered by ecstasy's cunning motivation.

The critical thinking, which comes from our cerebrum, is very important because it is needed to make precise decisions in people's lives. However, with the seducing help of ecstasy, many repulsive and bad decisions will be made. Although, people, as well as myself, will make bad decisions at times in our lives, even without the help of drugs, however, when ecstasy meets the brain's decision maker, it will force people to have unbalance thoughts, which will lead to making regrettable decisions. As your brain (cerebrum) is being influenced by ecstasy, many of your decisions made in life, will be choices that will cause you to break many laws. Ecstasy will never motivate the brain to have good thoughts. Do you remember the drug stage of action I clearly spoke about in the beginning chapter of this book (Chapter 1- The Power of Violence and Wickedness Is in the City?

After drugs are inhaled, then comes violence, and then comes the attempt to murder. Ecstasy users may seem cool and in control at the present moment, but soon, wrath and rage will become a mental and physical ongoing habit.

Heroin- this drug is first a seed to be planted. A man dug a hole in the dirt (ground), and dropped a seed of heroin therein. Then this human being poured water into this hole, so that the seed would grow. By God, dirt was used to make a man. Nowadays, humans are using dirt as a substance to make heroin.

Usually, flowers, fruits, and trees grow from the ground to bring beauty upon the earth. However, this seed, Heroin, after it grows, it brings no beauty upon the earth. This seed brings deceit and wickedness.

Once this seed grows into a bean, it is now ready for usage. The bean is called, "Tar". The tar is pitch black, and is hard. The tar is then handled by a human, and then placed inside of an electric blender to be grinded up. As the tar is being grinded up, seconds later, it is changed into a brown or white substance of powder. After all this has taken place, the drug is now available for wicked and pathetic individual's to use for his or her own personal pleasure.

Ever since humans have fastened their hands on heroin, they have used it for personal mental satisfaction. Personal mental satisfaction is nothing but a work for self-pleasure. Self-pleasure is now the reason for heroin usage. Heroin or any other drug should not be used as a method to inherit self-pleasure.

Wickedness has caused many different people to do anything just to fulfill a mental rush. Why do people put drugs in their brains for mental pleasure?

Well, the suitable answer is simple; wickedness is the psychological power that strongly persuades people to seek pleasure from drugs. Little do heroin users know that the drug, heroin, which gives birth to wickedness, has caused user's to seek pleasure from it. Therefore, when people intake heroin for pleasure, they are actually getting pleasure from wickedness.

This drug, heroin, was discovered in a country outside of the USA. Although, heroin began its growth and discovery in another country, somehow, someway, it cunningly made its way into the United States. When heroin was brought into this country, a demonic deceiver and murderer now lives here. Whether it was by plane, or by ship, the wicked predator and killer (heroin) is here, seeking a brain to devour. This killer (heroin), just like ecstasy, is upon the earth being passed around from city-to-city, and state-to-state. Yep, the killer traveled from across seas, and can now be located in all 50th states of the USA.

Heroin's natural use and purpose was probably for killing extreme pain within the body. In other words, heroin was once known as a legal medicine. If there was any pain in the body, heroin was used as a treatment, to take a dose of, and the ingredients from it would search and attack the area where the pain is. Actually, the plant, heroin (Pain Killer) was for general practitioners to utilize for medical handling.

A medicine as potent as heroin could probably only be handled when prescribed by physicians. License physicians wrote prescriptions to clients, so this drug could be handled. Nevertheless, heroin's seductive power has caused many people to become self-willed practitioners, because they go and purchase this drug at their own will.

Once the brain and body has been filled with the ingredients of heroin, usually, the user's brain is sent into a nodding mode. Minutes later, the heroin user is cast into a mild and sometimes a deep sleep. This sleep is called a mode of wicked subjection. A person does not have to be tired, exhausted, or anything of the like, heroin with its potential power will create a sleep mode within the brain. People actually become mentally addicted to a drug (heroin) that puts them to sleep.

The limbic system in our brains deals with sleep. When heroin cast a sleep mode into the user's brain, the limbic system and brainstem is being persuaded to do the abnormal. Heroin will cast a sleep mode in the brain, as if a person limbic system is charging it to go to sleep. Actually, the limbic system's performance is to alert the brain when it is ready for sleep. But heroin, with its manipulative power, will send sleep to the brain. Since heroin forces the brain to fall into a sleep mode, the normal time for sleep to take place has been cast away. A person could have slept 15 hours last night, however, once heroin has been put into the brain, minutes later, the individual will be sent right back to sleep. It is so crazy to become addicted to a drug such as heroin.

Not only will heroin motivate users to nod, but also, a bad attitude into the emotions comes about. The user's attitude is quick to jumping from being friendly, to acting as if he or she is your enemy. Therefore, a change in emotions, which are controlled by the frontal lobes, are ignited by this drug's evil and influential power.

Just the other day, I heard on television, that heroin killed more than 40 people in one month. Not only did heroin kill more than 40 people, but also, those deaths occurred in one city. Wow, heroin is dropping and killing people like houseflies. Wow, heroin stopped those people's heartbeat, and sent their bodies into the chains of death. Many of those people were probably heroin users for years. Then, suddenly, one day, heroin acted against their brain, and murdered them all. Drugs are never for you; they only have the power to work against you. The Power of Drugs will not only destroy communities, but it will also murder living beings.

People never know when their city is going to get a batch of dope so powerful and potent that it kills. On the other hand, people never know what a drug seller has mixed with the dope, as he or she tries to make it more potent, and a longer lasting high. You just cannot trust anyone these days, let alone a drug.

Heroin and other street drugs go through a great number of hands before reaching you. Those people (the 40 that heroin killed) put heroin into bodies expecting to feel pleasure. However, heroin did a work beyond their expectation. Heroin went over the limit, and now 40 lives have had a funeral session. Right now, today, 40 bodies are now buried in the ground, covered in a casket, because of the power of heroin.

Well, actually, wickedness is the power that killed them all. Wickedness comes to life after heroin or any other street drugs have been exposed to a person's anatomy (brain and body). As I said before, "The murderer and predator" is now in our country. Who will be the next victim killed by the character called, Heroin?

Codeine pills, **morphine**, **crystal meth**, and **heroin**; all will cause serious harmful mental effects. Therefore, every drug just mentioned in this paragraph will influence the brain to operate in negativity.

Marijuana- just like heroin**,** marijuana is a plant that grows from the ground. Although, this drug is a plant, it does not bring righteous characteristics upon the earth. As soon as the seed of marijuana grows into a plant, a stem of deceit has just stuck its face out of the earth's soil.

A great number of people once believed marijuana was harmful, but from the populations' daily use, they now believe it is not so harmful after all. Since people do not believe marijuana is harmful, their minds have been twisted into believing in an imaginary tale, rather than non-fiction. Marijuana has many people in the world mentally fooled. This drug creates within the mind of its users, thoughts on why this drug should be legalized. People use the phrase, "God made the herbs", therefore; it can and should be used at will.

So many food products can be substituted for the name "herb". What makes people believe that marijuana was one of them? Well, you might be right; *John 1:3- All things were made by him; and without him was not anything made that was made.* The bible says, in *Genesis 1: 29- And God said, Behold, I have given you every herb bearing seed, which is upon the face of all the earth, and every tree, in the which is the fruit of a tree yielding seed; to you it shall be for meat.*

God said, "Every herb shall be for meat". Meaning herb is a food product. Herb is for eating, not inhaling and exhaling. Every time a marijuana smoker says, "God made the herbs on the earth", tell that individual, "the herbs are for meat (to eat), not for inhaling and exhaling". People have allowed the herbs on the field to make their inner being perform look like a chimney (blowing out smoke).

When people are trying to justify why marijuana is truly here, they conjure all kinds of reasons. Their reasons have become so profound; they can almost make you a believer of their philosophy. It has become a pathetic shame. Just because people in other countries smoke marijuana at will, and has legalized it, that does not mean God made it right for them to do so. We all need God in our lives, so we will know the truth for ourselves.

This drug, marijuana, has dumfounded many people in the world. People actually believe there are no chemicals in marijuana. When it fact, marijuana has more than 400 chemicals. When it comes to marijuana, we have become so ignorant; it's a pitiful shame.

Hey ignorant folks, anytime you put something in the brain, and it changes its normal ways, that's a work performed by a chemical. The brain is made up of chemicals itself. Only chemicals have the ability to touch another chemical. We are so quick to put things in our bodies, before learning anything about the facts. I do not care how you try minimizing marijuana's power; it is still "a chemical controlled substance". In addition, it is also called, "a mind alternating drug". I do not care how dumbfound we are, God is still against this drug called, marijuana. We so ignorant that we rather learn from experiences first, rather than learning through knowledge.

Tell me something, who gave you the insight to know the next time you smoke a blunt that your brain will not trigger off into the wrong direction? People do not realize that chemicals changes the brain's normal ways of functioning. God intended the brain to do a certain work, but people are allowing chemicals to make it do something else.

People think marijuana's power is weak. Marijuana might not be as deadly as the other drugs, but it still has power to confuse all users somehow. Once marijuana has been put into the brain, any of the head organs are up for harmful grabs. If God uplifts his mercy for a split second, your brain can completely become dysfunctional. Then, your brain will be unstable for a long time.

To get the effects from marijuana, a person must inhale it into the brain. The brainstem is being utilized, because inhaling and exhaling is in motion. After the brain stem has inhaled this drug, the chemicals from it then settle into the blood. Very quickly, the chemicals interact with the blood, and then travel throughout the entire region of the brain and body.

Teenagers are quick to try marijuana. Marijuana has become the teenage party enhancer. There are so many areas of the intelligent human brain marijuana and other drugs tamper with; a person never know which of the brain's organ will soon lose its normal ways of functioning.

The limbic system is your motivation and hunger awakener. Once the limbic system becomes addicted to marijuana, it then hungers or becomes motivated for satisfaction from this chemical. When hungry, the limbic system motivates you to seek a meal. However, once a person's limbic system has been introduced to marijuana, and has become addicted, it then seeks for that drug (marijuana) to satisfy the craving hunger.

It is said that marijuana effects a person's memory and emotions. Since marijuana targets memory; the procedural, declarative, and short-term are being hit and distracted. When people inhale marijuana's formula in the brain, they have magically thrown the intoxicants into their memory center. Just as a dart is tossed in the "dart throwing competition", when you inhale marijuana into the brain, you have just tossed its chemical elements at your memory bank. Oh yeah, once a person has inhaled this drug into the brain, that same individual has also inhaled unrighteousness. Now his or her memory is under the influence of disobedience.

Things people may have done wrong to you in the past, marijuana will keep those events on replay mode, until you get pay back. While being high on marijuana, you might not remember where your keys have been placed, but you will always remember your enemy.

Steroids- are known to enhance strength, endurance, and performance in the athletic world. Many athletes use this drug, so they can get physically buff. Not only that, but also, to perform in game play at amazing levels. Since that is so, this drug is used to elevate the cerebellum (limbs mover and controller). Athletes who use steroids might become physically stronger, but muscle strength is not the only enhancement given from this drug. As this drug enhances the user's physical strength, not only will it do just that, but also, at the same time, it works against the operation of the brain. When any man use steroids, yes, he will become stronger, but the strength of wickedness will soon prove it is most powerful.

When athletes put steroids into the body, they often become sick. At times, these athletes think a sickness is from eating certain foods, when in fact, it is because of steroids strategy.

Steroids are put into the anatomy in two ways. This drug can be inserted into the veins by needle injection, or it can be swallowed. Whichever way this drug is used, it still takes a physical movement to get it activated.

Just like any other drug, when steroids have made a contact with the brain and body, the intoxicants travels to the head through the blood. Just as a person in a boat floats on the water, the chemicals from steroids float throughout the entire body. Just as water fills up the bathtub, however, when steroids are put into the body, the ingredients from it fill it up. Now the user is walking around with a body filled with this drug's seductive power.

Steroids affect memory, problem-solving skills, and can cause aggressive behavior. I did not write too much about steroids, but I do want to let you know, this drug has killed many athletes throughout the years. Only a few deaths from steroid usage have been spoken of over the news. But I wonder how many athletes have been murdered by this drug, and the event has never been broadcast. I am sure there are a great number of deaths that had not been spoken of. Whether you have heard about it or not, steroids can and will destroy.

Alcohol- is a liquid substance that can be purchased from your local store. In every city and or state where a store has been built from the ground up, alcohol can probably be purchased from there. Not only can alcohol be purchased from all over the world, but it is also advertised daily on your television screen. Somehow, someway, you will see an ad promoting alcohol.

I read an article the other day. The article was about "people becoming sick after drinking alcohol". The article called alcohol abuse a sickness, but I am going to call it being poisoned. As I was reading the article, all I could think about was the word "poison".

When a person has been drinking, then goes to sleep, and cannot be awaken, he or she has been poisoned by alcohol's ingredients. Doing things that you normally will not do, such as vomiting, is a sign of poisoning. Vomiting takes place after too much alcohol has been consumed into the anatomy.

Nowadays, a person only need a dollar and a few cents to purchase a container or bottle filled with liquid dope. Yeah, that is all it cost to purchase liquid dope. A person actually goes into his or her pants pockets, pulls out hard-earned money, and then gives it to the store's clerk, trading it for liquid dope. I call alcohol, "legalized liquid death".

When you purchase liquor from over the counter, and then drive under its influence, you are asking the creepy character called, "death" to come into your life. Although, everyone is appointed to one-day die, however, when people drink and drive, death can come sooner than suppose.

A date and time is appointed for us all to die one day. However, when you drink or put dope into the brain, it will create a time and day for death to come. In other words, many people in the world die before their God given date, all because of drugs and alcohol abuse.

Drinking alcohol and driving at the same time is like buying a farewell ticket to leave the earth. Just as a traveler buys tickets to take a trip by plane, however, when people drink and drive, they just might take a trip to death. That is what chemicals, and wickedness wants to do unto you; it wants to kill you before your God given date.

When a person dies, or has been killed, two different types of events has taken place. When a person has been killed, or when a person has died, those two deaths approached the person's life from different aspects. A person that dies at 100 years old, most of the times, that individual has died when it was his or her time to die. That's called a normal death. On the other hand, when a person's life has been taken, because of drinking and driving, that individual has been killed or murdered. That type of death was experienced before his or her God given date. Therefore, dying, or being killed, takes the meaning of two different types of death.

Pouring alcohol into your brain and body, and then driving a motorized vehicle is practically like playing the college game, "spin the bottle". Spinning the bottle is a game college student's play, as they make up their personal set of rules. For instance, after a student spins the bottle, whomever the bottle stops and points to, that individual has to do something that he or she would not normally do. Whether it is to kiss an unattractive person, or strip naked in front of a group of people, the rules say it must be done. Once the bottle spins and points at you, you must do what has been agreed upon.

Round and round the bottle goes, where it stops no one knows. Once the college student, with the hands spins the bottle, he or she never knows whom it will stop and point at. At the same token, when people drink and drive, they never know when death is going to spin into their lives. Therefore, obey the laws of the land, by not drinking and driving.

Driving a vehicle while intoxicated from alcohol has caused many car wrecks that lead to death. Drinking and driving automobile accidents occur, because a person's thinking center has been deceived. People begin to believe that they are not too intoxicated to get behind the steering wheel of a vehicle. When intoxicating alcohol makes a contact with the brain, the limb's controller (the cerebellum) receives the intoxicant effects, and all physical movements are being hindered. Also, drinking and driving accidents are caused by drivers having blurry vision, due to the occipital lobe (sight) impairment.

The "frontal lobe" is the quick judgment center. When alcohol is put into the brain, it bothers and hinders the ability to use accurate judgments. Many vehicle accidents occur because of the minimization of accurate judgment. Therefore, the cerebellum and the frontal lobes are being distracted when trying to make a driving task a complete success. When too much alcohol gets inside the brain, the cerebellum (limb controller) and the frontal lobes (judgment authorizer) are just a few effected areas of the brain's system. Not only are those two brain components under the influence of alcohol, but also, from the help of the brainstem this drug is swallowed into the body.

We have seen many things happen to people when they have consumed too much alcohol. A normal walk would be for a person to walk on a straight line. But when too much alcohol makes a contact with the brain, a staggering walk will be earned. It becomes hard to walk on a straight line, after alcohol has the brain under its influence. The cerebellum, which controls the balancing in a person's walk, is being persuasively afflicted at that particular time.

Once the limbic system becomes addicted to alcohol, it will hunger for liquor as if it is food. Not only does the limbic system awaken hunger, but also, it arouses your thirst as well. Once you become addicted to alcohol, your brain's limbic system will thirst after it, rather than healthy water. After becoming addicted to alcohol, however, in a short time, the body and the brain will become depressed if alcohol or liquor has not been poured into it.

Cigarettes & Coffee- I bet all users of cigarettes and coffee don't want me to expose facts about these mentally craved products. If I had left out the two legal and most craved products, this chapter would have been lacking. This chapter would not be a fulfilled chapter, if I had left out the world's most highly craved products.

Although, these two products (cigarettes & coffee) are cheapest chemicals to purchase, yet, they are rich in addictions. Cigarettes and coffee both performs great works of negativity within the brain. Cigarettes are high in nicotine, and coffee is filled with caffeine.

Let me explain and define nicotine for you, so that you will get a better understanding of what you are putting inside your brain and body. From study; Nicotine is first an oily substance found in tobacco leaves, and it acts as a stimulant, which contributes to addictions. Nicotine is a substance that works in the brain.

Nicotine, which is made from the tobacco leaves, is also used as an insecticide. Insecticide and alkaloid both are put into cans, that we call "bug spray". In other words, insecticide and alkaloid is used to kill insects. Well, nicotine, which has insecticide ingredients, is a part of the formula when making cigarettes.

Insecticide, which is in all cigarettes, is being inhaled by humans today. Humans are actually inhaling bug killer (insecticide) into their brain, and they know it not. If insecticide is used to kill the lives of insects; then what do you think it will do unto the brain. Your brain and insects both have the same ending results in life, when it has been touched by insecticide.

When you spray insecticide on an insect, the bug usually never dies right away. It usually dies minutes or hours later. In the same sense, when you inhale insecticide (cigarettes), the brain does not die immediately. But years later; the brain will experience a growth of mental organ decaying, which will soon lead to a sickness unto death. We as a people, we really need to be careful about substances that are put together by human hands.

When a person becomes addicted to cigarettes, he or she might be led to try other mind alternating chemicals, too. One chemical addiction opens the door for another chemical addiction. Just as a person can "oops", slip and fall on a wet floor, a person can "oops", slip, and fall into another chemical addiction. Not only does smoking cigarettes lead people to other chemical active products, however, cigarettes have destroyed the mental minds of many people over the past number of years.

Cigarettes have cleverly killed more than 100,000 people in one year. Wow, that is a great number of brains being sent to the graveyard because of smoking cigarettes. Wow, that is a great number of brains becoming sick, and then suddenly appearing in a rectangular box during a funeral session.

As people smoke cigarettes for lengths of time, they soon inherit a rough cough. The brainstem is the breathing operator, and it is falling into contamination, because of smoking of cigarettes. I sat and watched a person cough for approximately 5 minutes, trying to re-gain normal breathing. Once the normal breathing came back, he put the cigarette right back to the mouth, and inhaled it again. The brainstem, which gives life, is slowly being destroyed, but the cigarette user knows it not.

Many people have actually smoked cigarettes their entire lives. Although, many people have begun smoking cigarettes in their teen years, however, if you are over the age of 40 and still smoking, that's practically your entire life in which inhaling nicotine has been in action.

It is crazy because many people can be on their deathbeds, and continue to smoke cigarettes. Can you imagine a person on his or her deathbed, and crying out, "I need a cigarette"! You would think that a person in the hospital would have the mental empowerment to flee from the physical activity of smoking cigarette. However, the chemical addictions that the brain has become captivate to, will keep the erg and desire to smoke cigarettes, even while lying on a deathbed.

People do not believe that smoking cigarettes will lead their bodies to experiencing future illnesses. As people, for years, we have overlooked the negative effects cigarettes cause. People often hear about sickness and diseases that smoking cigarettes can plague the body with, but they smoke them anyway. Everyone thinks he or she is hidden from illnesses created by smoking cigarettes. Nevertheless, if people continue plaguing their brain with cigarettes, their brain will unexpectedly receive a reward, which will be a mental illness.

The law does not force people to refrain themselves from smoking cigarettes. Therefore, anyone can purchase as much as he or she desires. However, the brain has a law against cigarettes. The brain's law is: "neither nicotine nor caffeine I need". The only stimulant the brain needs is its maker, and that is God. Nevertheless, we disobey our conscious center and cause our bodies to experience the negative habits cigarettes creates.

Most cigarette addictions begin after the age of 13. Most coffee addictions begin after the age of 19. That is just my own personal assumption. One addiction (cigarettes) comes from teen stress and ignorance, while the other addiction (coffee) comes from not having proper brain needed rest.

Okay, I have a question for you. Is there an answer for your stress problems, and your non-resting habits? There has to be another solution besides shoving caffeine and nicotine in your head to bring about a mode of "relaxation".

Cigarettes are substances that have the ability to cause premature death to come into the user's life. In other words, a cigarette smoker can face death before it is truly his or her time to die. Just as a woman can have a baby earlier than 9 months, a person can die before his or her time by smoking cigarettes. Every person, who has died on the count of smoking cigarettes, has died from an illness that found its way into the organs of the head.

Usually, cancer is the illness that comes from smoking cigarettes. When such an illness has found its way into the body, the individual is actually feeling the motions of death. Although, no one really knows that death can be felt, however, when a recorded sickness has attached itself to body, if death is with it, then death is being felt. Have you ever heard anyone say, "I felt myself dying"? It is so true that chemical usage and abuse will force a person's life to experience a death that can be physically felt, and emotionally aware of.

Every time people purchase cigarettes, they have just bought their own personal killer. If you go to a store, and buy a pack of cigarettes, you have willingly purchased for yourself, a pack of brain killers. You have actually walked or drove to the store and bought 20 death sticks. Therefore, for you, it only costs less than 10 dollars to start the process of self-destroying your own brain and body. This killer (cigarettes) does not have to stalk you, nor follow you down the yellow brick road, because you, on your own went to the store and purchased it. With agreement from your mind, you have just purchased a three -inch (cigarette size) murderer. Remember, every time you smoke cigarettes, you are inhaling an inner being illness creator.

Cocaine- is produced from the leaves of the coca plant. Cocaine grows out of the ground, just like marijuana and heroin do.

Cocaine was once used as a numbing to certain areas of the body. If cocaine is shot into the body with a needle, or put on the tongue, it will numb that touched area within seconds.

The lobes in the brain that deals with touch are the parietal lobes. Once cocaine has caused a part of a person's body to feel numb, the parietal lobes in the brain have been hit. Cocaine, by its cunning power, will take the sense of touch from its users.

There are three ways cocaine can be put into the body. The first way to utilize this drug is to snort it through the nostril, which is a work done by the brainstem, because inhaling is being performed. The second way to use this drug is to inhale and exhale it through the mouth, which is the brainstem job again. The third way to activate this drug is to use a syringe and inject into the bloody veins, which the hands controller does.

People who put cocaine in their brain and body often times experience nervousness and paranoia. Nervousness and paranoia are attached to emotions (frontal lobe work). After cocaine has traveled through a person's emotion and paranoia center, it has that individual's feeling in its crafty power.

Cocaine will cause its users to walk up and down the streets night and day. All during the day, cocaine users will not take a bite to eat. Once the limbic system becomes addicted to cocaine, it will ignore the need for food. Cocaine will become the limbic system's new food for flavor. The appetite for food will not be the limbic systems satisfaction, because cocaine will. However, in a short period of time, the brain cells, neurons, cerebellum, cerebrum, hemispheres (left and right), the four lobes, brainstem, and memory, will all be controlled and demolished by this chemical control substance.

Inhalants- are substances that can only be inhaled. As a person inhales inhalants, vapors of air chemicals dashes into the brain. Inhalants come in a variety of products, such as gasoline, cosmetic sprays, household cleaning products, paint thinner, nail polish remover, and many other products.

When inhaling this drug into the brain, it starts to operate immediately. It is believed that inhalants cloud up the entire brain after inhaling it. Since the brainstem does the inhaling, it performs when this drug is used. Therefore, inhalant users are brutally murdering their own brainstem activity. If you have willingly submitted to inhaling the product, then you have willingly submitted to destroying your own brain's organs.

Years ago, it has been recorded that close to 10, 000 people have been led to visit the local hospital because of inhalant usage. In a one-year span, more than 100 inhalant users have died due to its usage. Of course, that's in one city and state. I suppose the vapor and ingredients from this drug choked the brainstem (breathing regulator), and death became the user's reward.

It is said that inhalants will destroy learning ability, memory, and cleverly distract problem-solving skills. Well, short-term, procedural, and declarative memory will be destroyed after long periods of using inhalants. Since the frontal lobes deal with our problem-solving skills, that section of the brain is being affected during every inhalant usage.

When people first try drugs, they have persuaded their selves to do it. It's a mental persuasion thing. As people continue using drugs, they do not realize a tolerance level is soon created. Meaning, when you once were satisfied with smoking one joint, you will be led to smoke six for the same psychological effect. You will never reach a level satisfaction. You can already be high as a kite, but you will still desire to puff-puff pass.

From the information I have written unto you concerning drugs and their power, now we understand why people are performing so many law-breaking deeds. Now we know why wickedness is on the up rise in our land and community. It is all because of the way drugs alerts and controls the brain and body. Well, maybe I should say, "wickedness is so exalted, because of what drug intoxicants do to the thinking system of the brain". If people do not use drugs, their cerebrum will not think about committing a murder. If people do not put drugs into their thinking processor, then thoughts of murdering will not be a consideration. Nor will the cerebellum control the hand to pull the trigger.

All drugs are like wicked dice; once a person put drugs into the brain and body, the ingredients from that chemical-controlled substance roll throughout the anatomy, and soon the lucky 7 will soon be hit. Once a person has been killed, due to drug affiliation, the lucky number 7 have just been rolled. Eventually, the gambler's dice will hit the number 7, and eventually, the drug user will be hit with the penalty of death.

Once drugs effectively leak its negative habits into your life, it already has its unseen grip on your brain and body. Well, after you have finished reading this nonfiction story, you will learn the true plan of drugs.

SAY NO TO DRUGS, AND YES TO THE LIVING OF YOUR BRAIN!

Chapter 6

STAYING IN SCHOOL, AND MY BRAIN'S FIRST DRUG EXPERIENCE

Now you are about to see if chapter 4 (The Intelligent Human Brain) and chapter 5 (Drugs Controlling The Intelligent Human Brain) is true information. I suppose it can be said, "Brian Irons is the test dummy" God used to alert a world of people that such a hurting experience can happen, due to becoming addicted to drugs. I believe, I am the person who has the testimony, which will reveal unto the world that drugs can manipulate, influence, control, and destroy hopes and smash dreams. Not only that, but I am the person who was used to show the world that wickedness is associated with drugs. It is time for me to get to the tangible point of why I call this particular nonfiction story, <u>I Did Not Know.</u>

After basketball practice was over, it was time for the players and me to go home. Practice lasted for a few of hours, and our bodies were tired. The bus was filled with nothing but young black high school basketball players. We all lived in the city of St. Louis where the streets are rough.

Many times, on the activity bus, the basketball players smoked marijuana. Lighters, cigarette papers, and everything needed to smoke marijuana was on the activity bus. The more people on the bus that smoked marijuana is the reason why everything smoked marijuana was here. If one person did not have a lighter, someone else did. Probably, 2 to 3 times out of the week, the players smoked marijuana on the activity bus.

Soon, the basketball players began asking me to take a puff of the weed. After being asked, my brain immediately compelled my mouth to say, "No, that's ok". The players asked me to take a hit of the marijuana on several occasions. Each time I was asked, my brain would control my mouth to say, "No, that ok". It did not take more than 2 seconds to decide if I wanted to participate in this marijuana-smoking event.

The limbic system (a brainworker), which is my fear regulator, did what God created it to do. In fear, my limbic system rejected participating in smoking marijuana. Although, the cerebrum (the thinker in my head) made the decision to say no. However, the limbic system played a key role as well. People turn down many things because of fear. My limbic system showed its God given power, by elevating me to fear smoking marijuana.

I did not have a thorough understanding why the players inhaled marijuana into their bodies anyway. Therefore, the desire to smoke marijuana was not even a chance of thought. Smoke it for what? My dream in life is to become a professional athlete. To me, it was useless and meaningless to inhale and smoke anything. My health is far most important. Also, I am dreaming of showing my talents and skills to the world of sport viewers.

Smoking marijuana in high school was the grand performance to do. Most of my high school friends were addicted to marijuana. I believe, their limbic system (the appetite arouser also) was addicted to the flavor of marijuana, because they smoke it very often. I suppose not one player was thinking about the health of the body. To them, it was all about the mental rush marijuana provided.

One day, as the basketball players and I were traveling home, it happened. The fellows (team players) asked me again saying, "Irons" take a small hit of the marijuana. This time, I gave in. I extended out my hands, and did grab a hold onto that joint. I suppose, I finally empowered my mind to agree in participating in inhaling marijuana. I took two willing puffs. After so many seconds passed by, I replied, "I don't feel anything". Then the players said, "wait for a minute, then it'll kick in'.

Well, about 3 to 4 minutes later, the operating chemicals from marijuana leaked into my entire head. The chemicals hit me unexpectedly. While this marijuana was operating in my head, it made me laugh until I exited the bus.

Marijuana was the first street chemical that enter into my anatomy. I actually caused my brain to decide on saying yes to smoking marijuana. As of now, during high school, the door of drugs has just opened in my life. Not only that, but my feet are about to walk down a pathway that only leads to ignorance.

The uncontrollable laughter was the first effect marijuana brought into my mental existence. While I was laughing, the players were laughing at me. The players knew this was my first time getting "high" from a chemical control substance. As they observed how silly I became, while this drug was operating in my anatomy, I became the comedy show of the hour. Every small reaction performed by me was entertaining to them all. Nevertheless, my brain had been kidnapped from mental freedom to a condition of being controlled by a chemical substance, and <u>I Did Not Know</u> it.

Indeed, my brain has truly been kidnapped. Just as a kidnapper captures and abducts a child and takes the infant away from his or her known surroundings, my brain has been abducted in the very same like manner. Kidnap means to captivate someone and hold him or her as a living hostage. Seizing a person and taking the individual against his or her "will" is called, kidnap.

Kidnapping or abducting someone is against the law. Although, I was not kidnapped by a human being, my mind has been abducted by marijuana. My life is about to be taken forcefully on tours of negativity. My life is about to go to places which I never intended for it to go. Hell, and back is where I am about to go. My brain is about to travel on an ignorant mission; and I have no idea where I'm going, nor do I know what is about to happen next.

My brain became captivated to marijuana's pleasure. Marijuana imprisoned my brain. Therefore, I am using the term "kidnapped" because my brain had been taken out of freedom. Although, I was not physically snatched by a person, however, my brain had been taken from the norm.

If marijuana is on the school bus, then wickedness is on the school bus as well. Wherever there are drugs, wickedness is always the reason why it is in the presence. Wherever there is wickedness, a law or two has been broken. Therefore, every person who smokes marijuana on the activity bus is handling a substance that gives birth to wickedness.

Not only am I a breaking the law, but also, I have performed a deed of wickedness, too. Not only did I inhale a substance that is against the law, but also, I inhaled the seed of wickedness into my anatomy. Since a drug is now in my brain, wickedness is in it as well. As of now, my brain has tasted a substance that exposes a person's life to wickedness. Wickedness (marijuana) I saw lying on the ground in the projects, and the same substance can now be found inside of me.

1st John, chapter 2: 16- for ALL that is in the world; the lust of the flesh, and the lust of the eyes, and the pride of life.

When I finally decided to smoke marijuana, it was something within me that empowered me to do it. It is almost like having sex for the first time. Once a person has sex for the first time, his or her mind had been empowered to do it. That is exactly how I felt when I first tried marijuana. My brain's high intellectual censor (the cerebrum- the brain's thinking member) was lifting up itself and persuading my mouth to say, "No" to inhaling marijuana. However, as I continued viewing the team players smoking marijuana, my mind obviously said, "try it one day". Moreover, I did.

My flesh obviously lusted for that same feeling the players had. My flesh desired to have that drug encountering experience, too. My eyes viewed the amusement the team was having after smoking marijuana, and my flesh eagerly wanted to become a partaker. No matter how long the basketball players have been inhaling marijuana into their brains, whatever it was that influenced them to try it for the very first time, was the same force that persuaded me. I am sure that, when they first tried drugs, they watched someone intake dope, too. Nevertheless, by my first drug usage experience, I immediately became one of them. I once used to look down on these marijuana smokers, but now, I have actually become their equal. Some of these guys have been smoking marijuana for years. Although this is my first time, I am still looked upon as one of them.

Just that fast and just that quick, my brain and body had been cunningly exposed to the evil scheme of marijuana. In the twinkling of an eye, in the blinking of a moment, my brain and body was wrapped up in the magical ways of this chemical controlled substance. I am sure I've done many evil deeds before this, however, from my first substance usage experience; I have actually met the author of wickedness (marijuana). Yes, the author of wickedness, which is marijuana, is now operating in my life. From the first few puffs of the joint (weed), I have given my life and brain to the power of dope and wickedness, and <u>I Did Not Know</u> it.

After inhaling weed into my brain, my body became impure from the first contact. This entire drug process became active, because of the lust of my flesh, and the lust of my eyes. Pride had not visibly kicked in yet, but soon, it is going to break into my life, and set me up for the righteous visitation of God's judgment. Marijuana has visited me, and God's judgment is soon to visit me, too. So here I am, with a chemical controlled substance operating inside of my brain and body. Not only have I just been exposed to drugs, but also, God's anger is after me, and

<u>I Did Not Know</u> it.

When I first smoked "marijuana", I became disobedient unto three rules. First, I became disobedient unto the laws of God, because it is against the law to have drugs in my possession. Although, I am not the person who brought marijuana on the bus, however, as soon as my hand touched this drug, I became disobedient to the laws of God. Secondly, I became disobedient to my parents counseling, because they verbally told me to stay far away from people who use drugs, and if offered, "walk away". Third, I became disobedient to my brain's conscience center, because my mind told me on several occasions not to smoke the weed.

Therefore, when I first smoked marijuana, I disobeyed the cry of my brain's conscience center. Whether I realize it or not, my conscience center cried and cried from within not to put dope in it, but I did anyway. The brain is so intelligent, on it's on, it knows what is good, and what is not so good for it.

To all drug users, when any drug has been used, it was done through an act of disobedience. Teenagers as well as adults have overstepped or disobeyed their parents counseling, and their mental God created fear. No person has ever used a chemical controlled substance, without his or her brain displaying a percentage of fear. Every human being that has ever tried drugs, before trying it, a movement of mental fear was active first. Actually, when I first tried marijuana, I disobeyed every lobe and organ in my human brain.

I wonder how my parents are going to feel; if or when they find out their teenage son is inhaling marijuana. My parents prepared the time to tell me about drugs being bad for the body. My parents gave me talks and talks about staying away from drugs. Yet, here I am inhaling weed into my brain. Although, my parents have spoken unto me saying, "drugs will kill", which I did believe, but nevertheless, *the lust of the eyes, and the lust of the flesh* won this battle. Nevertheless, I needed help becoming free from this chemical control substance even right now, but <u>I Did Not Know</u> it.

Although the basketball players offered me the dope, it was my own personal will to accept it. I am the individual to take the blame for participating in this puff-puff pass event. When the dope had been offered unto me, it became my own judgment to take part in this activity or not. Since I've inhaled marijuana into my brain, my mental status has truly become contaminated. My brain immediately went from not knowing what marijuana feels like, to effectively experiencing its amusement, and its negativity.

Whether I realize it or not, I have actually introduced my brain and life to a different world. My physical being is still on earth, but my mental body is located on Mars. I was 14 years old, still a young boy, so <u>I Did Not Know</u> that I had just exposed my life to a completely new style of living. Actually, I am a changed man as of now, because of putting this chemical into my life. Although I am still the same person, however, deep down inside, I became a different being.

I must confess, "I did enjoy inhaling and smoking weed", because of the inner feelings it "charged" within me. I became so addicted to this plant called, "marijuana" that I never sought the chance or the opportunity to rescue my brain from its damaging power. My brain spent more time trying to find ways to get high, than it did trying to find a technique to be freed from it.

If I had not liked nor enjoyed the feeling marijuana produced within my brain, I would have been coaxing myself to cease or discontinue using it. My days of seeking to intake marijuana would have been days seeking to uproot the seed of this addiction out of me. Finding a way to refrain myself from applying this substance into my brain, would have been my global authorized deed. However, nevertheless, I enjoyed the feeling; therefore, I continued using and directing marijuana into my brain. It seemed as if I was pulled by some unknown power, which kept me actively replenishing this chemical craved substance. So here I am, a freshman in high school living with a brain that has become addicted to marijuana.

Now that I have marihuana in my brain, my physical limbs have been hired to do works of evil. Wickedness is now in my brain and body; therefore, it has permission to put me to work according to its own evil pleasure and purpose.

Wickedness will empower me to do tasks of evil to fulfill its demonic desires. Just as any drug does not operate until it is put in the brain, well, wickedness does not work until a person has been hired to do evil. Wickedness is the boss, and all its employees are commanded to do actions of evil. Nevertheless, just by smoking marijuana, I have been hired to perform at a position to do evil, and I Did Not Know it.

People and even myself have absolutely seen from watching digital television how chemical control substances destroy lives. I did have a great level of fear within me before trying marijuana. I guess from repeatedly observing the basketball players inhale marijuana into their bodies, I reckoned that it could not be that injurious. Once I caused my brainstem to immediately participate in inhaling marijuana, every bad spoken word about it departed from my mind. From my first usage of marijuana, all the counseling that my "declarative memory" once retained had been blotted out. My brain now has a new fact about marijuana, which is, how good it truly feels. The dangerous and horrifying information I have heard concerning drugs have been overridden, by the fascinating feelings my brain and body had been exposed too. My brain no longer believes drugs kills; it now believes drugs will make you feel good.

Maybe parents should properly instruct, and counsel their children about the drug's addiction, and the controlling force drugs have. Well, not too many of us are knowledgeable about the brain and body, therefore, we do not teach on this issue.

I smoked marijuana through my brainstem my entire high school career. Smoking marijuana became a driven escort of guidance during my high school days. Things became so hectic; I began skipping school and classes. Most of the times, I skipped school and classes just to get "high" with a friend or two. Sometimes, after smoking marijuana at school, I would not attend any classes. I would rather walk through the halls, and interrupt classes while they were in session. Skipping classes and bothering other classes were two ignorant performances I did while under the influence of marijuana. Believe me, it is so true, because I was mentally persuaded to do stupid things such as that.

As years passed by, dropping out of high school was heavily in my thoughts. I was having deep thoughts about not needing school academics in my personal life. My mind was thinking that I have a chance to become a pro-basketball player, so why do I need school? Since I am going to be a pro basketball star, I do not need the highest achievement award in education.

Take heed to this quote, which speaks about the painting of a house. A person owned a house, and the color of the entire house was white. One day, the property owner decided to paint the entire house light blue. That he did. Since the house was once white and now light blue, a new color has now been applied.

After smoking marijuana, that painting of the house process became my mind's procedure. My normal ways of thinking and reasoning had been overlapped by the persuasion of marijuana. Therefore, I will never know, if I wanted to drop out of high school from a normal thought mode or not, because marijuana was in my thinking system (cerebrum) and my reasoning worker (frontal lobes). Eighty five percent of teenagers, who did not earn their high school diploma, probably had drugs operating in their thinking system.

Marijuana is in my brain cleverly rambling from one component to the next. When any drug is inhaled into the brain, the dope becomes the brain's mentor and or tutor. Drugs will actually teach the brain how to become addicted. In other words, when drugs are put into the brain, they become your director and or counselor. Do not allow drugs to overlap your brain's normal ways of performance. God created the brain to do one thing, and that is to work on it's on without any lawbreaking help. The brain is made and created by God to work for Him.

During high school, I attended it more than four years. I was a complete clown in high school. I do consider myself an average student, but my grades proved otherwise. Well, I must not leave out the fact that, probably every report card period, there was an F or two printed on it. The classes I received bad grades in were classes I acted a complete "nut". Although, I did more than four years in high school, I was far from being, "dumb". Nevertheless, once I first started smoking marijuana that was the dumbest decision I could have ever made.

I had to go back to school to take up a summer course just to accommodate for the unearned credits. I had to go back to school for an extra semester. My mother was the reason why I completed high school. She was not supporting nor approving me dropping out oof school. My mother definitely wanted to see all of her children at least earn their high school diplomas, if nothing else.

Now that I have my high school diploma, it does feel good to have it nearby. Having my high school graduation achievement award is somewhat satisfying to my inner being. Just having it at home sitting on the shelf makes me proud.

If I ever decide to further my education by attending college, I will not have to waste time studying for a G.E.D... A high school diploma or a G.E.D. must already be in your possession, before being accepted to become a college student.

No matter how many years a person strays from school, a high school diploma gives you the ability to enroll in college immediately. Therefore, I advise all youths of any nationality to at least earn that high school diploma. Trust me; there "WILL" come a moment in your life that you will consider re-registering for school (college).

Most of times, people are urged or persuaded to go back to school to better their financial status. 85% of the people in the world return to school (college), just to escape the mental pain of having financial lack. Some people go back to school to better their financial status, just so they can do greater things for their children. Therefore, people of the earth, stay away from drugs, stay in school, and collect as much educational information as you possibly can.

In order for an earthly being to have a decent living, that individual will need to be able to read and write, which are activities learned in school. Learning how to read and write will help you to understand documents and contracts you sign your signature on. While learning how to read and write, you are preparing yourself for mental success, and less mental frustration. If a person does not learn how to read and write in his own native language, life on earth is going to be rough. Everyone needs to be able to read words on documents, and write complete sentences. How can you get a job, if you do not know how to read the application? So, stay in school, and as they say, "Learn the golden rule".

I've seen many foreigners in the U.S.A. These people are called foreigners, because the U.S.A. is not their home country. Some came to the U.S.A. seeking to live their lives on this side of the world. Many foreigners, who came to the USA, came unprepared. They didn't know how to read nor write in English. If documents aren't written in their foreign language, they are lost and have no adequate understanding. If they cannot read the English translation, then it is most likely they can't write it neither.

People who are from the USA will try to get over on the unlearned foreigner. When the opportune chance comes, that USA citizen will plot to do mischief. I hope a foreigner does not cross the pathway of people who will try to take advantage. However, since the world is full of ongoing wickedness, there's a chance someone has already plotted an evil work on a foreigner.

Also, little children take the time to learn mathematics. If nothing else, learn your basic math. Adding, subtraction, multiplying, and dividing will always be needed. Somehow, someway, math is going to approach you.

Many people hate mathematics. They can't dodge it, nor can they run from it. When you earn your cash, you need to know how to count it properly. If you can't count numbers correctly, your boss, or whoever finds out, will cheat you out of your money. Remember, there are many people in the world whose minds are operating in deceit and wickedness, and humankind will cheat you whenever they get the opportune chance.

Let me put it all together; mathematics, reading, writing, and home economics are considered basic essentials for survival. Those four subjects (math, reading, writing, home economics) are daily necessities you need, when trying to maintain an average living. Those subjects (math, reading, writing, and economics) are topics you will constantly learn all through high school. Actually, those subjects are learned in grade school, but high school teaches at advance levels.

We all need to know the basics in life, so stay in school and learn how to read words, write with understanding, and add and subtract numbers. When you learn those things, that information will descend into the brain's center called, "Declarative Memory". There will be things that your declarative memory will probably let go, however, when you learn how to read, write, add, subtract, and basic home economics, I guarantee you, you will never forget how to operate those four functions in life.

Although, I smoke and inhale marijuana throughout my high school career, I did learn a subject or two (actually more than 2). I learned my basic reading, writing skills, math and home economic skills. Right now today, I am living off those four subjects I learned in high school. I have not been in school for years, but those 4 subjects I learned in school are still with me. Therefore, here I am, years later, living from the teachings I learned in school. Although, this book might have a few errors in it, but as you can see, I learned and kept enough English/Grammar skills in my declarative memory to write a decent book. I am so glad that I learned the basic eight parts of speech. Nevertheless, I put marihuana into my educational background.

You know what? Just by writing the above paragraphs, I have caused hundredths of people to stay in school. That is my job, through writing, to encourage you all. This entire book might not teach you everything, but if one paragraph encourages you not to give up and stay focused, then my book has served its purpose. Now that you are reading this book, that means, you have learned the writing is English translation. Keep up the good work, and keep a positive attitude in life.

We fell to realize that education and God are very important while living on the earth. Never will I try to hinder you from getting an education, because without it, life will be so depressing. But God is more important than your earthly education. While reading this book, it will teach you why God is needed more than anything else.

When you are done reading this miraculous story, you will receive much knowledge to teach your children concerning the works of drugs, and the operation of the brain. The written words in my book, which speaks about my life's experiences, are recorded for your learning. Learn from it, and teach your children. Since most of us have already messed up decades of our lives, let's seek to better the next generation.

Chapter 7

SEARCHING FOR EMPLOYMENT AND STILL ADDICTED татроO DRUGS

My high school diploma is at the school waiting to be picked up. I drove my mother's car to the school to pick up my high school reward (diploma). My heart began rejoicing. While driving on the highway, I began talking to myself… "Thank you Lord for this high school diploma my hands are about to handle". It felt good to pick up something I earned.

It was a rough high school journey, but success has been fulfilled. It was rough, because I did not obey school rules, nor did I obey the law. Drugs caused me to hit many bumps on this journey, but I kept on rolling, and victory is now mine. The name Brian Irons is printed on a real high school diploma.

As I was driving down the highway to pick up my high school diploma, I inhaled the flavor of marijuana into my anatomy. By now, my brain is seriously addicted to this mind-alternating substance. As of now, for four and a half years, my life has been given over to marijuana. There I was, in my mother's car, driving down the highway high as a kite.

I received my high school diploma at the age of 19. I was schedule to receive it at 18, but I allowed drugs to consume many hours of my school time. Time is precious. If nothing else is based on time, you can believe that education is.

My high school days have now ended. Finding a job to earn a few dollars is my goal. I realize money is exceedingly necessary and important in our society and world. Without cash, a person will not be able to buy nice materials and products from the local department store. If something is free, in most stores, you can believe it is a sample size product for the company's benefit. Everything cost, and everything has been tagged with a price. Any materials you and I desire to own in life is stamped with a price. Therefore, I must proceed in life, by moving forward, and searching for employment.

I went out into the world and walked into a couple of business places. While being inside of these business places, I filled out applications. Thank God, I already knew how to read and write. Since I already knew how to read and write, I was able to fill out applications with a decent understanding. Yeah, the reading and writing that I learned in school is now paying off today.

While searching for employment, I did find an occupation. Someone hired a drug head like me. Of course, the boss knows nothing about my chemical usage. I did not have a criminal record; therefore, if the boss checks up on my history, my records will show nothing. Now that I have employment, I'll be earning a few dollars to put into my pockets. I am soon to receive an earned income or a financial payment. If I've worked for it, I must be paid for my services done.

This job is a restaurant business. This restaurant is located a few blocks away from the old neighborhood where I once lived. I am not talking about the neighborhood I grew up in as a child. This neighborhood is not in the projects.

At this time, my family moved toward the South City of St. Louis. Therefore, I met new friends, and my job was located five blocks from our hangout spot.

At this job, my duties were to cleanse and stack the dishes in racks. For 4 to 5 hours, Monday through Saturday, I washed the dishes.

Minimum wages is my hourly pay, which is $3.14. Of course, I did not want a minimum wage paying job, but I was led to do what I had to do. If this job requires washing and stacking dishes, then that's just what I'll do. Although, I did not want a job that started paying minimum wages, however, since I did not continue my education, I was forced to settle for whatever employment came first. Therefore, I hung in there, and took care of the dish room.

Since my high school diploma does not have specific qualification skills attached to it, walk on jobs, which did not require a certain skill is what I found. A high school diploma does not have any additional personal academic skill award printed on it. Although, a high school diploma is great to have, when seeking for high paying job positions, your search is widely limited. However, if you earn a college degree, your starting pay will be beyond minimum wages.

If your degree requires that you be worth a starting pay of $19 an hour, the company that hires you, must abide in the area of payment. The business must pay you the salary of what your degree is worth. However, there might be companies in your degree field that may want to start you at a couple dollars less. You might negotiate and accept that, or you might go and apply somewhere else, but the decision is all yours. Although, your college degree might require beginning payment at $19 an hour, however, making $17.50 is a nice bargain.

There is nothing like being in control of your own financial living. You took your brain through college, and became a winner by earning that degree. From all the mental trials and stress your brain went through, it deserves it's worth. By earning your degree, you deserve the right to make your own financial deals and decisions. But me, my power is limited, because I only have a high school diploma. Hey, do not get me wrong, because having a high school diploma can get you a decent job. But as I said before, with a high school diploma, your job search for high beginners pay is widely limited.

I cannot walk into a pharmacy store with the intent on applying for a job position. The doctor or manager or front desk clerk will ask, "Do you have a degree in Pharmacy". On the other hand, the front desk clerk might ask, "Do you have the minimum required hours in medicine training? Well, for me, since I have no continuing educational skills, or the required experience needed for the RN position, 9 times out of 10, filling out an application to be a RN would be a waste of time. They would not waste time handing me an application. By me having no degree, or hands on training, jobs that require a certain skill level, I became highly limited to applying for.

But hey, people get lucky all the time. Some people are hired at positions that require a certain educational background without even having the hours of training.

Now a day, if you want the job of your choice, you must stay in school, and earn that degree. Why not work for the rest of your life, at the job of your choice? You went to college for 4 years, and earned that degree, so go ahead and retire there. After 10 or 15 years of working there, you might become tired and bored, but think about the next promotion, and retirement benefits. It is not about being bored or tired, or having fun, it is all about God and your financial future.

My mom and dad both have been working at the same job for more than 30 years. I am sure there has been many times they wanted to give up and work somewhere else. But they hung in there, and thought about their kids, and the next year's promotion.

The job I been hired to work for payment plan is weekly. Earning cash once a week was cool, but the minimum wage pay was very weak.

After purchasing a pair of casual jeans or tennis shoes, and a bag of marijuana, my pockets became flat and empty. Oh yeah, I had to purchase my brain some marijuana, because it craved it. Inhaling marijuana throughout my high school career caused a heavy addiction to this chemical. My limbic system has been hungering for marijuana for a very long time. Every pay period, I bought a great number of Fred Quickie joints.

Here I am working at this restaurant, and marijuana is still working in my brain. If my brain did not get its food (marijuana), life would have been pathetically boring. Marijuana tricked my brain to believing in such a thing. It seems like my entire life is focused on the mental actions and pleasures marijuana provided.

Weed cunningly persuaded my friends and I into believing that marijuana brought all the "fun" into our presence. The power from marijuana had caused us all to believe, "if we didn't smoke weed, there will be no joy". We all inhaled weed, for the purpose of fun. To believe in such a thing, my friends and I are ignorant individuals. I'm an idiot, my friends are idiots, and every marijuana user is an idiot too. If you are a weed smoker, you are automatically a member of the idiot crew. Hello there, my name is Brian Irons, and I am an idiot; and who are you?

Every friend of mine smoked marijuana throughout their entire high school career. 75% of my friends dropped out of high school, and you probably know the reason why. Every friend who dropped out were quick marijuana smokers.

Even people on my job brains were addicted to drugs. Always, an employer yelled out, "I need to smoke something". The entire shift of workers had a chemical addiction of some sort operating in their brains.

One day, the restaurant was open to the public. One of the employees and I was smoking marijuana in the basement. The owner of the restaurant became suspicious about the scent that filled the air. Just as children smell the scent of weed in the home when the parents smoke it, and then become suspicious, my boss became suspicious in her place of business. The difference from children and my boss is the fact that, my boss knows exactly what the aroma is, but children do not. Therefore, the boss confronted us, and asked, "Are you young men smoking pot in my restaurant"? Of course, my friend and I nervously lied and said "no". We told the boss that some people were sitting on the back steps near the basement door of the restaurant smoking marijuana, and the scent blew inside the building from the traveling wind. The boss replied, "If I find out you guys are smoking marijuana on my property, I am going to fire the both of you".

Already, as you can see, I have been led or forced to lie about my marijuana usage. Marijuana almost caused me to lose my first job. If the boss had fired me because of drug usage, I would have felt very stupid. Nevertheless, there was not a day on the job, that my brain was not over flooded with marijuana's formula.

All the time, I thought about how I should be earning a check for playing professional league sports, not being financially rewarded for washing dishes. I should right now be in college playing basketball, creating moves on the court damaging the opposing athletes. By now, I should be on my way to play professional sports, but yet, here am being a professional weed smoker.

I thought about the professional talents and skills I still have. Sometimes, within myself, I still believed I have the chance to play professional basketball. However, since I'm not in college playing basketball, time is quickly winding down. I am still young, and I am thinking about going to college. Every time I thought about going back to school, I never move a limb towards doing so. Marijuana had me content with a living that will probably not take me far in life.

Since I didn't graduate on time, and no basketball scholarships were offered, I thought I messed up, and couldn't play ball for a college.

Since I made my high school years so hectic, my brain was not thinking about going back to school. I could not bear to think about carrying books and papers, and attending classes again. If you make your high school years hard, your brain will not think about continuing education.

Anyway, back to my employment. After a while, my mind became exhausted with this minimum wage paying job. So, I quit. Not only did I suddenly cease from working at this job, but also, I crept out the back door when I was out of the boss's sight. The restaurant was still in operation, meaning, customers were eating, and the dirty dishes needed to be cleansed. I walked out of this restaurant while the used dishes were being carried to the cleaning room. I did not care; I just wanted to be free from the sounds of stacking dishes. My friend, who was my coworker in the dish room, had to wash all of those piled up dishes by his lonesome self. I ran out on the dishes, and I ran out on my friend too. Hey, my good buddy, J, sorry I walked out and left you to wash all those dishes by yourself.

After I had ceased working at my first job, I soon began searching for another occupation. At least, I did have enough sense to remain active in searching for jobs. Besides, I needed to earn money, so I could feed my brain the substance it craved and longed for. Therefore, I am on a high pursuit searching for another job.

One day, I found another job. This job also was a restaurant food chain operation. As I said before, since I did not have any certified skills or advanced educational certificate achievement, walk in jobs were my primary leads. At this job, just like my last job, washing the dishes was my duty.

I worked at this job for a total of 8 months. My first job only lasted for 4 months. At this new job, the payment period was every two weeks. Monday through Friday, I worked 6 to 8 hours a day. My hourly payment was minimum wages. So I guess you know I was not making a whole lot of money. However, I was still able to buy my brain what it craved (marijuana) and a pair of Jordan's from time to time.

While working at this job, many times, I thought about my sport career. I began to realize that I really messed up my chance to have some financial stability in my life. Here I am washing dishes for minimum wages, when I should be being paid 50 times higher by playing professional sports.

Anyway, a time and day came when the owner of this restaurant had fired me. I was doing something in the restaurant I had no business doing, and that was inhaling and exhaling drugs on the boss's property.

Of course, it is against all job rules to use drugs on the property. Therefore, I was performing an act that was against the company's privacy and policy agreement. Not only am I breaking the laws, but also, I am breaking personal business's laws, too.

A few friends (employees) and I were smoking dope in the back area of the restaurant. We were getting high and claiming to have fun as we inhaled toxic substances into our anatomy. Then, suddenly an employee yelled out saying, "The boss is coming". We all scattered and went our own separate ways. Even though, we all scattered, the boss still smelled the strong scent of dope that filled the air in the restaurant. We all thought the owner of this restaurant was gone for the entire day, so we planned (frontal lobe scheming) to smoke a little dope in the back room. Nevertheless, I was the only individual who had been fired.

So there I was, feeling mentally stupid because I had been fired because of using drugs. Being fired from my job, due to drug usage, was very embarrassing. It is shameful and embarrassing because, if anyone ever asks me, "why did you get fired from your job", I must tell that individual, "I was smoking dope on the job site, and had been fired because of it". As of now, only a few incidents have happened in my life concerning drugs, but to me, they were embarrassing moments.

I honestly believe that marijuana is the ultimate reason, why I did not graduate from high school at my scheduled and appointed time. Not graduating from high school at my appointed time was a terrible and an embarrassing event to experience. Graduating from high school later than suppose, was the first embarrassing experience recorded in this book concerning "drugs and embarrassing moments". The second grieved or embarrassing moment is when I was fired from my place of work. For some reason, it never crossed my mind that dope is the "prime" reason for my embarrassing experiences. It also never came to my thoughts that I needed some serious mental help from the usage of chemical controlled substance.

Anyway, let me share with you more information in detail about the drug the employees and I were smoking which caused me to be fired. The employees and I were inhaling into our brains a drug that is called, "Pre-mo". Pre-mo is a drug that gives the brain its effects from inhaling. Pre-mo is craftily put together in the form of a joint. It is smoked as a joint, because cigarette papers are involved when activating this illegal product.

Normally, the marijuana is first laid on top of the cigarette papers, and then grinded up crack cocaine is carefully sprinkled over the marijuana. Then, both drugs are rolled up into a joint. Now that I think about it, the object I saw in the projects (marijuana) is now being used by me. Gas charges up the car; electric activates the iron, and drugs control's a brain. I have actually picked up marijuana and brought its power to life.

Now that I think about it, I was fired from my job because of smoking a mixed drug product. Even though, there were a few of us smoking this drug, I was the only individual who had been fired. One of the restaurant employees whispered the information to the boss, saying, "**Brian Irons** is the employee who brought this illegal substance on the jobsite. Therefore, since I was the only employee fired, I was the only person who received a verbal judgment. From the boss's mouth, this verbal judgment went forth.

As you can see, drugs have caused my life to receive a judgment from humankind. Yes, it was a judgment because I was found guilty, and had been charged for the act. In other words, in this situation, I suffered the consequences. Anytime you suffer consequences for your actions done, you have truly been judged. My life has just reaped from what I had sowed.

My life is now filled with nothing but satisfying the flesh. *Galatians 6:8- For he that soweth to his flesh shall of the flesh shall reap corruption, but he that soweth to the Spirit shall of the Spirit reap life everlasting.* Being fired from my job is sort of like experiencing corruption, because I am not able to work there anymore. My brain, which is where my spirit lives, is only seeking ways to find pleasure. Since the limbic system in my brain is the pleasure arouser, this head function is dealing with the addiction. If the scripture says, *For he that soweth to his flesh shall reap corruption*, I wonder what kind of corruption my future will see. I've heard about that scripture many times, and I wonder how true it really is or how it really works.

I would like to say, "Drugs attacks people's brains physically", because when the dope has been inhaled into it, immediately it charges the organs in the head. When anything charges at something, it goes after it physically. However, by charge and force, drugs will control your life. Just as a man physically attacks another person to do harm, drugs will also physically attack the intelligent human brain to harm it. Although, drugs have neither arms nor legs, but once the dope is inhaled into the brain, it moves violently throughout the entire system in the head. You might not feel drugs physically beating on you now, but one day soon, the physical beat down will be felt.

Drugs are putting scars and marks on your brain right now, but you cannot see them, nor can you feel them. Trust me, when dope is sharing space in your brain, the organs are truly being physically bruised. Remember, your brain is the target, and drugs are throwing its power and might at it. You might not believe drugs are physically hitting your brain; however, unexpectedly, one day soon, you will feel the harsh pressure.

Let's say an enemy of yours is out to kill you, or is seeking to harm you. Your enemy will do whatever he or she has been plotting to do. The enemy's plan is to get close to you as possible. Once the enemy successfully finds a way to get into your presence, that adversary will do whatever it takes to physically harm or even kill you.

Well, think about this, drugs are your enemy, because their purpose is to do you harm. The unknown thing is this, your enemy, which is drugs, has you in its presence, and is so close to you, but you cannot see that the dope is working against you. However, me, and the people who are in the world are mentally blinded from the fact that drug's whole purpose is to kill them, and provide for them an early death date. Just as drinking and driving can give a person an early death date, putting drugs in the brain will do the same. Drugs have blinded all users from the fact that they lead people straight to a dead man's coffin. Yeah, drugs are powerful, because they put blindfolds on people's insight.

The clever work drugs does to the minds of people is this; they cause people to uplift them, rather than speak against them. If someone approaches you, and say, "the reason you are going through rough obstacles in life is because of your drug filled lifestyle. That individual will deny the fact that drugs are the prime reason. If someone would have approached me, and said, "The reason why you did not graduate from high school with your senior class is because marijuana hindered you". I probably would have replied and said, "That's not the reason". Then I would have said, "The reason why I did not graduate with my senior class is because I played around in school, and did not do the schoolwork". From those personal words of quote, I would have been uplifting the dope, rather than speaking against it. That is what the power of dope does; it hides every reason from all users to believing that it is the true reason why problems are occurring or have occurred in their lives.

People blame their problems on any and everything they can think of. People never admit drug usage is the reason for their broken-down situations and problems. People put the blame on their friends, their jobs, their co-workers, their kids, their wives, their husbands, Adam and Eve, but dare to blame chemical dependency. Drugs will cleverly hide the fact why many current problems in life exist.

The working of a drug is similar to the performance of a person wearing a black ninja suit. Usually, the person wearing the black ninja suit creeps, while plotting to do harm to the body of a living man.

Let me clarify unto you the evil plots, ways, and tactics a wicked ninja does when preparing to do business. A ninja, most of the time operates in dark or black attire, which is to hide his identity. The black attire hides the ninja's appearance from his enemies. When it is dark outside, that is when the wicked ninja does his best creeping. The wicked ninja does not want to be recognized by his target. While the wicked ninja is plotting, he seeks the right moment and time to creep on his victim. In other words, the ninja kneels down, squat, and hides himself from the presence of his enemies. Once the ninja is close to his victim, he then leaps out, beats the victim, and leaves him for dead.

That is exactly what drugs are going to do unto all dope associates. By drugs evil powers, you will be crept up on, beaten, and left for dead. The drug ninja" is good at its job. You cannot run, nor can you hide. When the wicked drug ninja finally gets a hold on you, nothing can be done, but to accept the scars and pain. Nevertheless, the wicked drug ninja (drugs) operates through your body, trying to kill your brain.

Actually, the wicked drug ninja already has my life. He is now plotting and waiting for the right moment to jump out and damage me. Remember this; the wicked dope ninja is slick, sneaky, and surely, drug chemicals are after your life. Another translation for the ninja is… "You reap what you sow". Even right now today, if you have drugs in your life, the wicked drug ninja is creeping up on you from behind, to perform a work of damage in your life.

Let me ask you a few questions; is the wicked dope ninja (any drug) operating in your local neighborhood or area? Did the wicked drug ninja creepily find a way to enter into your brain and body? Has the wicked dope ninja crept up on you, and has sneakily beaten on your wallet? If your answer is yes to any of the above questions, then nevertheless, the ninja either is inside you, or is lurking around you.

Every time a person intake a drug, that individual gives the wicked ninja (the creeper & killer), personal rights stop his or her heartbeat at any given moment. On the other hand, the ninja can and will brutally destroy your brain functions. The reason why I am using the word "ninja", to be equivalent to a drug is that, awful personal experiences are going to creep into all drug handler's lives one-way or the other. That is what a ninja does; he creeps and creeps until finding a way to injure his victim. Nevertheless, you just never know when the wicked drug ninja is going to jump out of nowhere and mess up your life, by adding more problems.

The wicked drug ninja did not kill me, however, when I willingly tried another drug product, that day and time crept up on me suddenly, and truly, it was unexpected. I mentally thought, and probably swore unto myself that I would never do any other drug, but marijuana. However, as you've already read, I was easily moved and persuaded into trying another drug, which is cocaine (pre-mo). As I just told you in the earlier paragraph, the wicked drug ninja is good at his job.

Anyway, after I had been fired from my job, there was no income coming into my possession. I needed some money in my hands to keep my male dignity. As I said before, money is a true necessity in this world. Without money in my possession, my mind began to plot eagerly on ways to make a nice amount of money, that does not require educational academics.

Come to think about it, I should have consulted with a job counselor, or signed up for a trading school. My city does not have many trading schools in it, but I should have searched until something was found. I should have at least stayed busy with education, rather than seeking more ways to get high. Nevertheless, a thought and vision entered into my mind, and it had me visualizing how to make some quick cash.

In this vision, I had seen many great things happening pertaining to earning money. The vision that entered into my mind was about selling drugs. Within myself, I felt if I operate it right, I could earn enough money to buy a few profitable businesses, and then step away from selling drugs. If I could earn a couple thousand dollars, that would be enough to purchase a business. Within this vision, not only did I see myself purchasing a business, but having fine clothes, expensive cars, and taking great care of pretty women were in it as well. Nevertheless, I was led to selling an illegal product just to keep money in my possession.

Drugs infested my brain, and became controller and ruler over my thoughts and actions. Since my cerebrum, which is my brain's thinker, is plagued with dope's formula, my thoughts of returning to the restaurant business had been cast off. While drugs were operating in my thinking system, they encouraged me to think from an illegal point of view. The organs in my brain have been given over to the power of drugs; my thinking system is what I really needed to make wise choices for my life. Since my cerebrum is soaked in the tactics of drugs, making illegal decisions became very easy. Thinking from a drug point of view, my brain was persuaded to doing anything there is just to earn cash. However, as a human being, I must delete and X out those law-breaking thoughts. Nevertheless, when drugs are controlling a brain, it is hard to escape the plots, and scheming thoughts of wickedness.

Anything positive, my brain didn't seek doing. My brain chose to break the law by selling drugs, rather than going back to school or finding another job.

Drugs filled my mind with ongoing law-breaking and wicked intensions. I now understand why God replied to the people who were on earth more than 2000 years ago.

Genesis 6:5 and God saw that the wickedness of man is great upon the earth, and that every imagination of the thoughts of his heart was only evil continually.

In this scripture, the word continually is the key to its understanding. I have actually become one of those wicked people God spoke about centuries ago. For the past 6 years, my heart has been fastened on the things of evil continually. All day every day, I broke laws, by indulging in drug activity. Ever since drugs came into my life, brain, and body, I have been filled with the power to commit wickedness on a continual basis. I am no different from the people who God killed centuries ago. The people who God destroyed by the flood, they're thoughts, and imaginations were on evil continually, and so is mine. In God's eyesight, those people back in the days, and **Brian Keith**, are like-minded.

My thoughts are on one wicked act to another. Not only that, but I am also doing one wicked thing and then another. I once was a drug user, but now, I'm a drug seller. My life went from being a drug user, to being a drug seller.

When I bought this product (cocaine) to sale, I was very nervous.

Nevertheless, I purchased a product that has an attachment to wickedness. I used to get high with wicked people, but now I am about to sell them drugs.

As I was selling cocaine, I could not believe the amount of money earned. Customers were purchasing cocaine back-to-back. After selling cocaine to a customer on my left side, I quickly turned to the right to sell dope to another. Customers were sometimes returning to purchase more cocaine in less than 45 minutes. My life has elevated from being a drug user, to being a drug seller. Not only has elevation-taking place, but also, I am on a new wicked level.

Just that fast, wickedness has given me a promotion. From wickedness to wickedness is what this promotion is all about. Nevertheless, from high school and even until now, God has been watching me since the first day law-breaking and wickedness through drugs has been operating in my life. Wow, you mean to tell me that God is watching every move I make. Yes, indeed he is. God is now watching me meet different people and sell them drugs.

I bought this cocaine product with my last paycheck. I had one last check to receive from the job I had been fired from. My paycheck was about $200, and I anxiously invested the entire check on powdered cocaine. I bought 2 separate bags of cocaine, and each one cost $100. I bought these two bags of cocaine from "D". Each bag of cocaine is called "teenager". From the power that cocaine possesses, the name, "Teenager" is an understatement.

Maybe cocaine should be called, "Strong Man", instead of Teenager, because of the strength and power it possesses.

All dope chemicals have the physical power and strength of a big Strong Wrestler. Once a "Big strong Wrestler" wraps his arms around you, it is almost impossible to break away and become free. A person might fight, wrestle, or try wiggling his way from the mental controlling power of drugs, but drugs magnificent power will "strong hold" the individual. Drugs will pin its ways into the user's life. The Big Strong Wrestler (the addiction) is stronger than you are.

The "Big Strong Wrestler" has control over my life. Cocaine is the big strong wrestler's left arm, and marijuana is his right arm. My life is now caught up in the strong arms of addictions.

I never thought my life would be so deeply caught up into drugs, that it would be so hard for me to say "no" to any of its law-breaking motives. <u>I Did Not Know</u> my life would hold on to drug habits or daily law-breaking ways for so long. These things crept up on me, and I have been persuaded to deal with drugs on a dangerous level. Meaning, I must meet hundreds of people who I do not know just to make drug sales.

Beware of what drugs has to offer, and exclude yourself from them. Hey, you just never know what kind of evil experience dope is going to bring into your life next. I had one small experience of smoking marijuana during high school, and my life is turning out to be like this. Never in a million years did I think that my life would be experiencing such events.

I want you to remember this quote for your life; one wicked act leads to another wicked act. Since I studied and learned math formulas, I have something mathematical to say. Take heed to this addition problem; a brain on drugs + wicked thoughts = performances of evil. If the wicked character (drug) is dwelling inside of you, it will bring about its power throughout your entire body, and the strength or power of wickedness will develop continually within your brain. I have another mathematical equation for you; a man + a woman = a baby soon to be born. College + a degree = financial stability.

Everything on earth is about addition. Also, remember this; what you do in today's society will always expose mathematics in your life/future. Whether you do good deeds or evil, there will always be addition in your life. As you can see, in my personal life, the mental usage of cocaine, and the physical activity of selling cocaine have been added into my living. Believe me, when drugs are in your life, wickedness, and other actions of evil will be added into your existence. Math, math, math, somehow, someway, it will be a prime subject in your life.

I have another drug experience I would like to share with you. In this experience, I was falsely accused. In other words, drugs and wickedness added another experience to my life. I was living with my parents at this particular time, and yes, I was a drug seller then.

One night, I went into the house to get some sleep. This same night I was getting high with a good friend of mine, whose name is G-Money. We both were in his car riding around together. Then, he drove me to my parent's house to drop me off. While walking towards the front steps, G-Money and I were having a conversation. After the conversation ended, I opened up the door, went into the house, and went straight to bed.

Well, after Gur dropped me off at my parent's house, he left. Minutes later, G returned to my parent's house searching for an item he had lost. The item he was looking for was on my parents' front porch. So G went on the front porch, reached down on the ground, picked up the item up, and left.

When Gur reached down to pick up the item, my dad was sitting in his truck watching the whole scene take place. My dad thought my friend, picked up a package of drugs off the front porch. I guess my dad thought a drug transaction just took place in front of his house. Nevertheless, my dad thought it was drug related, and he became upset about it.

When my dad came into the house, anger came along with him. He charged into the room where I sleeping, and woke me up immediately. He said to me, "Did you just make a drug transaction on the front porch". Then he said, "I want you to pack up your belonging, and be gone in the morning.

When my dad woke me up, and said that unto me, I was lost in mind, because <u>I Did Not Know</u> what was going on. I was sleeping, and all of a sudden, I am hearing words of commotion. When my dad commanded me to depart out the house, that was another verbal judgment cast upon my life.

Judgments do not only fall from Heaven. Judgments will fall from your own household. No one can stop judgment when one is to be pronounced. Wherever there is anger, there is always judgment. Anger operates first, then judgment charges in afterwards.

When I was kicked out of the house, prior to being fired from my job, I begin selling drugs to the point of no return. Now that I am on the streets with no home to go too, I felt like I had nothing loose. Being kicked out of the house did not make my dope habits too much of a difference, because my brain was heavily plagued with the venom of drugs anyway. Therefore, I kept on selling and using drugs, as if nothing serious just happened. I never allowed my brain to analyze these experiences; every time something bad happened in my life, I shook it off, and kept on living a drug-filled life.

When judgments fall upon us, we sometimes continue doing the same thing as if nothing truly happened. After any judgment has been pronounced, we need to pause for a moment, and analyzed the situation. Judgments are supposed to make people stop and think carefully about what's happening in our lives. We as individuals need to analyze our living, detail by detail, in order to discern why judgments are being pronounced. Nevertheless, when wickedness is living in human's brains, it will never let people analyze or inspect their living.

As you have just read, drugs have brought another grieving pain to my heart. My emotions were hurt when I was kicked out of the house. I drank and inhaled marijuana as soon as I left my parents' house. I was using drugs as a healing supplement to subside the pain of being kicked out of my parent's house.

Now that I think about it, if I was a hard-working person like my dad, and I thought my son was selling drugs out of my home, I would have kicked my son out too. However, the sad matter in this situation is that, drugs were not picked up off the porch, a gold chain was. Therefore, I was being kicked out of the house because of a gold chain, which my friend came back to the porch to retrieve. Nevertheless, this is the second judgment "humankind" pronounced upon my life because of drugs.

To my parents, this experience is more than 20 years old, therefore, there is no since in getting upset now. The reason why I said that is because; people can hear a confession from someone about an act that happened 20 years ago, and they'll become upset about it, as if it happened yesterday.

As I kept the ongoing affiliation of drugs, I still never thought that anything bad, nor anything unpleasant would ever happen in my life. I inwardly felt as long as I am taking good care of myself, then my life should be all right. However, as you have just read, I am not taking good care of myself because drugs are still bringing bad experiences into my existence. Taking good care of myself requires taking cautious actions in life, by not putting drugs in my brain and body. I must begin to do good things to my body, and not bad things. The only works I am performing in life are activities that bring ruin into my living.

If anyone is putting any kind of substance/drug into his or her body, that individual is not providing it with proper care. Every time a person put drugs into his or her brain, that individual is feeding it poison. Just hearing the word "poison" sends a great level of fear into people's minds. All drugs are dangerous! When people put drugs into their brain, the task of damaging one's health is in session.

Once the word "poison" is heard in our ears, we immediately become skeptical, frightening, and fearful due to the information we have heard concerning its work. Therefore, we keep our bodies far from its reach. We believe anything pertaining to poison is dangerous to the touch.

We also believe poison can bring sickness to our bodies, or peradventure kill us. We are so fearful and skeptical about drawing near or touching poison ivy, let alone, "true poison". I have been using drugs for a very long time. <u>I Did Not Know</u> or realized I had poisoned my own brain and body. As of now, neither am I providing my brain and body with proper treatment, nor am I expressing proper care. I am only poisoning it.

If you have ever seen a real snake on the outside or inside of your home, the first thought that comes to mind is, "not to get to close too that reptile's reach". Then you begin wondering if the snake is poisonous. You do not even think about becoming sick, you immediately think about dying from the lethal fluids the snake might be carrying. Over the years of hearing about snake's poisonous venom, you were taught to fear snakes to the fullest. Therefore, you keep yourself far away from wild snakes at a nice distance.

A snake's venomous poison and a drug addiction both have the same physical and mental affiliation. A drug addiction and a snake's venom both sickens a person's brain and body. They both lead people to experiencing mental and physical illnesses. Ever since I've been putting this poison (dope) into my brain, no physical effects have occurred yet, but only in my brain, which is the addiction. Although, I do not feel any physical sickness or pain, however, my mental body has many ailments. However, I do want to let you know that I have been bitten and poisoned by teeth marks of drugs. The day I became addicted to drugs is the day I became poisoned. It has not been manifested in the physical were it can be seen, but inwardly, the poison is slowly damaging my brain's organs for the kill.

If a snake, which has deadly poison in its fangs, bites down on a human being, and shoot its venom into the body, that bitten individual normally does not die immediately. It is the same performance with drugs. When a person puts drugs in the brain and body, he or she might not die immediately, but one day that person will be forced to die. However, I have read and heard about people being bitten and poisoned by a snake, and dying hours later. Also, I have heard stories about people trying drugs for the first time, and died hours later.

I know drugs are poisoning, because after putting them into my brain, my entire course of living changed. My life was once positive because I wanted to be a pro athlete. Now it is evil, because law-breaking habits have become my life's daily deeds. That is how poison works; it gets into the brain, and transforms the God given tasks from which it has been designed to do. God created the brain to serve him, but here

I am, serving drugs with my brain. You need to order my second book, "*Thou Shalt Not Have Any Other Gods Before Me*". Also be on the lookout for my 4th book titled, *Lord Forgive My Hands*.

I remember an old statement said by the older people, and it goes like this, "One thing leads to another". I now find that to be a true statement, because marijuana led me to alcohol, and then came cocaine. Finally, and crazier, I was led to selling drugs. I am a true witness that one thing does leads to another. Lord please have mercy upon my soul!

Since so many surprising events have happened, I began wondering, when will the dope madness end. I also began to wonder, "How can I be released from this drug filled living? As I can now see, things aren't looking too good for me at this point in life. For some reason, neither could I stop selling drugs nor could I stop putting dope into my brain. Yes, I do want to be free from drug money and drug usage, however, I've been poisoned, and my brain has been filled with the power of continual wickedness. My entire life is now surrounded by dope, nothing more, and nothing less. When will my personal affiliation with drugs end?

Drugs will always keep the party going. From the poison that drugs sprays into the brain, it makes the mind believe, that, without drugs, the party will not be fun. Every time people attend parties, the first ignorant question that come out their mouth is this, "what are we going to drink" or "what are we going to smoke" for the party. When the people finally get their drinks, or get the smoke in their possession, they begin to feel calm. Soon, the people become highly ignorant and begin saying, "We only live once, so let's get messed up and party all night". That is one of the stupidest "quotes", ever said. Since drug addicts say, "We only live once", they are acting as if it is okay to die today. How can you smoke or intake chemicals, and then say, "We only live once". Well, I cannot talk too bad about you because I have said it times before, too. Therefore, you and I both are ignorant.

The powerful drug addiction inside people's brain will cause their mouths to speak words of stupidity. The dope in the brain is causing the lobe that deals with "speech", to speak ignorant quotes such as that. Actually, when people say the quote, "We only live once", what they are saying is this; if this drug kills me today, then it is okay to die because "I'm supposed to only live once anyway". Now think how ignorant the quote sounds. There are many ignorant phrases and words drug users quote from their own mouths. Well, what do you expect to say or think when drugs are in your brain speaking and thinking for you? Stop putting drugs in your thinking and speech center. Stop being ignorant people, and become wise individuals.

People believe or think that weed or alcohol is the only product they will use in life. However, that is not true. Smoking weed or drinking alcohol is a door opener for other drug products to come into a person's life. From the entrance of weed, or the entrance of alcohol, other chemicals will soon become a temptation. When one door of drugs is opened, eventually, another drug of choice will become active too. Once you have used one drug, your mind will be empowered to try another. When you first try one drug, it then becomes easy to try another.

People try other drugs just to enhance that first mental "feeling" or "high". In doing so, people seek to make the drug "high" last longer. Whether you drink on occasions, or smoke dope every now and then, those chemicals are still going inside of your brain developing a hazardous addiction.

When people get involved with drugs, their careers and goals are up for grabs. Unexpected situations will always appear in one's living, when drugs are a part of it. Whether you are a drug user or a drug seller, unexpected situations will always arise into your living. Experiences of evil will continually find ways to fulfill your commercial living.

Hey people, stay in school, stay away from drugs, and keep a positive attitude in life. Work hard for the things you desire to have. Accomplishing your dream and goals will make life easier. Keep your mind on the adventure of your dreams, and stay free from mind alternating chemicals. Since drugs are classified as mind alternating chemicals, then surely, they are dream changers.

Every living person on earth will reap whatever he or she sows. If any man sows it, guess what, that man shall reap it. Every human being in the world is a true planter and farmer in life. Whether he or she realizes it or not, sowing and planting will always be a part of your living. You, the farmer, will either plant good seeds or seeds of evil. Whatever you sow (plant) in your life, you will reap from that very same seed.

Let's say, you, the farmer, own acres of land, and have many empty planting areas in your field. In one area of the field, you dug many holes into the soil, and put tomato seeds in them. Then you turn the water hose on, and begin watering those seeds.

While the seeds are in the soil, you expect tomatoes to grow in the day of harvest. Once the seeds grow into ripe fruit, they have just experienced a moment of harvesting.

Another example: let's say, you've planted apple seeds in the field of your farm. You patiently expect to grow apples in the day of harvest. The word harvest means to reap, receive, or gain from your actions done. Anything you plant or sow will grow in your future as a result. Once the results are seen, harvesting has just been exposed.

Therefore, while I am sowing (inhaling) drugs into my brain and body, my experiences are my life's harvesting. I sowed drugs into my anatomy, and I am reaping negative results in the day of harvest. My evil experiences are growing and growing, just like a branch does on a vine.

To all farmers (living humans) who plants drugs into their bodies; your body is a field, and when you plant drugs in it, negative results grows into your life. The reason why our bodies are an actual field is because our bodies are made from dirt. And once people in-take drugs, the intoxicants take root within, as a seed does when planted in the soil. When you plant anything, it will grow. Whether you plant seeds in your field, or drugs into your body, one thing that is for sure, your experiences are the fruit. The body might not grow apples and oranges, but when it has been judged, that's your fruit right there.

I have another scripture for you to read: *Galatians 6:7 be not deceived; God is not mocked: for whatsoever a man soweth that shall he also reapeth.* As I was pointing out unto you, whatever you sow in life, especially in the body, you will reap true results in the day of harvest. In other words, a judgment from the law or biblical prophecy will be pronounced upon you. Without being summoned to go before a judge in the court of law, a judgment can still be pronounced upon you. It does not matter where you are right now, you can reap at any given moment.

A person can even reap on the day of his or her marriage. Meaning, on the day of marriage, the spouse found out that his or her companion has been cheating. A person can reap at a family reunion. A person can reap at the baseball game. A person can reap on his or her job. A person can reap on the street corner. A person can reap wherever the feet are standing. The "reap what you sow" law, loves proving its power. A person never knows when the day of harvest will be brought to the light. Therefore, I advise the people in the world to get their life in order, and stop sowing seeds of wickedness (evil), into their lives.

As I was still involved with drugs, from them, a tight grip had been clamped on my brain. At this particular time, I have been bound to drugs more than 6 years. That is a very long time. It was as if drugs had a tight grip on my life. I thought I was only going to give marijuana a first-time trial experience, but years later, here I am still messing around with this dope stuff. More than 6 years of my life has been under the command of chemical control substances. The seed of drugs sprouted great strength, and its power stayed connected to my body, as a branch does while attached to its vine. The net of drug's had every organ in my brain wrapped up in its power. Drugs are trying to kill me, but I Did Not Know it.

Although, I planted the "seed" of death (drugs), inside of me, I decided to go back to school (college). Drugs are still operating in my thinking system, but I fought and fought, and a thought of doing something positive contacted my mind. Going back to school was a positive thing to do. Instead of doing negative things, I decided to do something positive. It was hard trying to do something positive, because my life has been operating in negativity for the past 6 years.

When I went back to school (college), my high school diploma had already been earned. Therefore, I did not have to sign up for G E D classes. I did not have to take extra tests to begin my college courses. The only test I had to take was a test that will decide what level of courses or classes I need to take first. Even while I was taking this college placement test, my brain was high as a kite then. Yep, the seed of drugs were still planted in me because it had taken root many years ago. I might be a farmer, but I have not the power to hoe this seed of drugs and wickedness up out of me.

The main reason why I enrolled in college is because I wanted to give my basketball skills another chance to make it to the professional sport world. Within myself, I felt as if I still have a chance to present my talents and skills to the professional sport world. If I get the chance to present my basketball talents and skills in college, then I'll have a chance to be free from selling drug. Besides, my vision is to show my basketball talents and skills to the world on camera. I did not want my talents and skills to go down the drain. Although, drug poisoned my mind, my basketball skills were still top-notch. However, my decision-making in life was bad.

After being accepted to attend college, the college administrator told me "I signed up for college too late to play basketball". I had to wait until the following semester to participate in basketball. I signed up for college two weeks too late. I had to wait for about 2 months to play basketball. Therefore, I realize I needed to take those college classes, until it was time to sign up to play basketball.

Patience is always a test in my life. In order for me to play basketball, I needed a rush of hard-core patience. With drugs working in my patience center (brain), it's going to be hard for me to abide with the rules of waiting.

While I was attending my basic college courses, it seemed as if the drug money had a mouth, because the cash spoke to me through my pager. In class, once my wristwatch pager beeped, my mind became very distracted. When my pager beeped, I look at the screen to see who it was. Many of my customers punched in a code of the amount they wanted to spend. After seeing it, I boldly escorted myself out the class, and went to get that wicked money.

Sometimes I left class while it was in session. While the instructor was explaining how to do certain assignments, I would get up and escort myself out the class. While the teacher was explaining how to do certain assignments, my mind was focused on that money. Therefore, I walked out of class on several occasions just to go and serve dope to a customer. Sometimes I left just to get high. My brain could not handle doing righteous things. When a brain is on drugs, and patience becomes a test, from the chemicals in the drugs, they will always win. The human mind itself cannot defeat the awful choices that drugs will cause it to make. Your choices in life might not be the same as mine, but I know you have made many regrettable decisions while being under the influence of a chemical.

One day, I decided not to go back to college. College was hindering me from making money. Well, there I went back on the streets with no more sport hopes. Actually, I was planning to play college basketball and sale drugs too. At least that's what I thought! As you can see my reader, my entire brain is highly plagued with getting high, and making that wicked money. Nevertheless, I went back to the streets, and left my mental education, or a definite chance of making it in the N.B.A.

I truly believe, if I would have stayed in college, and waited patiently for basketball to become available, I would have been the star player on the team. I am so sure, I would have been a starting guard. Most definitely, without any doubt, either a bigger college, or N.B.A. scouts would have been observing me as the season toured to the end. I am so sure I would have made it to the N.B.A. With the talents and skills I possessed, someone, somewhere, would have caught a glimpse of my court performance. The only thing I needed was for one "big timer" (basketball scout) to watch me play one game, and that's it. Nevertheless, once again, drugs have unexpectedly performed another stunt in my life by causing me to quit school. Truly, drugs and the money are the direct blame for me quitting college.

As you can see, drug's influences were in my thoughts, and there I was again, making bad decisions in my life. When I quit going to college, it was because of the wicked drug ninja jumped out on me again.

Now I understand why people say, "I wish I could start life all over again". That quote is in my mind right now. I am actually thinking, or wishing I could start life all over again. I wish I had chosen another path in life, instead of choosing the road of drugs. Once I committed the act of engaging into drugs, I became guilty of the actions that they led me to commit. When I first began smoking marijuana, the hands of time (clock) will not go into reverse mode and change already experienced events. Although, I am alive and healthy (so I thought), I still wish I could start life all over again.

Hey, you, my reader, the hands on the clock has one charge to do, and that is to go forward, and never return and swing backwards. Once your actions have been committed, time shows neither sympathy nor pity. Time has one duty to perform, and that is to go clockwise forever. You do not have the power to go back in time, and correct already made mistakes. Therefore, I advise you to be smart and make wise decisions in your life. Stay far away from drugs, as far as you possibly can. I have warned you!

My usage with drugs can be compared to a person who has lost his or her virginity. The very first time a person has sex, the virginity stage no longer exist. Willingly, 95% of the people in the world have given up their virginity. They agreed to lie down with a human being, and then perform the pleasurable act of lustful sex. The mental side will always have the remembrance of what sex feels like. Because of the usage of drugs, my brain and body knows what drugs feel like; and from the virgin's first sexual encounter, his or her body knows what sex feels like too.

Let say that a female, who is a virgin, has been opened up for sexual pleasures. Once the barrier of virginity has been broken, there is no way she can ever go back to being a virgin again. Her womb has been opened by sexual admission.

That is exactly how my life feels. Once I opened my brain to marijuana, I can never say, "I never did drugs before". Because of using drugs, my mind has become impure. My brain and the virgin have become impure from two different types of mental and physical pleasures. The virgin's mental and physical pleasure was sexual activity, and my brain's physical and mental pleasure was the act of slandering dope intoxicants into it. The reason why I said, "the virgin has become impure, is because, every person is supposed to give up his or her virginity on the night of marriage. I'll tell you more about the virgin and marriage subject in a different chapter.

Sex and drugs both have similarities when it comes to performance. The virgin, who was once sexless, has lost the testimony of being called, "chaste" or "pure". Eventually, the once known virgin will become sexually active with another partner. Losing your virginity is the same physical and mental reaction as losing your once known to be drug free brain. Once you lose your drug free mind to one drug, one day soon; you will be pressured and apt to try another. In the same sense, if that once known virgin be not careful, he or she will have more sex partners over the years. Just like I went from one drug to the next to have mental pleasure, the once known virgin will go from one sex partner to the next to have mental pleasure as well. Therefore, sex and drugs both have similarities in mental and physical performances (the addiction).

In our world today, sex and drugs are like wicked twins in action. They both are highly craved for. By their pleasures, many hearts and minds have become captivated. The people in the world have allowed sex and drugs to become a high priority.

Here is another fact about them both; sex and drug are the two dominant killers in the land. Yeah, drugs can kill you by its powerful addiction, and sex can kill by its given disease (aids).

Let me write an update of dope experiences I have encountered. Ever since drugs have been number 1 in my life, I've experienced nothing by sadness.

1st my brain became addicted to marijuana.

2nd I did not graduate with my senior class in high school.

3rd I was kicked out of the house from living with my parents.

4th, I quit a job.

5th I was fired from a job.

6th, I quit going to college.

7th I became a drug seller.

8th I began using cocaine.

Those are the many experiences, which chartered into my life, while using drugs. Whether you believe it or not, drugs were interceding with my brain's decision maker, causing unprofitable choices to be made.

Anyway, I am sure I am not the only person in this world that street drugs have hindered and have mentally influenced in a very negative way. I believe and know there are many people in the world who are wrapped up in the net of drugs. If people are not wrapped up into the mental pleasure of putting drugs into their brain, then they are entangled with pleasures of making that wicked money. However, whether it is the drug money, or the drug mental high, I am sure that drugs pulled a few awful tricks on you too. Nevertheless, with me, I was physically entangled with them both, the drug high, and the illegal money. My brain has been swimming in the aquarium of chemical additions for a very long time.

Chapter 8

MORE ADDICTIONS WITH DRUGS AND THE CONSEQUENCES

When people are selling, they advertise the dope as if it is a legal product. As I was advertising and selling this illegal controlled substance (cocaine), financial gain became my daily mission. Filthiness of the flesh and lucre is now operating in and through me. Soon and very soon, I became more addicted to money than I did from getting high.

Anytime a person (**Brian Irons**) quits a job just to earn money through breaking laws, that person is addicted to money. Anytime a person quits college, and messes up the chance to possible become rich the right way (becoming a pro athlete), just to sell drugs, that person has an addiction with money. When a person has an addiction for money, he or she will do whatever it takes to have the cash in their possession.

Earning hundredths of dollars a day had spoiled me rotten. Every day, I thought about more and more money to stash into my pockets. This sounds like the same "mind set" I had when I began smoking marijuana. Just as I wanted more and more marijuana to smoke, well, now I want more money to stash into my pockets.

Although, I was earning money from selling drugs, however, every dime earned serves one purpose. Of course, the money earned from a job, or earned from selling drugs; they both grant payment from different resources. The money earned from a job is legal; therefore, no laws are broken, nor is the anger of God aroused. The money earned from selling drugs, about 4 to 5 laws are transgressed. When the laws have been transgressed, God's anger then awakens.

Whichever way you earn your money in this world, whether legal or illegal, an act of God's righteousness will always be rendered. Whether God punishes you through his laws, or blesses you from doing what is right, righteousness from him will always be rendered. There is nothing righteous in selling drugs. However, when God judges you according to your law-breaking deeds, he did that through His righteousness. God will spill and expose truth through righteousness into your life one way or another. Therefore, the righteousness of God will always be proven through his judgments. If you do not allow God to make your life a righteous living, God will step his righteous self into your life with judgments, and make his righteousness be seen anyhow.

Let me share a biblical verse with you before moving on. *Psalms 19:9 The fear of the Lord is clean, enduring forever: The judgments of the Lord are true and righteous altogether.*

I wanted you to read a verse from the bible that speaks about God's judgments being observed as righteous. Your life might be filled with all manner of deceit, falsehood, and darkness, but the spotlight from God's righteousness, through judgments will be seen. Every time you go in your kitchen at night and turn the lights on, you do it so you can see what you are doing. In the same sense, every time God judges you, he does it so that his righteousness can be seen. You cannot get away from the righteousness of God. Even when the law convicts a person with the death penalty, that is from a righteous judgment. When God destroyed by drowning all those people in the days of Noah's, his judgments through righteousness was pronounced upon them all. If you read your bible, you will see that the death penalty is in there too. As I said before, humankind cannot judge or sentence anyone without God's righteousness (the law's conviction).

Anyway, the more dope I sold in the neighborhood, of course, the more money earned. The neighborhood I sold drugs in, I call myself expressing love to every soul that dwelled in the area. Although, I did not have much, however, the name "Lightskin" became known as one of the greatest throughout the entire neighborhood. Other people were known as well, but Lightskin was on another level. In playing sports, Lightskin was on another level, and when it came to selling drugs, Lightskin was on another level.

Selling crack cocaine actually became my financial means for survival. It seems like I am cursed by this cocaine business. I could not fully perform my heart's desires (sports) that were once in my life. Ever since drugs entered into my life, it was all about dope and the money it provided.

The neighborhood I dwelled in is called, "Grape Street" or "Grape Hill". Andre and Rico gave the hood that name. Those two guys walked around in purple clothing representing Grape Street. And as they say, "Only the strong will survive".

There was not one friend or person who dwelt in the neighborhood that I did not provide a helping hand too. If someone in the hood needed a financial hand, Light would be more than happy to fulfill that individual's need. Of course, I could not help the entire neighborhood at once, but as time passed by, everyone received something from my hands. Not too many days passed by, in which I did not dish out money to someone for some apparent reason. Even if a person did not live in the hood, if he became cool with the fellows, and me, he received a gift from me as well. Although, I am a drug dealer, I still had a decent compassionate heart. Well, I think I can say that.

In addition, I have given hundredths of dollars to help people with their housing bills. I bought shoes for people. I have given money to people who did not have the finances at the particular time to put gas in their cars. Almost every female in the neighborhood, I freely gave them money to get their hair done or just to put it into their pockets. Fingernail and toenails I paid to be done. I bought clothes for people. I happily gave away money at will, as if I did not care. Although, I was earning money through selling drugs, when it came down to it, I was never stingy or kept the money all to myself. Actually, money is charitable, good to have; and I will never watch an individual person, or an entire family suffer hunger or need, if I can make a difference. Money was not a big issue to me. I mean, I did love to have money in my possession, as you can see, but to be stingy with it, my heart was not filled with that hideous mess. My heart was pregnant with charity, and when charity gave birth so that I could give, I spread the money throughout the entire neighborhood. I know that making money from selling drugs is horribly wrong, but as I said before, "all money does the same thing"; it spends. However, the money did not cause me to look down on people who did not have any. It only lifted me up to help the person that had a need.

As I was selling drugs and earning that unlawful money, there came a time the police had caught me. The cops caught me with cocaine in my possession. In my life, I had been charged with three drug cases in a 4 or 5-year span of selling narcotics. The three drug cases that were cast upon my crime record were two possessions of cocaine, and a cocaine sell to an undercover cop.

After the police officers caught me the first time with cocaine in my possession, they handcuffed me, put me in the squad car, and drove me to the city jail. In the city jail is where I registered my name. The name **Brian Irons** has now been registered in the criminal judicial system, along with other law-breaking people (individuals that performs wickedness).

After my name had been registered in the judicial system, I was sent to a cell until further notice. This was my first offense; therefore, I was able to leave jail less than 24 hours. Before leaving jail, I was given a sheet of paper that had a court appearance date on it.

Since I had been summonsed to appear in court to stand before the judge (the law), my mind wondered greatly. Thinking about what could possible happen unto me when I appeared in court was bothering me mentally. I walked the streets, thinking, I could actually be sentenced and convicted to serving jail time. I Did Not Know too much, or anything about the law, nor attending court service. However, I was given a court date, therefore, I must show up at the appointed time.

After I had been released from jail, I was happy to see the outdoors again. I felt free like a bird loosed from its cage. My mental body (brain) felt relieved. Being in jail, which means being behind bars, made me feel like an animal at the zoo. Just as animals at the Zoo are caged in; in jail I was caged in too. Being physically trapped behind cell bars was a torturing mental experience. Those few hours in jail were the roughest isolation I ever had to cope with.

For about 4 or 5 months, I was traveling back and forth to court presenting myself before the judge. At this particular time, a public defender represented me in court. On the last day of court, which was the day for me to hear a judgment, I pleaded guilty to possession of cocaine. I was caught red handed, and there was no way of escaping. Therefore, there was no need to take this case to trial. After pleading guilty, I was then openly sentenced in the court of law.

When the Judge, through the law, pronounced upon me a sentence, it was required that I serve 3 years on probation. The 3 years on probation is supposed to be ample amount of time for me to get my life on the right track. Being put on probation was a substitute for being sent to jail.

So far, I've been judged by two voices from mankind. The first voice of judgment came from my boss, and the other from my dad. Well, this time, I have just been judged by the voice of God, through his laws. Since God spoke laws into existence, when a person has been judged by the law, that individual has been judged by the voice of God. My dad spoke a judgment upon me; my boss spoke a judgment upon me; and God has spoken a judgment on me too. I can now see that a person does not always have to be hit physically to feel a judgment. From the tongue, which speaks out words of judgment, your life can be hit. If you read my second book, *Thou Shalt Not Have No Other God's Before Me*, it will teach you more about spoken words of judgments. This book will be published one day soon.

While living in St. Louis, and under the law's provision (probation), I went back to the streets to sell more crack cocaine. My cerebrum (the thinker in my brain) was highly saturated with the poisonous asps of drugs. The thoughts and the intents of my heart are devoted to doing wickedness continually. The only thing my brain knew to do was things pertaining to breaking the law.

Drugs and wickedness have truly poisoned my mind. The venom from wickedness (drugs) kept my thoughts connected to law breaking activities, which were the desires of my heart. I sold drugs as if I had nothing to worry about. The law could not stop me; being on probation could not stop me, nothing had the power to stop me. I sold drugs for about a year or longer, and then I caught another cocaine case.

This is my second time going to jail because of selling cocaine. Well, again, here I am, in jail being fingerprinted. Well, here I am, having my name (**Brian Keith**) processed into the law's system again. After the processing was done, I was escorted to a jail cell.

Well, again, here I am, about to hear another verdict from the laws of God. Now, it is possible for me to serve a little jail time. I thought for sure God's law was going to declare me guilty, convict me, and then sentence me to serve time in jail. I was so sure that the laws of God were going to send me to the penitentiary for an X number of years. I suppose, I can use this as an excuse, "it is all because drugs allowing drugs to become number one in my life". All because of making one bad choice and decision during high school, my life has been on a wicked road. My heart and life has now been hit with the bull's-eye misery.

About a year later, I caught another drug case. This time, I was charged for selling crack cocaine to an undercover cop. I sold dope to a cop who was dressed up like a dope feign. He was an undercover police, and I Did Not Know it. The cop had dirty clothes on, and a full-untrimmed beard, which was a work of disguise. The beard actually caused him to look like a dirty crack head. As I said before, I must meet and sell drugs to people whom I Did Not Know. Most of the people I sold drugs too, at first, I Did Not Know them. Over the years, I am sure I sold drugs to hundredths of people I Did Not Know. Nevertheless, I sold drugs to an undercover cop, and I now have three cocaine charges on my criminal history report.

Well, I was bonded out of jail again. Again, I was given a court date. Again, I was summons to appear in the presence of court. This is my third time having to appear in court for drug charging issues. Therefore, I was summons again to appear in court, to listen for name **Brian Keith** to be called.

As of now, I realize the judge, through God's laws, is about to pronounce righteousness (a sentence) upon me. Justification is about to be performed. God's law, through the judge, had mercy on me the first time. Here I am again going before the laws of God, for the very same wicked deed (selling drugs). I am about to face God's law in court for this same act, and now God's law is about to present a righteous judgment upon my living again.

If any man is caught breaking the law, the laws of God are set to render him or her a desert. The laws were sent to help us, however, on the other hand, the laws are sent to break your heart. Of course, the laws were sent to provide protection unto the world, but if any man breaks the law, the law will act completely against him. Not only are the laws here to help us out, but also, if any man breaks them, God's laws becomes his enemy.

Actually, if you break the law, God himself becomes your enemy. Oh yes, God does become your enemy. If the law is against any performances you do, then God is against you as well. For example: if God says, "Thou Shalt Not" do a certain deed, and you do it, then who becomes angry, and is against you? If I command you not to walk into my house without knocking; that is my rule. If you do enter into my house without knocking, you have just broken my rule. Then you have to deal with my anger. God is the same way.

The law was also sent to condemn your heart. When judgments are pronounced on a person's life, it hurts the heart. Who in their right mind boasts about being judged or condemned? People fear judgments. They sometimes would rather miss a court date, and have a warrant issued in their name. People break laws all day every day, but I am sure no one wants to be caught and sentenced.

When a judgment has been pronounced, it makes the heart sad. Then the countenance of the face transforms to looking bitter. Therefore, after experiencing judgments, your life will be ruled by it, until time served. Actually, one conviction from the law can be on your record for the rest of your life. No one wants to be under the court laws and rules for the rest of his or her life.

That will make a person's mind (thoughts) be stuck on what can and cannot be done. People do not want to be under the law's judgment for one hour, let alone the next decade or longer. Judgments never feel good to the mind, they only bring worries into the brain. When a person has continual worries, that individual's current living is messed up. I will explain to you later in the story concerning, "the law messing up your life". My advice to the people in the world is this; cease yourselves from committing wickedness before the law through judgments takes control over your life.

When I went to court for my first charge of cocaine, a public defender represented me in the court of law. The public defender helped me escape a sentence that probably would have shipped me to the penitentiary. Well, I now have 2 new cocaine charges on my criminal history report. However, this time, I felt within myself that I needed a paid lawyer, rather than a public defender. Therefore, I searched for a lawyer to pay, so I could be represented in court.

While being tried in the court of law, concerning these two new drug cases, I pleaded guilty. Of course, I spoke with my lawyer before pleading guilty. My lawyer told me, "He can squeeze all my drug cases together, and that 5 years of probation will be my judgment. I replied, "Yeah, that's cool, I can handle that". When I agreed to the 5 years' probation, the judge immediately beat the desktop, and sentenced me to 5 years probation".

After the judge sentenced me to 5 years of probation, I then walked out of the court building. I was so happy to leave the courtroom on my own, and not by the escorting of the police. As every individual in the world says, "I thank God for his mercy upon my life". So let me get my thanks on too; "I thank God for his mercy upon my life".

After this sentence went forth, I knew I could not get into any more trouble with the law. Most definitely, I do not need another drug case added to my criminal history record. <u>I Did Not Know</u> how much longer the laws of God are going to hold back its awaiting conviction.

Even after my second judgment, which added more years to my probation status, I went back to the streets to sell drugs. Every time I went to court, and had been sentenced, I always had thousands of dollars worth of crack cocaine somewhere hidden. Therefore, I was led to go back to the streets and continue selling crack cocaine. Wow, the thought and intents of my heart, is continually on wickedness.

After being sentenced to deal with 5 years probation, the judge assigned my name to a system of probation officers. I must go to a place and register the name **Brian Keith** where probation officers are gathered. A probation officer is a person who supervises people who have been caught breaking the law.

I went to Cherokee street, which is the road where the probation office building is located. When I walked into the probation building, I saw White folks, Black folks, Chinese folks, Mexicans, Hispanics, and Italians. I even saw a real Indian. As I said before, drugs do not discriminate color, race, creed, nor beliefs. When people (any nationality) give drugs the opportunity to prove its power, their lives are at risk. Drugs care nothing about ethnic background. Nevertheless, there were about 5 to 6 different nationalities in this building, waiting to see a probation officer. Therefore, not only has my name been given to a probation agency, but other cultures names had been assigned here too.

After finally meeting my probation officer, she gave me all the rules and tasks required to complete the program. One of the requirements was to visit her at scheduled and appointed times. My probation officer told me, "I must not be caught breaking the law for the next 5 years, because it will violate my probation. If I violate my probation in any kind of way, I might have to serve my remaining probation time in jail.

In the beginning stages of reporting to my probation officer, it was required to see her once every two months. As those 5 years began shrinking, my probation officer was getting more and more strict. She started scheduling appointments to see her two and sometimes three times a month.

Throughout the years of visiting my probation officer, my brain stayed filled with drugs. My brain and body was swamped with chemical controlled substances. The limbic system in my brain has been hungering for chemical toxicants for many years.

The brainstem is my survival kit. However, ever since it has been introduced to drugs, it has been made to believe drugs are needed for survival.

The love for the feeling of drugs was in my heart and body drastically. Chemical controlled substances has been operating through my brain for many years. From high school, even until now, drugs have been operating inside of my head. That is a very long time. Nevertheless, after having 3 drugs cases and being sentenced to serve probation time, my brain never deleted the acquaintance of wickedness that operates from drugs.

Just as practicing sports everyday will promote or enhance a better athletic performance, well, in the same sense, using drugs on a daily basis also enhances wickedness. I once played basketball every day, but now, I sell drugs on a daily basis. Yeah, every single day, I am doing something pertaining to wickedness. The more I used drugs, the greater the addiction became, and the longer I activated wickedness.

As I was using drugs, <u>I Did Not Know</u> a skill was in effect. The first skill drugs perform in any brain is the cunning addiction. Here I am, on probation, because drugs performed its skill (the addiction) in my brain.

Whether legal or illegal, all drugs have skills. When you have pain in the body, a pill sometimes heals the acing. While the pill sits in the body, it tries deleting the pain with its skills. Once the pain leaves the body, the pill has performed its skill.

Drugs have the most cunning power in our world today. Throughout the world of cultures and races, they all have the same brain structured figure. The one and only difference in all brains is the IQ level.

Even a brain diagnosed with a high IQ can lose its intelligence when drug intoxicants become its contender. Drugs are not afraid of educated brain smarts, or high intellectual intelligence. Actually, drugs are stronger than a person's IQ. Once any drug meets the brain's IQ or mental intelligence, that IQ level is destined for doom. As you already know, I do have a little education (high school diploma), but drugs have cunningly made me look like a man who has no understanding at all. Although, I perceive my IQ level to be decent, however, from my usage with drugs, my IQ level has tremendously dropped. Here I am, on probation, because I've allowed drugs to work its cunning skill through my entire central nervous system.

In this world, a person's IQ level is based upon his or her smartness. However, I have another theory. An IQ is based upon a person's mental intelligence, not so much upon the A's earned in school. Do not get me wrong, because being smart does play the highest role in the IQ business. However, just by making wise decisions in your life will rack up IQ points too.

While on probation, it was required for me to find employment. Having a job will prove to my probation officer I am trying to better my living. Therefore, I went into the public to find a job. While searching for employment, I still had drugs in my brain, and in my possession to sell.

I needed to be high, because I could not take the mental thoughts of the things I am dealing with. However, I did find a job, and you probably already know what kind of occupation it is. Yep, you've guessed it; it's another restaurant job. I figured I should get any kind of job just to keep my probation officer off my back.

As I was working at this restaurant, of course, I knew I could not leave the occupation at will. I have a job to do, and I must do what is required. Although, I was hired, I really did not want to be there.

As I was working, beep-beep, there goes that evil pager. The pager beeped during college classes, and now it is beeping while I am at work. What shall I do? A decision must be made. Maybe I should not look at the pager. Maybe I should keep the pager in the car. Since I am addicted to money, I had to look at the pager. It was powerfully rough watching people post hundreds of dollars on the screen, and not go and collect it.

One day, as I was cooking fish sandwiches, a thought came to mind. Not only was it a thought, but also, I obeyed the thought. I walked out of the restaurant. Yep, there I go again, walking out on another employment. I quit this job because I did not have the patience to work on a real job. At this point in life, an employee's check could not mount up to the payment that selling drugs provided.

My reader, as you've just read, drugs are really in control of my life. Drugs have provoked my cerebrum to make another awful decision again. This is the second job I walked out on, and quitted, while being under the influence of drugs. I worked at this job (McDonalds) for only two days. My brain could not take it; I had to get out of there. I didn't stay in college for the sake of financial freedom, and I didn't stay on the job for the sake of personal freedom.

I know I am doing what is called stupid things. Walking out on a job again, is another payment drugs provided me with. Even in this situation, I reaped from what I sowed in my brain many years ago. Not only that, but drugs have performed another stunt in my life by its skill.

After quitting the job, an appointed time had come to visit my probation officer. When I walked into the probation building, I signed my name on the sign in sheet. Soon, my probation officer came to the seating area, and called my name. I followed her to her office. As I was following her, I was very nervous. Saying in my mind, "I hope she doesn't ask questions about this McDonald's job".

Here I am, sitting in my probation officer headquarters high as a kite. Actually, every client in the building appears to be high as kites. As people, we think these probation officers do not see how high we are looking. The eyes of a person tell it all. When chemicals are in the brain, they cause the pupils to look red and glossy. When the eyes of a person look high from drugs, the occipital lobes in the brain are feeling the chemical's power.

While visiting my probation officer, she begins questioning me. She asks, "How are you doing at the job? My reply was a big lie. "I told her everything is going just fine". "I really don't want to work there, and I am looking for a new job".

Then she said, "I want you to come see me next week". She also said, "I am going to do a drug test on you, to see if your system is clean. Uh oh, another drug screening has just been scheduled.

Many probation clients were escorted by the police out of the probation building. Normally, the probation officer schedules a day and time for the police to appear at the probation building. While the parole or probation officer is speaking to the client, the police suddenly walks into the room, handcuff the criminal and takes him to jail.

Well, another day for drug testing was scheduled. I was scheduled to go and visit my probation officer again. Mentally, I feared going back to see her. My body's system is drug filled, and I know the test results will show positive for drug use. Another thought came to mind, and it was about not going to visit my probation officer. Well, yeah, I never visited her again.

When I decided to stop visiting my probation officer, I made another dumb decision. My decision-making in life is horribly bad.

Negativity is what my life is experiencing. Nevertheless, when a brain is on drugs, many stupid and compulsive decisions will be made.

Wow, unexpectedly, drugs have performed another skill in my life. Already, I have quit two jobs; I quit going to college, and now I quit going to see my probation officer. Again, wow, what great skills drugs has. Or shall I say, "What great skills drugs and wickedness have".

You might think I cannot blame my ignorant decisions on drugs. From what you have read so far in this story, it has been revealed to you. I feel the need to blame someone, because I know I am not this ignorant. Oh, maybe I am. No one admits being ignorant. I already confessed being an idiot, and now I am confessing being ignorant. An idiot plus ignorant, equals one dumb wicked man.

Below is an update of events that the skills of drugs performed in my life.

#1 – An addiction from drugs developed within my brain.
#2 – I did not graduate from high school at my appointed time.
#3 – I was kicked out my parent's house.
#4 – Started smoking cocaine.
#5 – Police caught me with cocaine in my possession.
#6 – Police caught me with cocaine in my possession again.
#7 – Sold drugs to an undercover cop.
#8 – I was placed on probation.
#9 – I quit attending college.
#10 – I quit going to visit my probation officer.

Those were the many experiences my life encountered, while being under the influence of drugs. Those 10 events became my life's experiences, because of drugs performing their skills. You would think that enough is enough, but when drugs have heavily plagued its evil power in a person's thinking center, it is hard for deliverance to prevail.

When drugs are in the brain, the human head becomes a device of ignorance. Now that I think about my drug usage and experiences, my brain is nowhere near intelligent.

When I quit going to see my probation officer, my living became a big secret. I am now on the streets ducking and dodging my probation officer. Not only am I dodging her, but also, I am hiding from the law. Actually, I became a fugitive, because the law is now hunting for me. The law is the voice that placed me on probation. Therefore, the law is after me to convict me and complete its work. I am not on the run from the judge, nor from the probation officer, I am truly running from the voice that sent the law. Now that I am on the run from the law, actually, I am running from God himself. God holds the power to convict, and his laws are chasing me to perform its judgmental act.

When a person is on the run from God, what makes the individual think that a place of refuge can be found? Running from the law, which means running from God, a place of isolation can never be found. Well, actually, 95% of the people in the world have not the mental understanding of knowing, when they run from the law, they are running from God himself. Neither do people realize, when they disobey the law, they disobey God. Here I am on the streets running from God Almighty, and <u>I Did Not Know</u> it. Do you think God, or his laws are going to catch me?

When people run from the law, they become ignorant like Adam and Eve. Adam and Eve broke the law (God's command) and after doing so, they tried to hide. God is the one who planted the Garden of Eden, and Adam and Eve actually considered hiding in it. How can a person hide from someone who made the earth? Just like I can look down at the ground and see hundredths of ants working, in the same sense, God looks down from heaven, and see millions of people trying to hide. Adam is ignorant, Eve is ignorant, and Brian Irons is ignorant too.

If you are running from the law, then welcome yourself into the ignorant crew. You do not need to sign up; we need not to hold hands; the only thing you have to do is run from the law, and automatically you are grafted into the family of ignorance. We might not share the same bloodline, but due to our actions, we have become one.

While I was on the streets ducking and dodging my probation officer, she assigned a warrant in my name for an arrest. In other words, my probation officer signed papers, and sent out sheets for the law to come after me. The name, "**Brian Keith**" has become a fugitive to the world. No matter where I travel in America, the law has the ability to find me in any state. Wow, it is so true, you cannot run, nor can you hide from the law's Day of Judgment.

As of now, the police are looking for me. I dodged the law enforcers as long as I possibly could. Even when I did not have drugs in my possession, I still had to duck and hide. My life is now in a horrible situation of mental conflict. Every day of my life, I must hide. Because of another ignorant decision I made years ago (in high school), it caused my future to see this.

One day, as I was driving my dopeman-dopeman car, the police drove up from behind. When the police (the law) had driven up on me, one of them shined the bright light on my car. The cops walked to my car, and told me to get out. They both searched my body for drugs and weapons. Then they searched my car for the same.

After the searching was over, they handcuffed me, and escorted me to the squad car. I am now on my way to the city jail again. As I was being driven to jail, I was hurt from within. The law finally caught me, and there I was looking and feeling stupid. This is now my fourth time visiting the city jail.

When I arrived at the city jail, I was then taken to a room, and there I sat all by myself. While I was in the city jail, my mind began replaying all the pass hurts and failures drugs caused. Every drug experience flashed through my mind quickly. Usually, things flash through a person's mind one by one, but with me, things flashed through my mind, 3 by 3.

I am now in a position where I can't do anything, but sit, relax, and grope. Every time something arose in my life, I was able to leave immediately and attend to that business. Now that I am in jail, I have no pager to answer too; I have no chemicals to put into my brain, and my brain really needed its stress reliever. This day was really a brain-stressing day.

When I became a prisoner in the city jail, I sat in a cellblock for two whole weeks. It was so depressing to be in a place where only walls and bars could be seen.

In the city jail, I slept on a hard bunk. The bunk was made out of metal. My entire body pained until the morning time. This is the most uncomfortable moment of sleeping I ever experienced. A cot with a couple of blankets would have been more comfortable than this metal bunk. As I slept on this iron bunk, it did not give in; it stayed solid and sturdy. Therefore, my body could not sink into it, as it would on a real bed/mattress. My neck, back, and shoulders suffered intense pain. Crooks began to develop in my neck. My days in the city jail were rough on both my mental status, and my physical being. I hope I never experience jail again.

The food was okay. I ate breakfast, lunch, and dinner. I even met my favorite snack in this prison, which is a honey bun. Faithfully, the inmates were fed honey buns every morning. The honey buns were tossed into the cells, as keepers toss bananas to monkeys at the zoo. My meals were given to me on a tray. Every cell had a tray stand on it, that worked as tables for inmates to eat on.

So here I am, sitting in the city jail waiting patiently to hear what is about to happen next. The C.O. told me they are waiting for papers to process, and then I will be told what to do next. I am in the jail cell, praying God have mercy on me one more time. "I will do right in life, if you get me out of this one".

When the time came for me to be released from this cell, an officer called out my name. This officer came to the door of my cell, and said, "**Brian Keith** get up, it's time to go". Then the officer turned me around, and put both my wrists in handcuffs. At first, I thought I was going to court to hear the judge. However, this officer escorted me to a van that already had about eight sad looking men piled up in it. It did not take long until I realized I was on my way to the penitentiary. As I was being escorted to a van filled with criminals, I said to myself, "I just know this is not happening unto me". Well, yes, it is.

As I was walking towards the van, those prisoners looked like pitiful men. Every one of them (and me) had handcuffs clamped around our wrist. Myself, along with these fellow prisoners, looked like slaves or animals wrapped up in devices of chains.

The van was filled with criminals from all over the city. We were so close to one another that sardines in a can had more space than we did. As I was in the van with these law-breaking men, my eyes wanted to let loose some tears. I knew I was on my way to the penitentiary, and my mental power was getting weaker and weaker. The only reason I did not break down and cry is because, there were other prisoners in the van as well, and I felt it was time to either look tough or become tough. Although, one prisoner in the van cried like a baby, I still held in my true feelings, and never dropped a tear.

Going to the penitentiary was truly unexpected. I never thought I would ever be a victim put in a penitentiary. From the things I was doing, I knew there was a chance I could go to prison. However, I still never imagined myself going to a real penitentiary. Here I am going through another awful experience because of dealing with wickedness (drugs). Yep, again, I am going through this because of a skill performed by drugs.

I am willing to bet my life on the fact that, every man going to the penitentiary, was going because of something pertaining to drugs. Meaning, their hands were involved in an act, which caused them to receive a convicted judgment that sent them to prison.

When I finally made it to the penitentiary, there were more than several nationalities serving time in this camp. Wow, drugs have a world of brains trapped in its evil net. Wow, drugs have performed the ninja mode on every nationality. Somewhere in life, the wicked drug ninja crept up on them, too.

When I was a child, I was afraid of going to the penitentiary. After viewing movie scripts and television scenes pertaining to prison, it looked like a horrible place. I never wanted to be sent to a place like that. Examples shown from television have displayed the penitentiary to look like a bad place to be. Mentally, I was afraid of the penitentiary, but my mental fear did not mount up to preventing me from earning a spot in one.

Sit back and think about this; every penitentiary is filled with people who did evil deeds. Murderers, serial killers, thieves, rapist, forceful acts of sodomy, armed criminal action, and drug handlers are all crammed up in one facility. All those people, who have done evil with their hands, are gathered amongst one another. Since all those type of people (murderers, rapist, and drug handlers) are crammed up in one facility, then that is a place full of wickedness and evildoers. The penitentiary should be a place we should all fear. Although, I have not used drugs for more than 3 weeks, my mind still thinks from a negative point of view. These people in the penitentiary are wicked, and so am I. Who in their right mind can trust a bunch of wicked men? From the wicked deeds I have done with my hands, I must sleep in a prison every night, surrounded by a bunch of wicked people.

This scripture, *Psalms 28:4*, which says, *Give them according to their deeds, and according to the wickedness of their endeavors; give them after the works of their own hands; render to them their desert.*

If anyone is in the penitentiary for murder, the hands performed an act causing him to be placed there. If any man is in the penitentiary for rape, the hands performed an act in sexual abuse. If any man is in the penitentiary for robbery, the hands performed the act. If any man is in the penitentiary for aggravated assault, the hands did a work of bruising. If any man is in the penitentiary for property crime, the hands were in session to fulfill that act too. If any man is in the penitentiary for larceny theft, the hands did it. If any man is in the penitentiary for vehicle theft, the hands did that. All these men who are in the penitentiary, the scripture written in *Psalms 28:4* is talking about them.

Psalms 28:4 also said, "*Give them according to their deeds, according to their wickedness*". Yeah, it was God, through his laws that pronounced a judgment upon us prisoners. Therefore, everyone in the penitentiary got what he deserved. In other words, every man in the penitentiary performed a wicked deed; therefore, the penitentiary was their paycheck. If a man's hands perform the evil act, and the penitentiary became his home, he earned the ticket to get there. Wickedness and evil has made every prisoner a winner, because the penitentiary became their prize. There is no second place, nor are there third place winners, however, when any man is sent to the penitentiary, he has won grand prize.

If brain chemical infested people are all crammed up in the penitentiary, then violence and killings are committed in prisons on the regular. Since I am here in the penitentiary because of wicked deeds done with my hands, I have become one of them. We all have been sent to prison for one reason, and that is because performing wickedness with our own two hands. Although, I did not commit a robbery, nor performed a murder, I am still considered their equal. We are one!

Going to the penitentiary is like going overseas to battle and fight for your country. Just like a person joins the army to serve his time, and then fight for his country, well, going to the penitentiary, you have to serve your time, and may have to fight to save your life. A man might travel far away from home to fight in a war, and never make it back home to see his family, because of being murdered in battle. In the same sense, a man can be sent to the penitentiary, and never make it back home to see his family, because of being murdered by an inmate. Anytime a world of law-breaking people is dwelling together in one facility, wicked actions and experiences will occur.

It is 75% possible for you to end up in the penitentiary, if you keep involving yourself in drugs. I advise you to stay far away from law-breaking activities. If you stay far away from drugs, it will be easy to stay free from law-breaking activities. If you do not stay away from drugs, you just might end up in the penitentiary with us.

If you ever find yourself in a penitentiary, you are in a place of war.

From all of the past hurts and failures inmates have encountered, one of them is liable to mentally snap, and physically harm someone very badly.

One day, I was observing an inmate being released from prison. While he was packaging up his belongings, a big smile was on his face. This inmate was happy to be on his way to be re-united with his family and friends. All over his face was the message of joy. He had been here for a year and a half already. This very same day of being released, another inmate attacked him.

The inmate who fought him beat him badly. I saw the entire incident take place right before my very eyes. The wounded inmate went home to his family with a swollen black eye. His eye was sticking out so far, I couldn't tolerate looking at him. Nevertheless, both of these young men were in the penitentiary due to drug cases, which was a work performed by their own hands (fingers of evil).

The wounded inmate went home with a bruised-up face. I bet, when this wounded inmate finally arrives in his hometown, all of his friends and family will think that he's been getting beat up all the while during his jail time. Wow, that's a sad way to go home, and be united with friends and family, with a disfigured face. When you live in a place full of wicked people, awful experiences will come into your physical existence unexpectedly.

Although, I was in the penitentiary, life kept on moving. In the penitentiary, we had many dancing contests. So, I entered the breakdancing contest. Yes, I would win them all. I was a great dancer. I was one of the best dancers around. In high school, I even won a trophy in a dancing contest. But the best break dancer in the world, is Corey J.

If only you could have seen my dancing skills, you'd think I was a great dancer too. In the neighborhood, people called me "Turbo", who was a dancer from the movie "Breaking". As I said before, when my brain participates in anything, and likes it, it performs amazingly.

I played basketball every day while in the penitentiary. The entire penitentiary of inmates told me I was one of the best basketball players in the camp. This other person, Ernie, was a great basketball player, too. Ernie and I were considered the star basketball players in this camp (penitentiary). But my man Bill was a defensive threat.

Ernie and I both grew up together in the Vaughn Projects. We both lived in the area where wickedness cleverly took over. For the both of us, as we performed works of wickedness, we both had been caught. Suddenly, our names were added to the criminal system of the world. When I first entered into the penitentiary, Ernie looked out for me. Actually, when Ernie and I lived in the projects, we were cool friends then.

I have not seen Ernie in over ten years. However, from the performances of wickedness, it caused us to reunite in the penitentiary. If you have not seen certain people in years, and if you are sent to the penitentiary, you just might bump into those unseen people. You would be amazed who you might bump into at the penitentiary.

In the penitentiary, a few inmates were able to get their hands on some marijuana. The same drug, marijuana, which started this whole ordeal of wickedness in my life, is actually in the midst of this camp (penitentiary). I have not smoked marijuana or used any other kind of drugs for about a month; therefore, my body's system was somewhat clean.

Well, yep, there I go again, willingly causing my cerebellum to control my hand to grasp that dope. Yep, there I go again, causing my brain stem to inhale marijuana. This is truly crazy because I am in the penitentiary-inhaling reefer into my brain's organs. Something has to be wrong with me mentally, but <u>I Did Not Know</u> what it was. I should have been coaxing my brain to rehabilitate itself. Nevertheless, here I am in the penitentiary performing wicked deeds.

Of course, I was not the only idiot-smoking weed in the penitentiary. Ninety-five percent of the inmates were here smoking dope. The Penitentiary became "a neighborhood" full of wicked idiots. We were smoking marijuana in the penitentiary as if we were gathered in "the neighborhood". If any of us would have been caught with marijuana in our possession, more jail time could have been added to our sentence. I thought I was the only person who did ignorant things just to get high. I now see, I am not the only ignorant person in the world.

Every drug related inmate in this place shares a mental status of the <u>I Did Not Know</u> title. As these inmates allowed drugs to come into their lives, they have earned true rights to say; <u>"I Did Not Know</u> that drugs would cause me to serve time in jail.

Before I went to serve time in the penitentiary, here are some names of all the drugs I've experienced using. I smoked marijuana, which was my first substance of choice. I have snorted cocaine, and I have smoked it in crack form too (pre-mo). I tried "water" which is called "whack". I have crushed Tylenol 3's and 4's, and mixed them in cough syrup. I have swallowed volumes. I have snorted heroin. I have drunk beer and hard liquor. I did just about every drug there is, But never did I jack needles.

With all the drug chemicals I've put inside of my brain, do you think I have a normal brain operating mechanism (system)? Even though I felt and thought I was normal, however, it is impossible to be normal, after all of those chemicals have operated in one brain. That is too many chemicals one brain has been dealing with. Even right now, many of my brain cells have been destroyed, but <u>I Did Not Know</u> it.

Because of my drug addictions, I actually became a killer to my own life, brain, and body. When I started putting drugs in my anatomy (brain and body), I was feeding myself death. While putting drugs into my body, I was literally giving death an invitation to come unto me and swallow me up. Every person who puts chemical control substances in his or her brain is asking death to visit them soon. As soon as a person becomes addicted to any drug, death will be on is on his or her trail. Either death will come sooner, or it will come later. Just as a person cannot run from the law's judgment, a person cannot run from death. You cannot dodge death. How can you dodge the killer, when you are inhaling the murderer into your brain? For many people, drugs are going to unexpectedly choke their brainstem and creepily kill them.

Remember this: the drug ninja is after your life.

People, listen to my counsel, and receive this message! No matter what great things your friends tell you about drugs, do not be an idiot like me by submitting unto their words. Words are cunning, and they have the power to seduce you. You need to make up your mind, and be strong by saying "No" to drugs.

A friend of yours might be speaking to you in your left hear, saying, "give it a try, it will make you feel good". However, I am your friend speaking into your right ear saying, "drugs might feel good to the body, but it's not worth losing your sobriety, peace, and happiness in life". Do not give your life over to an addition. That is exactly what I did; I gave my entire life to an addiction.

Your friend in your left ear is not telling you the entire story about drugs. However, I am your friend speaking in your right ear telling you to stay away from drugs, because they will fasten a heavy and deadly addiction to your brain. I have told you the repercussions concerning drug usage, and not just the good feelings. So, which friend should you listen too? Are you going to listen to the one who informs you with only half the story (friend in left ear), or the one that tells you the whole conclusion of the matter (right ear friend, me)?

The only thing the left ear friend is telling you is how good drugs make you feel. However, I am telling you how your life is going to become a living mess. Even in this book, I am not hiding anything from you; therefore, I am telling you everything you need to know about drugs. Take heed to this book, and say no to drugs, or you'll be the next individual experiencing a lifetime of <u>I Did Not Know</u> tragedies.

If you know or hang around people who use drugs, you must decide immediately. There are two options for you to take. The first option is to disappear from their presence every time they put drugs into their brains. The second option would be to find new friends. There are many people in the world who do not use drugs. Therefore, you can always find new friends. When you leave the presence of friends who are utilizing drugs, your brain made a wise decision. Do not feel bad, because you have just saved your life from experiencing trouble. If the police pull up on you and your druggie friends, the both of you will be searched.

One day, I had a bag of marijuana stashed away in my pants pocket. In the bag, there were ten fat rolled up joints. I was planning (brain's frontal lobe scheming) to smoke this bag of weed with some close friends.

You know what, every friend of mine, has put at least 4 or 5 drugs into their brains, and that's a shame.

Drugs have manipulated the lives of many women who are in this world. Some women have allowed drugs to be their tour guide upon the earth. Being filled with dope, many women's feet have been led to walk up and down the streets searching for men to sale their bodies too.

Drugs have empowered many women to prostitute their own bodies. They actually take their clothes off; have sex with a man, in exchange for some dope or money. To all the women who give up their body (sex) to get high on drugs, that is an act of wickedness. Just as I sold drugs to make money, you sold your body to make money as well. You have shamed your body just as I have shamed mine.

Most of you women are just like me. Most women first got high just for the fun of it. But none of them realized drugs would take their life to highway limits. Just as I had no idea that I would turn into a drug seller; you had no idea that you would turn into a prostitute. Right now today, I know dozens of women who have been prostituting their bodies for years, just to get high. The reason why I know this is because, I gave drugs and money to many women to have sex with, more than the number of times I can remember.

In this life, we view women as being the weaker vessel in physical strength. Well, that is true, because she is physically weaker than a man. No matter how weak a woman may be, or how strong a man is, when it comes to chemical addiction, drugs do not care about the physical strength of human sexuality. Drug's addiction will beat a woman's facial appearance into the dirt, as if a man did that.

Women, get some heavenly help. Free yourself from the subtle force that drugs have plagued on your life. Go get your mind cleansed. Ever since some women have been on drugs, they have been hired by wickedness. Not only that, but wickedness has given them new names. These women new name is, "prostitute". Therefore, ladies, stop, drop, and roll out of the drug game and earn back your name. You and I both need to earn our names back. If you follow me, I will take you a place where names and lives are given back. Not only will I show you how to get your name back, but also, I will take you to a place where lives are granted peace.

Many women have once lived lives of beauty and glamour. Many were once crowned as "Prom Queen" or "Miss Beauty". If any of these women are caught up in using drugs, their beauty and lives will slowly change. It won't change for the better; it will change for the worst.

Drugs will perform its skill on any woman's brain, and will cause her facial appearance to go down. No matter how beautiful a woman appears to be, the power of drug's addiction has the ability to modify it.

Yeah, the brain is the worker that makes the face, and drugs have the power redesign it. Yep, God gave the brain such a power to make its own face. Because of smoking so many blunts, many women, as well as men, lips has been blackened.

Still as of yet, <u>I Did Not Know</u> or realized this drug addiction was setting me up. Once a person intakes dope, a certain path will be walked on. There are certain paths only people who use drugs will walk down. If I had not drugs in my living, my legs would not have experience walking down certain roads in life.

I have walked through many violent neighborhoods just to buy some drugs. Then suddenly, out of nowhere, rapid gun shooting appeared on the scene. You just never know what you are walking into when you are on a pursuit for dope. Here I am ignorantly seeking to purchase drugs, and walked into violence, wrath, and random gun shooting. What I am trying to say is this, if drugs had not been in my brain, many of the places I've visited, would not have been a walking ground for me. My footprints would have never been marked on certain pavements.

Check this out: A hunter goes out to the field seeking to capture an animal. The hunter takes along with him bait and a trap. The same way the hunter sets bait to lure and trap animals is the same way drugs lure and trap people.

After the bait and trap has been set, if an animal bites down on it, it then slams shut. Now the animal is trapped with no way of escaping. As this animal is trapped with no outlet, the hunter tosses a net over the creature's body.

Just as the hunter set bait on the trap to lure animals, drugs have done me the same way. Yes, I fell into the net of drugs. I am now trapped, and soon to be destroyed, and I Did Not Know it. The hunter catches animals to eat them as meals, and drugs have captured my brain, and are eating my brain cells.

A fisherman took a few rods with him to the sea. Along with the rod, he took a variety of hooks. Once the fisherman gets to the bank of the river, he pulls out his fishing rod. Then he puts bait on the hook, and launches the rod into the sea.

On the hook is a live worm. The fisherman sticks the hook through the worm's body. Just imagine how much pain the worm is having, while this hook is inside its body. The fisherman uses something (a worm) that is alive to catch another live creature.

The worm is used to capture the fish attention. The hook is for the big catch. It's a plot. It's a setup. Nevertheless, in order to capture something, a plan for entrapment must be planned.

The fisherman launches the rod, hook, and bait into the sea. The hook sits idled in the sea, until a water creature bites on it. When a fish bites down on the hook, the fisherman yanks and pulls on the rod. The hook thrashes through the fish's mouth. The fisherman now has complete control over the fish life. Now the poor fish is in the water being guided by this fisherman's pull. The fish cannot go the way it desires to go. The fish tries it's hardest to swim away, but the strength in the hook has its life captured. This fish could have been swimming in this water happily for weeks or perhaps months. Now all of a sudden, his life is being controlled by someone or something else.

The water is the fish city; it's his hometown, and it's his place of dwelling. Once the fish has been taken out of the water, it has been taken out of its city. In order to capture this fish, the fisherman has to launch out a rod with bait (worm) on it. Once a fish has been captured, and pulled to shore, the fisherman places the fish into his net. Once the fish has been placed into the fishermen's net, the fish has been taken from its habitat and from among its peers.

The fish has no idea that death was in the view. The fish did not know the hook and bait was a set up for its life. If this fish was able to speak for himself, I am sure it would say, <u>I Did Not Know</u>, the worm and hook was a set up for my life.

The living fish does not know what is about to happen next. My life is now a reflection of the captured fish. Just as the fish was captured by the fisherman, my brain has been captured by drug's addiction. Just as the fisherman tossed hooks into water to capture its prey, in the same sense, I tossed drugs into my brain, and the addiction has truly captured my life.

A biblical text I would like to share, concerning the fish. *Ecclesiastes 9: 12 for man also knoweth not his time: as the fishes that are taken in an evil net, and as birds that are caught in the snare; so are the sons of men snared in an evil time when it falleth suddenly upon them.*

As I have just said, I feel just like the fish, which has been captured and placed into a net to be killed later. Just as the fish did not know the worm was used to lured, captured, and then be killed. Yet, <u>I Did Not Know</u> drugs were the bait to lure me, capture me, and then have the opportunity to kill me. Most definitely, <u>I Did Not Know</u> drugs were the setup bait for death. Just as the captured fish was enticed with fish bait, in the same sense, I was enticed with drug bait. Now the fish and I both are battling for our own lives.

However, the fish has more sense than I have. The fish is squirming, and wiggling its body trying to get free. However, I am not doing anything but cramming more drugs into my brain. Even the fish realizes it has been captured. But I didn't realize a thing. I guess the fish's brain is smarter than my brain, huh.

If you are on drugs today, and not seeking to become freed from them, then a fish brain appears to be smarter. The fish has detected or realized that something foul has taken place. Although, a fish does not have mental knowledge of knowing anything about life or death, however, it has the ability to detect when something unorthodox is going on. Therefore, the fish panics and tries to become free. The fish does not want to be taken out of the water. The fish knows, if it is taken out of water, it will be taken out of what preserves its life. However, my ignorant self, <u>I Did Not Know</u> that life is in my brain, yet and still, I am smothering it with chemicals. Wow, in so many ways, a fish is smarter than human brains.

I've dealt with many drug addicts who were financially stable. Sometimes, they would spend 1 to 2 hundred dollars day on crack cocaine. Since that is so, the crack cocaine addict would spend $700 on crack per week.

The addiction lured and empowered the addict to travel back and forth to the bank to withdraw money. The money is withdrawn out the bank to buy more cocaine. The drug user does not know the chemicals are slowly forming such an event to file bankruptcy. Before the drug user realizes the addiction has caused him or her to spend close to $10,000 on cocaine in 4 to 6 months, filing for bankruptcy is in the making.

Filing bankruptcy is a devastating blow to the minds of the people who have been led to do so. Once filing for bankruptcy occurs, a person's feeling becomes hurt. Everything that once meant something has been taken away. When the money should have been used to pay bills or other important necessities, it was spent on drugs to feed the brain it's never satisfied addiction.

Having nice and comfortable furniture in your home will make you feel somewhat good from within. Nevertheless, if you allow your brain to stay chained to the addiction of drugs, all your rightfully earned money will be spent on wicked dope. Instead of buying things that will replenish your home, you bought drugs to feed the brain a chemical controlled substance. If you are not careful, drugs will create a moment to spend 90% of your biggest check (income tax).

As I was in this dope game (selling drugs), I experienced being involved in physical battle with other men. These battles were 1 on 1 fistfights. Of course, somewhere in life, quarrelling and disagreeing with people was in my life. I have been in so many fistfights that you would not believe. Frequently, I had to pay attention to my surroundings, and to those who were approaching me on a daily basis. These fights were also from works of personal judgment.

The craziest thing about my fighting battles is the fact that, every person I had an altercation with had drugs in their brains too. Whether their brains were filled with alcohol's ingredients, cocaine, or marijuana, a chemical control substance represented us all. In other words, drugs were in their cerebrum (thinking center) and cerebellum (hands coordinator) controlling its God created system. Yeah, we all are violent men. Drugs have waxed our minds with evil. If drugs are controlling your life, then God is not in control of your living. Do you see the difference?

I remember having eight fistfights. Each fight, of course, I was the winner. In all my fights, I threw a couple of combination punches, and the fights were over. Therefore, I had eight different fights, and all eight of my opponents ended up on the pavement. I am the greatest, I am the best, and there is none like me. But I must admit, a guy dropped me before too.

A human being does not fight against my body; he fights against my amazing talent, skills, and techniques my brain possesses. Although, my hands are the tools used when fighting, my brain is the vessel in control of it all. My opponent does not know that my brain has the ability to control my arms like identical twins.

Once I viewed how an opponent holds his guards, and how coordinated his punches were thrown, I already envision the moment to speedily rush at him and throw my lethal combination punch. Remember, in basketball, I can shoot 3 pointers with either arm. Remember, I can pitch a baseball with either arm. Remember, I can throw a football at a nice distance with either arm. Therefore, when it came to fighting, the same 2-hand talent and skill still applies. By my arms being both perfectly coordinated one to the other, it was easy throwing combination punches, and afterwards watching my enemy fall to the concrete pavement.

As you can see, my talents and skills are awesome in boxing (fighting) too. The people in Grape Hill began calling me, "LIGHT THE KNOCKOUT ARTIST".

After many of my fights were over, my friends named me after many pro boxers. Lord have mercy, in my life, when it comes to sports, I have been called every professional athlete's name under the sun.

Here I am in life, pronouncing judgment on people as if I am God. The people in the projects were handling situation by their own personal means, and so am I. The bible says, in *Romans 12:17 recompense no man evil for evil.* That is exactly what I was doing; I was using evil tactics trying to solve evil situations.

It's been more than 10 years since my family has moved out of the projects. In the projects, I saw much physical violence, gunplay, and random shooting. However, more than 10 years later, when drugs became a part of my living, I performed those same events. In the projects, I witnessed people running, and handling deadly weapons, such as guns. However, when drugs came into my life, I became a person who ran from the police and carried gun, too. As I said before, wherever there are drugs, violence will become an active force. Just as the Vaughn projects was an area filled with violence, however, my brain and body became the area filled with violence too.

I remember, one day, a friend told me that a particular individual was walking through the neighborhood searching for me. This individual was known for robbing and shooting the pistol. After I had been told, the first thought that popped into my head was him plotting to rob me. This person has never robbed me before, but I felt that an attempt was about to be done. Then I saw one of my friends in the hood, and asked him for his gun. Then I put the gun in my pants.

Then I went into this gangway, which is the spot that gives me a good view where his location. While the gun was in my hand, I stood behind a corner wall in this gangway. I plotted and waited for this guy to come outside. I stood in the gangway encouraging myself to pull the trigger.

This particular time, I was high as a kite. I was high from heroin, and only God knows what other kind of drugs were active in my brain. My brain's cerebrum (thinker) was filled with heroin, and it created strong illusions of actually pulling the trigger of this gun.

Drugs were talking to me big time. Although, I was talking to myself, however, drug intoxicants were in control of the entire mental conversation. Drugs told me, "As soon as the guy opens the door, wait till he get off the porch, and empty the clip. I never felt this way before in my life. But I felt like, enough was enough. Drugs caused me to become so upset, that they almost caused my cerebellum (hand mover) to pull the trigger of this pistol. If this person was seeking to rob me, I knew he would have had a gun, because nobody wants to get into a physical brawl with Lightskin. However, he never came outside, but if he would have, my brain was truly about to be tested.

I have been robbed 3 times already, and to be robbed again, I was not about to allow it. When a human being has been robbed at gunpoint 3 times, the only statement of words needed to be heard is that a known robber is looking for him. When I heard that this known robber was on the hunt for me, my drug filled mind clicked, and suddenly I became defensive. However, just that fast, and just that ignorantly quick, a 1st degree murder or aggravated assault with a lethal weapon was almost committed, and I would have been the chemical led victim.

If I would have murdered that man, the case would have been

called premeditated and non-self-defense. Execution by the law could have been my sentence and final judgment. Since only the law can give the death penalty, and God is the law, then God through his laws would have probably killed me. There is no telling, what other broken laws I would have had to face in court for that particular crime case. As I said before, God has a law's judgment for every wicked deed done under the sun. Another work of wickedness had almost prevailed in my life. Drugs almost performed another skill. My drug-filled body almost performed another work of ignorance.

Genesis 6:11, the earth also was corrupt before God, and the earth was filled with violence. Genesis 6:12, And God looked upon the earth, and, behold, it was corrupt; for all flesh had corrupted his way upon the earth.

Yep, I am one of those people's whose flesh has corrupted its way upon the earth. God is now looking at me, and watching me do wickedness continually. When people live lives full of drugs, their living is truly on a corruptible path.

Wickedness, wickedness, wickedness, how can I get help from the power of wickedness? Lord have mercy! Where can I find help? I need a doctor. I need someone to operate on my mental section. My brain has a real sickness within it, and <u>I Did Not Know</u> it.

Chapter 9

DRUGS FINALLY DAMAGED MY BRAIN FUNCTIONS

So, I served my time in jail, and freedom has come. Being released from prison, and not having to get physical with an inmate, was so relieving. I'm also glad did not have to use my brain's fighting talents and skills while in confinement. Although, at times, tempers were flaring on the basketball court, however, no fighting took place. Many of these inmates' bodies were solid and hard as a brick. I am glad I never had to wrestle with any of them. I came to the penitentiary in one piece, and I left it in one piece. However, I thank God for his mercy again, during those months of being in detention.

After I was released from the prison, I was then driven to the City of St. Louis. I went right back to my old neighborhood. Yep, I was so happy to be home again. It felt so good to see the intersection of Rutger and Ohio again. As I made my presence known in the "hood", many of my friends began greeting me. Although, the sun was beaming, the heat felt good, because I was in the "hood". Yep, here I am back in "Grape Hill". Yeah, I am home again.

Suddenly, one by one, my friends began approaching me. As they were approaching me, they began putting money into my hands. Maybe, my friends felt led to supply me with money, because of all the financial "love" Lightskin" showed them in the past. As I said before, there was not one person in the neighborhood that I did not give a helping hand too.

Anyway, after being acquainted with the neighborhood friends, I had to report to a place called, "The Halfway House". Although, I had to report to The Halfway House, it felt magnificently great to be in St. Louis again. In the movie, The Wizard of Oz, Dorothy said, "there's no place like home". That is so true, because when I stepped foot into the neighborhood, I felt just like that. Indeed, there is no place like home.

Also, there was no place like home so I can get into some sex. Sex is another addiction I had, oh so bad. My limbic system was addicted to drugs, and it was addicted to sex. I have not had sex in 10 months, and when I arrived in St. Louis, I had to get it.

Now it was time for me to sign in at the Halfway House. When I entered into the halfway house, I register my name (**Brian Irons**). After registration, I was then giving a room where I had to take my possessions. Once I sat in the room alone, I began counting the money my friends gave me. They supplied me with the exact amount of three hundred and fifty dollars ($350). That is a lot of money to receive, after being locked up in prison for 10 months. That truly shows that I was one cool person to the neighborhood dwellers.

Anyway, I slept in the halfway house for a total of 3 months. When I was released from the halfway house, I had to report to a parole officer. Therefore, I had to register my name to a counselor again. The name **Brian Irons** has been under the court's judgment for many years now.

At this particular time, I was living with a friend. My parole officer came to my friend's house, and attached a house arrest box onto his phone line. I had to wear a box around my ankle, which is a device associated with the house arrest plan. After a certain time of the day, I had to stay within so many yards of the house arrest box. If I'm farther away than the maximum length required, the house arrest box will record it. I think this house arrest assistance lasted somewhere around 4 to 6 months. The whole time, while I was stationed in the halfway house, and while I was on house arrest, I was getting high as usual. I allowed drugs to cunningly enter into my life again. I allowed drugs to find its way back into my brain and body again. This drug stuff has to be some sort of witchcraft; I must be under some sort of voodoo spell that I cannot break.

Before advancing any further in my story, let me submit unto you a scripture concerning "pride". *Proverbs 16:18- pride goeth out before destruction and a haughty spirit before a fall.* In other words, when a person has pride, a haughty spirit develops from it. When a person is filled with pride, he or she will somehow someway walk into a pit. That is what that scripture above is saying.

A person who has pride lifts himself so highly in self-pleasure, that it is all about self-achieved accomplishments. Anytime, you have "pride" operating in you, you are always on a mission to do things your very own "way". God hates the character called, "pride". Pride seeks to please itself, rather than exalt God. Pride is a self-motivator, and will always lift up itself in you. When you have pride in you, you only think about you, you, and more of you. Pride will cause you to put others down, just because they are not on your level.

Pride kicked into my life, and elevated itself as I was selling drugs. As I was making more and more money, I became the "man" filled with pride. I do not know how many years pride was operating in me, but it was there all the time, and I Did Not Know it.

Let me submit another scripture for you to receive. *Psalms 7:11, says, God is angry at the wicked every day.* If a person is doing anything, on a routine or daily basis, and it is against the laws of God, consider that person as being "the wicked". If you are living a wicked life, consider yourself an individual whom God is angry at. Most of those people who were living in the Vaughn Projects are called, "the wicked".

The penitentiary of inmates is "the wicked", and since I have been living this illegal lifestyle, I am "the wicked" too.

We as people always think God is happy with us continually. The scripture said, "*God is angry at the wicked everyday*". The scripture did not mention any names; it only said, "The Wicked". What you do on a daily basis will determine if God is angry at you. Also, what you do every day will determine if God categorizes you as "The Wicked". We think God doesn't get angry at us; we think he is only angry at other people. Later in this book, it is going to reveal unto you if God is angry at you, and if you are labeled "The Wicked".

After coming home from the penitentiary, while selling drugs, I reached a high standard. I went from profiting hundredths of dollars a day, to earning $2500 or more daily and faithfully. I had finally reached the point in my drug selling life where I was making top-notch money. Collecting and gathering so much money, my mind again became open to the thought, "You only live once".

As I was collecting so much money, I started a personal celebration. I have celebrated hundreds of times while using drugs, but no other weekend is in comparison to this one. This particular weekend, I sold a nice weight of cocaine. I sold whole ounces, half ounces, quarter ounces, and teenagers, which turned out to be nearly or more than $10,000. Actually, the celebration started Friday, and carried on until Saturday night. I did not have $10,000 in my possession all at once, but my hands handled that much money in two whole days. Actually, to me, this was a great and prosperous weekend.

I was sitting on the passenger side of a friend's car. We were both getting high, and selling drug to customers from the car. I probably sold drugs to about 10 different people this particular weekend, and no sells were 20-dollar crack rock. I moved up in drug rankings, and selling 20-dollar rocks to dope heads became outdated.

Saturday night, I was in a friend's car getting high. It had gotten late in the day, and was time for us to go our separate ways. I suppose, this guy drove me to my vehicle, so I could get in it. However, in his car, I had fallen into a deep sleep. Heroin and pills caused my brain to be overly exhausted. Right now, my brain is in a spell. I suppose the fellow who I was riding with, attempted to awake me, but I never woke up. Although, I was not aware of what was going on, my brainstem was still active because breathing was still in action. Nevertheless, the drug ninja snuck up on me again, trying to finish his work.

I suppose, at this particular time in life, I was slowly dying. Yes, this is truly, what the power of drugs has been trying to do unto me for a very long time. From the powerful stoke of drugs, I never made it to my car to drive myself home. Usually, after getting high, I would awake from a push or shove, but today; a punch in the face probably would not have worked.

Since I never woke up, I was then driven to a friend's house. However, when we arrived at my friend's house, I was physically carried inside of the apartment. I was carried because I was in a comatose state of mind. I was in a situation where I Did Not Know what was going on. The brainstem, which is the worker that gives life, is the only organ doing its job (helping me stay alive) (keeping the inner being operating).

When the people carried me into the house, they carefully laid me on the living room floor. It is possible, the people in this house thought I was probably drunk and knocked out cold, due to over drinking. However, I was not drunk. I was "high" from using drugs.

As I appeared to look drunk or high, this day was like a moment of disguise. From this household's visual experience, they all knew I was a heroin user, and as they watch me being carried into the house; I could have passed for being "drunk". While I was being carried to the living room, this family probably did not know what to think.

The long sleep patterns my friend and his family witnessed at times, after a night of me using heroin, was nothing new unto them. After a night of me snorting heroin, I slept heavily until the next day. Sometimes I slept until the next nightfall. The only difference remains to be seen is the fact that I was carried into the house. Other than that, sleeping overnight and halfway through the next day was a normal event.

As I laid on the living room floor unconscious, I strongly think my friend's family thought I would wake up the next day. However, I did not wake up the following day. I stayed on the living room floor sick and dying.

Death is now trying to enter into my brain, and cause it to become inactive. Anything dead cannot move, and death is trying to stop my brain from reorganizing itself. My cerebellum, which is my limb motivator, became forcefully inactive. Therefore, my limbs were on lock down. The only actions my body could do, was to lie on the floor, and obey what drugs had to offer. I never wanted drugs to put me in a situation that I could not wake up and do the norm.

When the next day came, it was about 4-pm, and I was still lying unconscious on the living room floor. The Collins family, whose living room I had overlaid in, soon realized I was probably in that same position and spot all through the night. I do not know the time in which I was laid on the living room floor the night before, but I heard I had lain there overnight until 4-pm, which is the next day. I suppose the family whose living room floor I was in walked by to check on me from time to time. I am sure my countenance was not looking normal.

My friend's family probably came to the living room, observed, and could not do anything but watch. As this violent drug scene was taking place, the family did not have the ability to help me out. I call it a "violent drug scene" because my brain had been knocked into a mode of unconsciousness. Anytime something knocks you out, the way it did me, that's a physically violent encounter. I may not have felt the physical encounter on the outside of the body, but my mental body felt the aggressive attack. My brain is now being manipulated by drug's power.

A member of my friend's family called my parent's house to inform someone about the scene that is now taking place. When my friend's family phoned my parent's house, they must have spoken to my mother.

This violent incident occurred on a Saturday night, and kept it's raging until Sunday evening (about 4pm). My mother was on her way back to church to hear some gospel preaching. She was on her way to hear a preacher speak on the oracles of God.

When my mother arrived, she called the church right away, to alert the saints about her son's incident. I am sure church service was immediately interrupted, and special prayers to God went forth. Within this church, the name **Brian Keith** is being lifted up in prayer.

Can you imagine the thoughts that are floating through my mother's mind, after hearing what has happened to her only son? The only words or news my mother could have heard is this; "your son laid on our living room floor all night". "We tried awakening him, but he is not responding.

A loving mother will always go and see about the condition of her offspring. No matter how light or heavy the condition is, a caring mother will make it her business to show up.

I have always known my mother to love me no matter what. I knew she loved me because of the passionate feelings and close relationship we have. I am confident that, when she arrived at my friend's house, as she beheld me, she put her hands upon my body. She probably knelt down on her knees, while viewing her son's body.

She, not really knowing, that she was watching drugs mistreat her son's brain and body. She has no idea; she is watching her son die. However, once she realized my condition is far beyond what her physical capabilities could do, she dialed 911 for medical assistance. She called the paramedics to come to the rescue.

While the paramedics were on their way, I'm so sure my mother began talking and praying to the God she knows. Mother probably said, "Lord, have mercy on my son".

My mother has been walking with God for quite some time now. Although, my mother's God (Jesus) did not answer prayers right away, as she may have desired, however, her God had a plan through his mercy. Since that is so, she already knows if God does not answer prayer right away, then keep believing, keep praying, and keep the faith.

Not only does God have a plan for righteous folks, but also, he has a plan for the wicked ones too. God will use you according to the lifestyle you live. If you live in wickedness, God will use your life through his judgments. If you live in righteousness, God will use your life in blessings. According to the lifestyle you live, will be the reason why God is doing to you what he is doing unto you.

In the neighborhood I grew up in (Vaughn Projects), there were gunshots, drugs, and violence that brought the police, and medical assistance to cater the area. However, in my situation, drugs performed a brutal physical attack upon my body all by itself, and caused emergency help to come cater to my illness. The projects became a place of illness, and my inner body became a place of illness, too.

When the paramedics arrived at the apartment, they immediately went into the living room to provide me with urgent care. Here I am, lying on the floor in my friend's apartment. Just as the person in the projects was lying on the ground after being shot in the Projects, I was put on the ground after putting drugs in my body. The man in the projects, which had been shot and killed, his incident was probably drug related, and so is mine. Somehow, someway, wickedness knocked us both down to the ground. We were both knocked to the ground by a performance of wickedness. Someone shot him, which was a performance of wickedness, and I put drugs in my body, which was a performance of wickedness too. We both were on the ground because of something that is illegal to have in one's possession. A bullet from evil struck his body, and my brain was struck by the evil power of drugs. On the ground, we both experienced the power of evil. Yes, the reason why were both were on the ground is because of actions of wickedness.

I suppose, the paramedics did CPR, while listening to my heartbeat. The paramedics placed me on a mat, while performing all their experienced skills to save my life. They picked me up and carried me to the emergency van. I am now on my way to the hospital to check in. The name **Brian Keith** is about to be submitted to a hospital for mental and physical treatment.

As I was on my way to the hospital, my breathing was lethargic (operating very slow). My brainstem was having a problem with performing its normal breathing. In other words, my brainstem is putting up a good fight. My breathing is fighting against the power of drugs, and the battle to survive is not yet over.

Right now, my brain's head organs are in a battle. I'm in the open field, and my breathing has been hit. Nowhere to run, nowhere to hide, my breathing is in a quarrel. Each intake of air is very vital right now. Breathe in, breathe out, it must be done, or I'm a goner.

This is so sad, too sad; it's nothing but the art of sadness. Yep, the name **Brain Keith** has just registered in another place on earth, in the city of St. Louis. My name has now been registered in a local nearby hospital. I registered my own name at the probation office; I registered my own name at the Halfway House; I registered my own name in drug programs, but my mom probably registered my name at the hospital. As of now, drugs put me in a position where I have not the ability to sign my own signature.

When the ambulance and I arrived at the hospital, immediately, I was transported to a special area. I was transported to an area called "critical condition". "Critical condition" means, "this is some serious stuff". When a person's injury is diagnosed as "critical condition", he or she is fighting to live. Just as it is hard to drive any vehicle in the snow, however, in the same sense, when critical condition is a person's status, it becomes hard to live. Lord have mercy! I am in a hospital surrounded by people, whose life, brain, and body has met the label of critical condition.

When the paramedics rolled me in the critical condition room, I was then pronounced "dead". My brainstem held on as long as it possible could, but the brutal strength from drugs overpowered it. My brainstem shut down completely, and stopped its natural use of function. I actually sent my God created brainstem through lots of ignorance, stupidity, and insanity. Nevertheless, the mercies of God are yet with me, even in this critical condition state.

As I was in the critical condition department, it was said and recorded that my heart stopped beating for 11 minutes. The emotions of life, which are connected to my brain, had just tasted death. In life, my emotions loved the pleasure that drugs released into them, but now, from the power of drugs, my emotion center no longer works. Drugs finally hit the target they been shooting at for years. My heart was the target, and drugs finally hit it.

I tossed marijuana's ingredients into my brain like a dart. After tossing marijuana into my brain, I tossed other chemicals into it too. However, on July 26, when I tossed heroin and pills into my brain, the bull's eye (the heart) was finally hit. The only sounds of celebrations being heard are heart-monitoring machines, which is to alert physicians of my heart rate, and other inner body activity.

Not only did my heart stop beating, but I went into a coma too. I slept in the coma for 10 whole days.

From all the talents and skills my brain possessed, I had the chance to shake up the sport world. However, as you have now just read, drugs shook up and messed up my world. Wow, <u>I Did Not Know</u> drugs would cause my heart to stop beating for 11 minutes. Wow, <u>I Did Not Know</u> drugs would cause me to be a patient in a hospital. Wow, <u>I Did Not Know</u> wickedness through drugs had a plan for my life.

After 11 minutes of no brainstem activity, suddenly, a heartbeat was found. Suddenly, there was a pulse rate in action. I suppose, while the doctors were working on my heart and body, the heart monitor machine showed breathing is now in action. If the lines on the heart monitor machine has ever gone flat line, they immediately turned into zigzags. My brainstem received unknown strength and went back to work. Yeah, my brainstem fought, and life came back in it. Just as a computer breaks down, and is able to be repaired; yeah, my brain broke down, and God's mercy repaired my breathing. Both my heartbeat and my breathing was turned back on. Therefore, when my brain was once pronounced inactive or dead, it now lives. I had no idea, or <u>I</u>

<u>Did Not Know</u> that drugs would do this to "MY" brain. I had no idea that the taste of death would be an experience for me. I have actually tasted a portion of death for real. I must tell you this; death does not taste good.

Although, my heart rate is now active, however, my cerebellum, which moves my limbs, is still inactive. The cerebellum is inactive because, I went into a drastic coma. In a coma, the body does not move, nor does it shift. The body sits still until it comes up and out of the coma. Although, my brainstem (mental alert center) is putting up a good fight, it had not enough strength to awake me from this coma. Therefore, I suffered going into a cardiac arrest. When I say "arrest", I truly mean arrest, because going into a coma is like being cuffed in a deep sleep. Wow, drugs finally brought damaged my brain functions.

The deep sleep (coma) that the power of drugs put me in is similar to the activity of two people in a fistfight. In my fighting days, I hold a brilliant record of 8-0, with 8 knockdowns. Easily, I handled each fight. I was able to see my opponent face to face, and duck or block any thrown punches. As I studied my opponent's fighting style, I used mental judgments before I threw my lethal combination punch. However, the opponents I am up against now are drugs. It's my brain against drugs one on one. I did not see the punch from drugs coming, and when it came, it hit me hard.

Drugs hit me with its one two-combination punch. The one two-combination punch that drugs hit me with is heroin and pills. Drugs hit my brainstem so hard that my heart stopped beating for 11 minutes. From the powerful punch of drugs, I was also forced into a coma, and stayed in it for 10 days. I have never heard or seen a man throw a combination punch, and from the punches, the opponent dies. However, when you allow dope intoxicants to operate in your brain, the dope will one day hit you with all its might. This incident was in the making for ten years, and I did not see this event coming. Another act from drug's power has just prevailed. Another act from the wicked ninja had just been performed. This is another act done by the skills in drugs. Drugs are powerful!

Drugs have a powerful punch; when they hit you, you will be hit at an unexpected moment. You might not be hit today; you might not be hit tomorrow, but it's a guarantee the punches from drug abuse will be felt soon. Sadly, to say, sometimes it takes a horrible punch from drugs and wickedness, for some us to get an understanding. When drugs punches on the body, there are no if's, and's or but's about it, you will know it was the strength and power from the upper cut of drugs. Take me as your prime example. When my heartbeat stopped, an unexpected uppercut from drugs did that.

While being in this coma, I had many dreams. For some reason, the dreams I had while I was in the coma, I thought they were events of reality. After awaking from the coma, my mind was in a confused state. After coming out of the coma, it was hard for me to determine between reality and fantasy. Many dreams can be fantasy, and some can actually be reality.

In chapter 5 (Drugs Controlling the Intelligent Human Brain), it says, when people intake Ecstasy or LSD, their brain can be sent into a state of not knowing the difference from reality and fantasy. In other words, when people intake Ecstasy or LSD, something can happen unto them, which might cause their thoughts to be to no different from mine. Yeah, the ecstasy or LSD user's thoughts will be the same as mine. A drug user does not have to awake from a coma to lose his mental awareness. The only thing he has to do, is keep-using drugs, and his insights will someday be compared to a man awaking from a coma.

More dreams I had while in this coma. While I was in the coma, I've had many dreams about being in a car wreck. For a very long time, I thought a car wreck was the reason I was in the hospital. When I awoke from the coma, those car wreck dreams I had while in the coma, I thought were reality. All the times, doctors would ask me, "Do you remember or know what happened to you"? Do you know why you are here in a hospital? After being asked, my reply was, "I was in a car wreck on Lafayette and Jefferson near the library. Yeah, my mind was really messed up in the days of being in St. Louis hospitals. I never knew the time, nor what day of the week it was. I was very confused.

I have a miracle to share with you. The miracle is about my coma experience. I was told my mother would ask me questions, while I was in the coma. My mother asked me to respond unto her by moving my hand. She asked me "to squeeze" her hand if I could hear her voice. I suppose, I did hear her voice, because family members told me I squeezed her hand when asked to do so. My cerebellum (limb controller) had just enough strength to perform that squeezing act. Of course, I did not squeeze her hand tightly, but she felt a slight pressure from the closing of my hand. I am sure the little squeezing of the hand brought great joy into my mom's heart.

Actually, since I did squeeze my mother's hand softly when asked, even while being in the coma, I still had enough sense to understand words. Maybe it was a sign from God showing my mother that her only son is going to be just fine. However, she still had to keep the faith, and keep praying, so that more miracles would be revealed and performed.

When a mother's child is facing death, there is no one on earth that will wail and moan to God the way she will. My life was under the power and decisions of my mother. My mother answered all questions from doctors concerning my health. If the doctors had horrible news concerning my condition and life, the weight of it, and pressure from it was cast upon her shoulders. I cannot leave out the fact that God's mercy has been the greatest helping tool of power in this situation. God's mercy has been brilliant unto me; and much of my health success thus far is because mother prayed to the God she now has.

When the doctors thought, I would not live to see the next day, or make it through the night, mother prayed, my family prayed, and friends prayed as well. When the doctors thought I would be brain damaged for the rest of my life, mother prayed. Everything the doctors thought would become a part of my life, if it was negative, my mother prayed against it all. When doctors told my mother horrible news, if it did not sound well to her ears, then it did not sound good unto her God ears. Remember, mother was praying, therefore, she was communicating with God, and hearing his voice.

The doctors questioned my mother; what do you want to do with your son? Do you want to take care of him for the rest of his life? Not only did the doctors say that, but also, they consulted with my mother about amputating my left leg. Wow, you mean to tell me drugs put me in a position were pulling the plug was a consideration. Wow, you mean to tell me drugs put me in a position where thoughts of leg amputation was a suggestion.

If my left leg would have been amputated, I have no idea how I would have handled that situation. However, I thank God I never found out what life would be like with having a missing limb. Nevertheless, if I did have to live life with one leg, I am sure that I would have adapted to it, because "**I am one strong man**".

In a sense, my mother was like a female Moses. Just as Moses went to God to get a word concerning the people, my mother went to God to get a word concerning her child's life. If her God said, "**Brian Keith** is going to be "well", it was a done deal. I think I need her God in my life too. Since God has given me a second chance at life, I think I need him in my life, too. I must grab a hold onto this God my mother has, and find out what he wants me to do.

While I was in the coma, the doctors thought if I do gain a little mental awareness, I would still live in a horrible condition. Meaning, I will be alive, but I will never know where I am or who I am. I will not be able to speak for myself. I will have to be fed by someone forever.

Let me clarify something right quick. All doctors who have earned their physician's degree, know what they are talking about. When doctors say, "A person just might live in a vegetative state, they know what they are talking about". Then, when the person comes out, and not in a vegetate state, that does not mean the doctor was wrong. Actually, from anatomy study, it teaches why people are in a vegetate conditions. It's just by the mercies of God, I am not in a vegetate condition.

People of the earth stop saying doctors do not know what they are talking about. Stop making our doctors look bad. God's mercy is upon the earth, and it can make any physician look like he does not know his study, when in fact he does. From saying this, "I've just empowered all physicians to keep the faith, and worry not. But I will also say this, hey Doc, you really do need to know your medical anatomy information.

While I was in the hospital, I Did Not Know why I was here in the first place. I did drugs with the fellows one day, and then woke up 10 days later. Imagine waking up 10 days later after being put to sleep for any reason. That is what the power of drugs will do unto its users. Drug users will put people in situations that will cause them not to know what is going on. Many people have already been put in horrible situation, but the worst is yet to come.

I remember when I was in the coma; many friends and relatives came by to visit me. They explained unto me I was looking like a person weighing more than 250lb. I have never weighed more than 165 lbs. in my life. Therefore, as I was positioned in the hospital, in this coma, I appeared to be a different man. I was so huge that a couple of friends did not recognize me.

I heard that, a group of friends came to the hospital to view my body while it was in the coma. They thought the front desk clerk gave them the wrong room number. The front desk clerk did give them the right room number; however, my body expanded and swelled up to the point that I was physically unrecognizable. Drugs actually altered my countenance. My reader, if you would have seen what my friends and family saw, you probably would have thought there was no hope for me. Truly, I looked like a man whose brain and life was going to be "out of order" forever.

Out of order! Did I say, "Out of order"? The last time I saw or read the phrase, "Out of Order", was on a vending machine filled with different flavors of soda. Well, I suppose the "Out of Order" phrase is the truth because drugs did knock my brain functions out of order. For the 11 minutes, when my heart stopped beating, my brain had broken, and became out of order. When people put drugs into their brains, they just never know when their brain will suffer damage, and be compared to a vending machine. Just as vending machines becomes out of order unexpectedly, your brain can become out of order unexpectedly too. Somehow, someday soon, drugs are going to knock a functioning part of your brain "Out of Order". Actually, if you are a drug user, I guaranteed you that many of your brain's cells have already been knocked Out of Order.

While I was in the coma, I was eating meals through a feeding tube. This feeding tube was attached to the navel of my stomach. For 3 whole months, I ate liquid food through this tube. Being fed food through a machine was weird, but it had to be done, in order for me to survive. Not only that, but also, my inner body was not strong enough to digest heavy foods, such as meat. Liquids became my food. I ate breakfast, lunch, and dinner through a feeding tube.

As of now, I feel like my life is completely messed up. I have to be a patient in a hospital because drugs thrashed my brain functions out of whack. Nevertheless, this harsh incident happened unto me, while I was under the tender mercies of God. I am starting to believe people literally need more than just God's mercy alone.

As my body laid in the hospital bed, there was a Foley Catheter connected to my body's private part. The Catheter drained urine from my body part. The Foley Catheter was connected to my private area because <u>I Did Not Know</u> when it was time for me to use the restroom. My brain lost the mobility of knowing when it is time to use the restroom. Drugs attacked my brain so badly, that the normal everyday bodily procedures, such as using the restroom had been stripped from my brain's knowledge. The doctors and nurses put pampers on a grown man (yeah, that is funny to me too).

Drugs deprived me of my young adulthood. Because of my usage with drugs, I became an infant all over again. Drugs sent a 24-year-old man into the mind and body of a 24-month-old baby. My physical strength (cerebellum) was going through the torture of what drugs had done unto it. Therefore, physicians, friends, nurses, and relatives had to do everything for me, and when I say "everything", I absolutely mean "everything". From all the fun I was having with using drugs, <u>I Did Not Know</u> so much fun would turn into so much disaster.

At this particular time, I was not able to do much for myself. The only movement, I was able to do was to lie down and allow nurses to clean my feeding tube, check my vital signs, and plug more operating devices to my body. About 5 to 6 machines were monitoring my condition. I was so sick and weak that I could not even move my own neck and head. I could not sit up on the bed to relax. I am sure there was pain in my body, but <u>I Did Not Know</u> what it was or where it came from.

While in this hospital, soon, it was time to start doing things on my own. My physical strength was still very feeble. The coma zapped much strength from my brain's power. Well, actually drugs are the workers that initiated this physical attack, because I am going through physical ailments all because of them. It seems as if my physical strength went into another world, and would never be found again.

It was hard for me to perform physical tasks, such as feeding myself. One day, while eating a bowl of cereal, my strength was being testing in a simple task such as this. Taking the spoon to the bowl to scoop up a little cereal, and then to my mouth to eat, was hard work and labor. When I scooped up a little cereal, and then raised it to my mouth, it would fall back into the bowl. I could not keep the spoon steady, to prevent it from tilting sideways. Slowly, I was able to lift up the spoon full of cereal, but guiding it to my mouth to eat it was the tough part. The cerebellum (limb controller) in my brain was still screwed up from the violent attack that drugs brutally spanked on it. At this particular time, I knew nothing about the functions of the brain, therefore, <u>I Did Not Know</u> which part in my mental was suffering from this brutal drug attack.

The occipital lobes in my brain deal with vision; therefore, since I was able to see the bowl of cereal, this lobe is still operating. Yes, thank

God I still have slight.

As nurses came into my room, I looked at them in a very strange way, because <u>I Did Not Know</u> who they were. I had no knowledge or understanding of knowing that those people were nurses. Drugs did my brain so bad to the point where, I did have sight, but I had no understanding of my present surroundings.

For so many years, drugs became a companion or a special part of my being. Wherever I journeyed, drugs went along with me. Either dope was in my possession or in my brain. Somehow, someway drugs were in my presence. Even when I went to the basketball court, drugs were either in my car or in my brain. When I went to see my probation officer, drugs went too. Even when I was attending court services, drugs were there too. There were not too many places or areas drugs were not afflicting its influential power around me. When a person does any kind of drug, the ingredients from the dope stays in the anatomy for days, weeks, and sometimes months. Before this incident occurred in my brain, I never went an entire 5 weeks of not having a chemical control substance operating in my brain. Well, during the 4 weeks I was locked up in jail just might be the longest time I ever went without surging drugs into my brain. Out of ten years of using drugs, 4 weeks was the longest time I can remember ever staying clean from dope.

Anyway, while in the hospital, I realized this was the worst incident that ever happened to me. No other experience I ever had is in comparison with this one. The process of having to learn everything all over again was hurting me from within. Not being able to leave the hospital at my own power brought great grief upon my heart and in my mind. I might not have to learn what 2 plus 2 is, but I have to learn many basics of life all over again.

While I was in the hospital, people told me I spat on many visitors. They said I spat on nurses, as they were providing me with care. In order for me to do something like that, it had to be a demon operating in my mind. Spitting on people is truly nasty.

I honestly believe a demon was in me, because of the attitude that proceeded from my mouth. Some people who visited me would stand far from my bed. I guess they were thinking I might spit on them too. At some point, it was as if the movie exorcist came alive in me.

I remember a certain commercial coming on the TV screen many years ago. This commercial talked about drugs, and spoke on what drugs will do to the human brain. The commercial was trying to shove fear in the minds of people concerning drug usage.

In this commercial, there was a frying pan, which had two eggs in it frying. The message the commercial was sending out to the world is this; when someone put drugs in his or her brain, the chemicals will cook and fry the brain cells, as an egg does in a heated skillet. People might not literally feel their brain cells frying, but the example is somewhat true. As people continue to use drugs, their nerve cells will gradually be destroyed. Obey the commercials on TV that speaks against drugs.

Actually, even right now, as you are reading this book, if you are a drug user, many of your brain cells have been destroyed. When certain brain cells have been destroyed, other cells in the brain accommodate for that which has been destroyed. The sad thing about it is the fact that you don't even know it. When brain cells have been destroyed, I am not sure if doctors can detect it. Millions of cells operate in the brain at the same time. Brain cells are probably smaller than atoms. Therefore, when a cell has been destroyed, how can it be detected?

When certain cells in the brain have been destroyed, other living cell go fill in the gap. The cell that deals with memory, if destroyed, another cell that deals with another function in the brain tries to fill in the gap. Cells that are for thinking needs to stay with the thinking. A cell that deals with memory should not go over to the thinking department to give support. The cells that leave its spot to help in another area of the brain, is in a place where it was not born to be. Just as it is hard to chew chicken with missing teeth, it is hard for a person to think properly when cells are missing from the cerebrum (the thinker). As a certain cell goes to help in another area of the brain; it soon becomes worn out, and then the person's mind is sent backwards. Say no to drugs, it is for the living of your brain's cells. Do not send your God created brain cells into phases of traumatic injury.

A person cannot hide from what drugs are soon to do to the brain. The only way to dodge drugs evil plots is to stop using them. As long as you are inhaling the death helper (drug) into your lungs, dope is going to get the victory out of your life. Do not think consequences or repercussions aren't going to contact your living. Drugs are your wickedness, and your wickedness must suffer the consequences. Your consequences are the tragedies drugs are going to bring into your life. From every drug encounter, a wicked experience will be chartered in the person's life.

When this harsh incident happened, I was 24 years old. 24 is a very young age for a person to suffer a tragedy such as this. Actually, any age is a horrible to suffer a tragedy such as this. If my brainstem and heart had not reacted again, I would have died at very young age of 24. If I now live to see the age of 90, that would have been 66 years of living, I would have missed from being present upon the earth.

Drug's job is to kill you, steal from you, and destroy you. At any given moment, those three activities (kill, steal, or destroy) can become your experience. If it concerns the drug money, or the mental addiction, one way or another, a person's life will suffer. The age of a person means nothing when it comes to being killed, stolen, or destroyed.

Even under the age of 13, drugs will hurt a young life. Drugs do not care about ages, nor do they care about personal background. Drugs have a program, and that is to make your life a complete mess.

Who would have ever thought drugs had the power to cause a person too suffer brain damage? Who would have ever thought drugs could be so breath taking, that breath would actually be taking from someone for 11 minutes? Who would have ever thought drugs would harm someone and cause that individual to stay in hospitals for months? Who would have ever thought heroin and pills would feel so good to the brain, then act against it, and send it into a coma?

Who would have ever thought drugs had the power to paralyze a person's limb? Who would have ever thought smoking one drug product (weed) would open up a door and empower the same individual to experiencing several other different types of drugs? Who would have ever thought drugs could take athletic talents that were once attached to a person's brain? Well, I never thought drugs could do any of the above actions just mention. But as of now, I am a true believer, because drugs did all those things to me. I am convinced that drugs can do almost anything that pertains to negativity. If you are engaging yourself into drugs, many of the above-mentioned experiences just might be yours. So, say no to chemical usage, because your tomorrow is counting on you to make positive decisions.

Drugs powerfully took a big part of my manhood from me; drugs have taken every bit of physical strength I once attained. If drugs have ever taken anything from your physical stature, consider yourself a victim who has suffered "drug assault". Anytime drugs take something away from your mental or physical status, you have been successfully assaulted. Assault means to do something physical force. Therefore, if drugs have ever taken anything from you, it was taken by force, which means you have been assaulted.

Usually, when an act of "assault" has been committed, they can be sued or prosecuted in the court of law. There are many laws in the script that cover charges for acts of assault. "Assault and battery" is one of the charges a person can be charged with. Well, I feel the need to charge drugs for "assault and battery".

If I could sue drugs, I'd tell the court to charge drugs for "physical abuse", which is "assault and battery". The assault happened when the drugs had violently beaten on my brain. Yes, it was a violent attack because drugs hit me and sent me into a coma. Not only was I assaulted, but also, drug's power went beyond a physical attack and abuse. When my heart stopped beating for 11 minutes, drugs actually performed a murder on me. During those 11 minutes of no heartbeat, I was considered dead, so murder is the case that drugs should be charged for.

Since I am the individual who put drugs inside of my own body, which caused my heart to stop beating 11 minutes, there is none to charge for the murder but me. There is none to charge for "assault and battery", but me. Yeah, my fingerprints were molded on every drug that has been put inside of my body. I am the guilty suspect to be charged with the "assault and battery" judgment. Death itself was truly my judgment. Nevertheless, God had mercy on me one more time, and here I am still in a land among the living.

Once a person put drugs inside the body, that individual has just made an agreement with drugs to become his or her physician. Once a person uses drugs, it goes into the brain and begins a task of surgical operation. Drugs will harm your body, rather than soothe or heal it. When you put drugs in your brain and body, you have just given drugs the amplified power to take care of you. Oh please, drugs will never take care of you; they will only bring more horrible experiences into your life.

When people go to the hospital for serious mental or physical issues, which may require surgery, usually a licensed doctor or physician is called upon. A license doctor is qualified to perform a number of surgeries. Surgery helps eliminate mental or physical distractions in person's body. Let's say, having surgery on a part of your body is required. Once a physician receives a verbal agreement or a written signature from the client, the doctor may then begin performing the operation.

Many surgeries require clients to be put into a deep sleep. After sleep has taken place, the physician then dives surgical devices into the body. Depending upon the type of surgery, which is about to be performed, anesthesia (numbness) to a certain part of the body might be one of the choices. Even a state of unconsciousness is required for certain surgeries. Nevertheless, when surgery is to be performed, the brain or body is soon to be re-configured.

Look at my situation; I allowed drugs to operate in my life as if they were a physician. Just as a physician puts his clients to sleep for surgery, drugs have put me to sleep (coma) in the same likeness. The doctor shoots dope (anesthesia) into the client's body, and I shot dope (inhaled or snorted) into my body. Just as a physician goes into the brain or body and reconstructs its functions, drugs went into my brain & body and reconstructed mine (brain damage) (paralyzed my left leg). This drug surgery was very brutal. I allowed drugs to become a physician unto me, and yes, surgery has been performed. Therefore, the doctor, which I call drugs, have damage my brain's functions by its surgical powers. Wow, drugs actually performed a surgery on my brain and body.

I realize a person does not have to be in the hospital to be declared sick. The only thing a person has to do is put drugs in his or her brain, and that is the sickness right there. Only sick people, such as myself, prances drugs into the brain. When I first put a drug (marijuana) in my brain and body, I was a sick individual to do something like that. I knew drugs were unhealthy for the body, but I used them anyway. Even before going into a coma, I was already sick in the head. I guess I was beyond sick; I was a psycho, because I introduced about seven different chemicals to my brain. If you are putting drugs in your brain and body, consider yourself a psycho, just as I once was.

When people in the world find out someone has committed a murdered or rape, they label that individual as a psycho. Well, in the same sense, if you are putting drugs in your brain and body, then you are a psycho, too. It is psychotic for anyone to put drugs in the brain, and then think to have fun while being intoxicated from them. People do not consider themselves as being psychos when putting drugs in their brain because they think it is a normal thing to do. Therefore, every time you put drugs in your body, consider yourself a psycho or a premeditated killer. That is exactly what you are doing, killing your own self. We are nothing but psychos because we are killing our own personal being. That is what psychos do; they seek personal gain to satisfy their evil desires. There is no good profit in using drugs. However, as people continue using drugs, psychotic tendencies will be their life's reward.

Chapter 10

Physical Rehab and Other Patients Injuries

The first medical building I was transported to was the St. Louis University Hospital. While being treated at St. Louis University hospital, things were very hectic. I was bedridden for about 2 months. At this hospital, my therapy needs were done while lying in bed. Although, I was a patient in St. Louis University for only two months, it seemed like I was there forever.

After two months expired at St. Louis University, I was then transported to a second hospital. This second hospital is called, "Bethesda". St. Louis University Hospital and Bethesda were both connected. My treatments in these two hospitals was my toughest times of coping. Many times, my eyes leaked tears in the presence of family members and friends. I was so hurt from within. My heart could not understand why.

After the two hospitals in St. Louis did their fair share of providing me with treatment, it was time to go to another place for more attention. I was then transported to a third hospital. The 3rd hospital is located out of town. It was still located in the state of Missouri, but it was stationed in different city. Therefore, because of the usage of drugs, my brain and body was scheduled to relocate to another city. Mount Vernon Rehab Center is my next destination for more physical therapy and mental rehabbing.

This is the second time I chose to do something and was sent out of town because of it. The first time my brain chose to do something, which was to sale drugs, I was caught doing it and was sent out of town to a state penitentiary. This time, which is the second time, I am about to be shipped to Mount Vernon Rehab Center.

All because of the performances of wickedness, through drugs, the name **Brian Keith** has registered throughout the state of Missouri. Wherever my brain goes, my name follows as well. The name Brian Irons was summoned to appear in court a number of times. The name Brian Irons registered in the prison system. The name Brian Irons registered in drug treatment centers. The name Brian Irons had a warrant for an arrest. The name Brian Irons registered in the Halfway House. The name Brian Irons became wickedly great in the City of St. Louis. Most dangerously, the name Brian Irons had registered in an 11-minute death experience. The name Brian Irons has been everywhere in the state of Missouri. It seems like names are very important in this life. However, follow me in this story, and I will explain unto you how important names really are. You need to know this. However, my name (Brian Irons) is about to check in at Mount Vernon Rehab Center.

From St. Louis to the Mount Vernon Rehab Treatment Center is a five-hour road drive. To me, it was far; it seemed like we'd never get there. My parents both drove me to this rehab center. The people (my parents) who told me to stay away from drugs are the ones taking me to sign up for more treatment.

Mount Vernon Rehab Center is a treatment center filled with skilled therapists. These therapist and doctors mainly deal with serious head or bodily injuries. I'm not saying that these therapists are different from any other, but since they have years of experienced dealing with brain-injured people, they learned how to treat intensive care patients. If this hospital cannot help an injured brain, then most likely, that individual's mental status is far beyond the help of earthly therapy. Although, my brain injury was far beyond the help of human therapy, God has performed a merciful miracle upon me. God has done for me what a human being cannot.

Finally, arriving at Mount Vernon Rehab Center, an evaluation of my condition was done. This evaluation is an assessment, which will determine the type of therapy required to get my brain and body in better condition. Not only will this evaluation expose my therapy needs, but also, the decision concerning the length of time to abide in this place was determined as well. After the doctors and therapists read over my medical report sent from St. Louis, they suggested I stay for 5 months. For the next 5 months, I will be living in Mount Vernon Rehab Center.

This drug encounter happened to me on July 26. I returned home on March 25. I was a patient in the St. Louis hospitals for 3 months and will now be in Mount Vernon for 5 months. For a total of 8 months is the length of time of being in hospitals.

As you have just read, I've lived in three hospitals for almost the total time of a complete year. ¾ s of the year I was stuck in buildings having mental and physical therapy. I was here in Mount Vernon on Christmas, and even on my birthday. However, I was not thinking about a birthday, I was only thinking about going home and getting better.

During my 5-months at Mount Vernon, the doctors and therapists were astonished after reading my medical report. The 11-minute heart failure persuaded the doctors and physical therapist into believing I was truly a "special" case. I suppose the 11 minutes heart failure is reason why I had two therapists walking along with me in the halls. I always wondered why the entire crew of therapists watched me closely, while walking in therapy. I guess from the conclusive report of my story, they were all so amazed to see me recover so fast. I felt like a celebrity in this place.

The reason two therapists were appointed unto me is because; while walking during therapy, I would lean too far on my right side. One therapist was on my left side, and the other was on my right. My right leg was stronger. I trusted the right side more than I did my left (damaged nerve leg). I was scared to walk on my left ankle, because I could not feel any pressure when stepping down on the pavement. My brain is not familiar with this kind of walking mode. I was very scared of stumbling or losing my balance, and then hitting the floor. Nevertheless, I thank God I never fell while walking in therapy.

Walking was a very hard task for me to perform. From drugs causing an injury to the sensation of my left leg, the left ankle suffered nerve damage. My walking balance was very poor. From this injury, the left side of my body is the side that needs the most work. The paralysis mainly attacked my leg left (knee down). My thigh muscles do flex, which is a good sign. It made me realize, if I can flex a muscle in this leg, then there is a chance for it to improve.

Walking long distance with damaged nerves in one leg, felt very weird. Due to this nerve damage, my walking has become slow, shaky, and uncoordinated. Even when standing upright, my balancing was being tested. When I realized my left leg is suffering from damaged nerves, I knew I had to work hard in order for it to get in better condition.

During my stay at Mount Vernon Rehab Center, the therapists were doing a great job. Not only that, but also, they were doing a great job at teaching me how to cope with life from a brain injured point of view. If it had not been for Mount Vernon therapists and counselors, I would not have recovered the way I did.

I want to thank a few therapists who helped me get my brain back together: Joe, Mary Lou, Betty, Patty, Melody, and many others, I thank you all for your support. Also, I want to thank God Almighty. Without his mercy, I would not have had the chance to participate in therapy.

Before this accident happened, I never had to think while walking. Now a day, I have to think before taking any number of steps. Before my brain suffered an injury, I walked willingly whenever desired. Usually, I stepped my legs out there, began walking, and never took second thought. Although, I now have to think before walking, my cerebellum is doing magnificently great.

Sometimes, on certain outdoor pavements, I have to think which leg to step with first. It's not that I'm confused; however, many pavements are uneven. Therefore, I need to be careful on which leg to step with first. On uneven pavements, I've lost my balance so many times, and almost fell. Actually, to be honest with you, I have fallen a few times. Although I have fallen a few times, I thank God, I never seriously injured myself.

Before attending Mount Vernon Center, the surgeons in St. Louis took the feeding tube out of my stomach. My inner being had gotten stronger. Therefore, my body was receiving great physical strength. During rehabilitation, as I was getting stronger, my mind was receiving strength as well. I began to eat normal again; meaning the food was not dropping back into the bowl after lifting it up to my mouth with a spoon or a fork.

While I was living in Mount Vernon Rehab Center, I learned that patience is a vital asset to physical recovery, as well as to everyday living. I had to learn patience on another level. Ever since this brain injury has occurred, I had to wait on other people to do things for me, and it was hard tolerating such. I was used to doing everything for myself. When I had gained mental sense to allow patience to endure, I became relaxed in heart. I realized, I must sit, be patient, and let the patience of life take its course.

My brain, as well as a few other clients in this rehab center, had suffered damage too. I sat and watched the therapist explain unto a man over the age of 40 how to ride a bike. This man's brain actually forgot the procedures on how to ride a bike. I am sure, before this grown man suffered a head injury; that he rode dozens of bikes in his lifetime.

However, in Mount Vernon Rehab Center, his head injury actually caused him to lose already learned bike riding information. Since past-learned physical activities are stored in the procedural memory, this person suffered an injury in that particular area of the brain. Wow, it is so true that one personal experience can turn a person's life upside down. If I can remember correctly, I think his brain injury was from a car wreck, driving while under the influence of alcohol.

There is another patient in Mount Vernon I want to write about. This patient is a young man. He was a patient in the rehab center before I became one. When I met him, he was 16 years old. His story or tragedy is very different from my tragedy. But his incident was so serious that Mount Vernon Rehab Center became a place for registration. No one goes to Mount Vernon, unless a person's brain, and or body has suffered from a horrible tragedy.

This young fellow rolled around in a wheelchair. Actually, 85% of the patients in Mount Vernon used wheelchairs. This 16-year-old fellow shared his story with us all. He told us that he was walking with two of his friends one day. As he and his two friends were walking, they all came to a bridge. When they reached the center of the bridge, his two friends physically grabbed him and tossed him off the bridge.

When this teenage child fell to the ground, he landed on his head and suffered an injury to the brain. The injury he suffered had caused him to be paralyzed in one of his arms, and in one of his legs. This young man's body was in bad shape. I felt very sorry for what happened to him. Nevertheless, he and his friends were both drug users, which wickedness lived inside of.

I suppose the two fellows who tossed this teenage boy off the bridge must have tried to kill him. This teenager was walking with some friends one day, and all of a sudden, he was attacked, handled, and tossed off a bridge. A case such as this, the law has about five convictions to charge those guys with. Just that fast, and just that quick, the power of wickedness led two men to perform an "assault and battery" but came close to committing a 1st degree murder.

I want to throw this paragraph in as a bone for you to bite on. My reader, "drugs will get you one way or the other". How can you trust a person who puts drugs in his or her brain? Your drug-filled friends are the ones who will set you up for the take down. Sometimes, your enemy is the same individual you are passing the dope too. You might think it's all about the puff-puff pass, but you just never know who is actually jealous of you, and giving you the evil eye all the while.

I never got the chance to hear the entire reason why he was tossed off a bridge. I do not know if his friends were robbing him, or if it was a payback for something he did in the past. However, I am going to throw my 2-cent in. Since he did confess he was a drug user, I am willing to believe the two people who tossed him off the bridged where probably drugs handlers of some sort. Yeah, their brains must have been operating from the cunning ingredients of drugs. Who in their right mind would toss a live boy off a bridge, as if he is a piece of trash? Honestly, who in their right mind would toss a man off a bridge, knowing there is a chance the young man could be killed or suffered tremendously from a spinal cord injury?

Well, let me tell you who would toss a man off a bridge. A person whose hand touches wickedness (handles drugs), will be led to do such a thing. A person whose thinking center is filled with the murder weapon (drug or wickedness) will be led to do such a thing. Once drugs elevate the mind to seek harm, it will soon cause the limb motivator to uplift violence.

A life filled with drugs will experience harm one way or another. Drug and alcohol usage will either harm its users, or provoke them to harm someone.

For example, the 16-year-old who was tossed off the bridge suffered an injury, but the people who did the tossing, never felt any harm. Therefore, drugs had empowered and encouraged two people to harm that young man, which is someone else other than themselves.

The reaping what you sow law covers every evil deed committed. No matter what evil deed you have done, the prophecies, and the laws from God have a plan. From the smallest act of evil, up until the greatest evil deed done, a judgment is measured out for you. The two men who tossed the young boy off the bridge will suffer because God has required it to be so. The prophetic scripture written in the book of *Psalms 28:4*, which says, *give them after the works of their own hands; render to them their desert.* This prophecy will haunt them down and provide punishment. The two fellows who tossed the teenage boy off the bridge, they might not be tossed from a bridge; however, they will reap from that evil act sown. They are living life, not knowing what's going to happen next in their lives.

Every person in the world says this; "what goes around comes around". Well, since that is true, maybe something has crept into those two guys' lives, and damage has come unto them. Actually, the said quote; "what goes around comes around", is not the phrase written in the bible. However, "you reap what you sow" is the true phrase to be said. Nevertheless, when we sow evil deeds in our lives, we just never know what type of judgment we will reap. Concerning the two guys who tossed the young man off the bridged, they could have been killed by now or going through harsh physical ailments right now today. Nevertheless, tossing a person off a bridge is an act of wickedness.

At Mount Vernon Rehab Center, I met another patient who had been wounded by acts of wickedness. Yeah, someone was guided by wickedness to perform an assault on this man. Someone used illegal firearm and shot artillery (bullets) at him. His leg was the prime area the bullets hit. When the bullet or bullets hit his leg, most of it became useless.

His leg was damaged so badly that most of it was amputated from the upper thigh area. In other words, ¾'s of this man's leg has been cut off. The knee is now gone. The ankle is gone. Only the stomp (upper thigh) of his leg remains.

The medical center he came from amputated his leg. For 22 years of this man's life, both of his legs were active while walking. He now has to deal with one leg for the rest of his life. Every day of his life, this tragedy scene will be reviewed in his mind. A tragedy such as his, and mine, and the kid who was tossed off a bridge, there is no way these events can be mentally forgotten. I am sure this one-legged man's heart was shattered, after the incident occurred. However, just like me, he must keep a positive attitude while living out the rest of his life.

I wonder what the doctors did with the parts of the leg that had been chopped off. As I now think about it, ¾ of this man's leg was probably thrown in the trash or given to charity. Or it was probably used for scientific experiment. Wow, acts of wickedness stripped a part of this man's leg from his body. Never will he attempt to put socks and shoes on one of his feet again.

This one legged fellow also uses a wheelchair just like the rest of us here at Mount Vernon Rehab Center. While we both were at Mount Vernon Rehab Center, we became great friends. We talked, laughed, and shared secretive experiences we've encountered in life. We shared stories concerning why we both were sent to this rehab center.

Hearing his story or testimony encouraged me mightily. After I told him my story, he became encouraged too. As the one leg man was sharing his experiences with me, it was revealed unto me through confession, he was a dope head too. Therefore, wickedness is the reason why he had been shipped to Mount Vernon Rehab Center. He is another witness who can profess and say, <u>I Did Not Know</u> drugs would prepare a scene, day and time for bodily harm to be my experience.

No one deserves to be tossed from a bridge; neither do I think a man will ask to have his leg amputated from his body. However, when drugs are in peoples' lives, the fullness of evil will be performed. Once drugs empower the mind to seek after harm, there is no turning back.

People in the world are harming one another all because of drugs being in their brains. As of now, three people have been sent to this rehab center because of wickedness and evil. Someone performed an act of wickedness by tossing the teenager off a bridge; someone performed an act of wickedness by shooting the man's leg off; and I performed an act of wickedness by putting drugs into my brain and body.

Nevertheless, wickedness is the blame for bringing bodily harm to our bodies.

I met two other people at Mount Vernon Rehab Center. At first, I did not remember who they were, until they both confessed, they purchased crack cocaine from me before. After their confession, I began to remember their faces. Therefore, they were friends of mine through dope transaction. They both were from the City of St. Louis. They both lived on the south side of St. Louis too. Nevertheless, because of the acts of wickedness, they both were shipped to Mount Vernon Rehab Center.

A horrible event happened in both of their lives. The event was so horrible that Mount Vernon Rehab became a place for them to check in. They both used manual wheelchairs while traveling through the hospital. One of them had been shot ten times. Ten bullet wounds were found on his body. Every bullet, which was shot into his body, left slashing scars. The slashes were once open holes, but they are now closed. His body is marked for life. Wickedness did this unto him. He said, "a few bullets are still in his body right now today". When I heard that, I thought about his inner being. Do you remember when I was a kid in the projects, wondering if bullets remain in the body? Well, after hearing his testimony, I now know that bullets can remain inside the body. If bullets are still inside of his body right now today, then those bullets are stuck to his inner being. He is another victim who can say, "I Did Not Know" that drugs would prepare a scene for damage to be done to my body". Since weapons of war (guns) are the true reason for his injury, then acts of wickedness is what caused him to be shipped to Mount Vernon from St. Louis.

The other person I knew from St. Louis had been shot too. Someone shot bullets at him, and one cruised into his neck. The neck bone and the spinal cord are the most important bones that keep the body upright while standing. Probably, immediately, when the bullet entered into his neck, the spinal cord immediately lost its power.

As you can now see, not only will a brain injury cause legs to suffer, but also a gunshot to the neck or spinal cord will take away limb strength as well. Even though the cerebellum in his brain is still operating, however, from injury done unto his neck, other parts of his body lost the power and strength it was once born with. When his neck became injured, the bones throughout his entire body became afflicted. As I said in the beginning chapter of this book, every bullet that is fired from a gun counts the number of wickedness. Therefore, not only did a bullet cruise into his neck, but also, wickedness proceeded into it too as well.

In the rehab center, I have met a number of people who had issues in their lives. Either the issue was physical or mental. If the issue was physical, the body had been beaten badly. If the issue was mental, the brain suffered an injury to the lobes. Every person in the rehab center needed to be provided with visual care. Since the brain is the duty of man's every reaction, most of these patients had to be hand fed. I was looking at people who were going through trying times I once experienced. Grown men lost the mental ability of knowing when it is time to use the toilet. When a person has reached a certain age in life and has lost the mental function of knowing when it is time to use the restroom, that hurts the heart badly.

As I said before, drugs do not discriminate. In the penitentiary, there were many cultures. At the probation office, there were many cultures. Now, at this rehab center, there are many injured races (people) here. At Mount Vernon Rehab Treatment Center, I saw more than seven nationalities. Many of the patients suffered from a tragedy that drugs had performed. Every nationality in this rehab center is no different from the other. Wherever there is a brain, and if, drugs become mobile in it, it becomes powerless. No matter what nationality these people are, drugs performed the same work on them all. Just as in the penitentiary, people were locked up because of what drugs empowered them to do, however, in this rehab center; drugs had empowered different races to check in. Drugs are not prejudice!

Many patients at Mount Vernon experienced horrible car wrecks.

From the car wrecks, many of these people's brains suffered damage, which caused their bodies to be in bad shape. It looked as if there was no hope for them. However, there was hope, because they were still alive. Many of the patients were pushed into the rehab center in nursing beds. They were in much pain, and loud noises of grunting I heard. As I looked into a patient's eye, I saw how his pain and misery. However, you just never know how far a person's rehabbing has come after suffering from a mental and or physical disaster.

Electric wheelchairs were their means of traveling through the rehab center. Moving their risk to control the wheelchairs was a skill used by these patients. They could not move or control their arms the way I could. They could not stand on their own two feet, nor could they move their legs. Some of these people had been driving while under the influence of drugs and alcohol. Drinking while under the influence of alcohol is a breaking of the law. Since many patients were in Mount Vernon because of driving while intoxicated, they brought condemnation upon themselves. Now they might have to use electric wheelchairs for their rest of their lives. When a person drinks, and then drives a motorized vehicle, he or she never knows if condemnation is in their driving lane.

Why do people exit bars or nightclubs thinking they are mentally okay to drive a vehicle? Many people believe it is okay to only drink a few drinks, and then drive a motorized vehicle. They think they are beating the system by only gulping down small portion of alcohol. Even after drinking small portions of alcohol, the brain's reaction is still off track.

When alcohol, drugs, or any chemical is released in the brain, never think you are in a good mental state to drive a car. When doing so, not only is your life in jeopardy, but also, other people's lives are at state as well. It's not fair for you to damage or jeopardize someone else's life. You might not be the person to encounter an injury, but while you are driving under the influence of alcohol, there is a chance you might injure an innocent being. Time after time, you've been driving while under the influence of alcohol, and nothing has happened on a serious note. However, your day of an evil experience is coming soon. If you keep driving motorized vehicles while under the influence of alcohol, there is a chance that your name might soon be on Mount Vernon Rehab Center registration list. Then you will become one of us. Either you will cause someone to check in for physical rehab or you will be in need of rehab yourself. I am not wishing anything bad to happen unto you, but that is just "how the cookie crumbles" when driving while under the influence of chemicals.

Just the other day, I looked at some pictures. These pictures were images of a beautiful young woman who had been in a horrible car wreck.

A man claimed to have guzzled down a few drinks. While being intoxicated from the drinks, he got into his car and began driving it. As he was driving to his destination, he hit the car of a gorgeous woman.

Her vehicle was hit so hard that all the doors became jammed. I suppose, from the impact, the car doors bent in such a way that they could not be opened. The beautiful woman was trapped inside the car with no way of getting out on her own. She could not move her limbs. It was almost as if the car became a strait jacket to her body.

As this beautiful young woman was trapped inside, she was being tortured. Her car caught on fire. The woman's body is feeling the power of flames. If her eyes opened during this horrible incident, I am sure her vision was impaired. I am sure she tried fighting the fire off, but who can win when fire is a contender. Even a person with great fighting skills as I have is no match against flames of fire. The car had not the power to fight the fire, and neither did the woman. The longer the woman stayed trapped inside, the more her life burning away.

The woman did manage to escape alive from the burning car. Rescuers saved her before her flesh burnt into a corpse. Although, she was rescued from the burning car, her body suffered major burn wounds from head to toe. Once fire hovers on a person's body, it shows no sympathy. Her entire head of hair, the fire burnt to the scalp. The hair holes in her scalp, will never spring forth hair again. She was burnt to the point where all her clothes had probably burnt onto her skin. She suffered greatly from the flames attack. Her beautiful skin was stripped from her body. She will have to use medicated lotion on her body for the rest of her life. Even unto this day, she is suffering physiologically and physically because of another person's law-breaking move.

I saw pictures of this woman before the horrible incident happened. While looking at her photographs, she appeared to be at the age of 21-25. She is very beautiful. She is a well-built looking young woman. She looked like the type of woman that never had difficulties finding a man. In fact, I am sure men fell at her feet, just to have a local dinner date with her. If you ask me, she is so beautiful that all the women in beauty competition would be fearful of losing their position. Yes, the girl is just that pretty, and she is one of a kind.

Let's just say, this young woman had gotten off work and was driving home to present her family with some joyful news. The sad and heart-breaking point in her story is that she never had the chance to walk down the pathway that led to her front door. She never got the chance to unlock the door and enter into the house. Actually, she never got the chance to drive her car down the street she lives on. She could have been 5 minutes away, and suddenly experienced a horrible car wreck. This car wreck prevented her from making it to her destination. Why, because, suddenly she had to be submitted to a nearby local hospital to be prevented from dying.

After her name was registered in a hospital, treatment and physical therapy was administered immediately. Hospitals became her home for the next several months. Medical attention became her nightmare. Another innocent victim's life changed toward the worst. She had no idea she would experience a horrible tragedy such as this.

Her body and facial appearance have been completely altered. Probably, before this incident happened, while looking at herself through a mirror, she saw something nice, pretty, and good to go. After the car accident occurred, she probably doesn't have a desire to look at a mirror. Within, she probably cannot stand the fact that the mirror reflects back to her a burnt face. For the rest of her life, she has to look at an altered face. All because someone broke the law by drinking and driving; her entire countenance has been changed.

How do you think it feels to have beauty, and then lose your glamour in uncontrollable "flames" of fire? That is sad, very hurting. Just thinking about this situation bitters my soul. Someone messed up her life and body just that fast. She has scars, burnt marks, and bruises all over her body that will never go away. The experience that unexpectedly arose in her life will be rehearsed in her brain for the rest of her earthly life.

People, stop drinking, and driving! Guess what, you can't stop drinking and driving. You are addicted to alcohol. You can't stop drinking and driving because you do not have the strength to do so. You have been poisoned. Your life seems to be cursed. The big bully has your mind, and the drug ninja crept up on you, and has captured your life. The hunter, the fisher, the strong wrestler, the reap what you sow, and every form of evil has your brain under their controlling power. You have bitten on the bait of chemicals, and the snake's poisonous venom is now in your brain. Now you need to go get some brain treatment.

The drinking driver physical situation is very distant from that of the young woman's. The drinking driver has neither scars, wounds, nor any harm done unto his body. He looks in the mirror every single morning and sees the exact same image (face). His heart might feel a little pain and resentment. However, his heart of pain will never mount up to the pain that has been compressed into the heart of the burning woman. Nevertheless, the drinking driver lives up to my title, too. He can actually say, "<u>I Did Not Know</u>" that I would cause damage to someone's life, while driving under the influence.

Now I am about to talk too all women of the earth. Ladies, you just never know what a man will cause to dissolve into your drink. Most women think drugs brings a calm mood while out on a date. Many believe drugs are the fun creator. Well, not only will drugs create fun on the date, but also, drugs can cause a heart hurting experience. For the rest of your life, an awful experience can be plastered into your thoughts. Just by using drugs while out on a date one time too many, you can unexpectedly be done in wrong.

Ladies, after meeting a man, going out on a date with him is a normal event to engage in. Dating is cool; it is our way of saying; "I am interested in knowing more about the person". Dating is one of the practices people do before entering into a real relationship. Dating is supposed to be clean and yet sober.

Now a day, people put drugs in the brain while the date is in session. We even do this on the first date. Not realizing it is a virtual mistake. I can only imagine the number of women who went out on dates and had in mind not to have sex on the first date. However, while being high on the first date, sex was performed. Most of the times, when people have sex on the first date, it turns out to be a one-night stand.

Chapter 11

SIGNS FROM GOD AND MY HEART IS IN PAIN

In this book, you have just read how my personal usage with drug brought physical and mental hurts into my life. From those physical and mental hurts, my heartfelt the shift of disappointments, and it travailed in pain. Instead of my mind operating in cheerfulness, it was stimulated by pain.

In life, I became a failure. My desire of becoming a pro athlete never happened. My sport career never touched the stadium of prosperity. Prosperity is a subject I only heard and read about. Never did I experience prosperity joyful ways. Actually, the only thing I can say I've accomplished, that might be a sign of prosperity, is earning my high school diploma. God's judgments through the law, and his prophecies did the most prospering in my life. As of now, the only thing I've earned was a horrible lesson.

It seemed as if it had fallen into a deep ditch. This ditch, which I've fallen into, was so deep, that human strength could not dig me out of it.

When this dope disaster happened, a partial victory it got. Never did I choose to be handicapped. The power of drugs made this decision for me. It was human strength (my strength) against drugs, and dope intoxicants won the battle. Although, I am alive, drugs still earned a high percentage of this reward.

After drugs tossed my brain into a coma, becoming a professional athlete was no longer a dream. Drugs did a whole lot of taking away in my life. Yeah, drugs defeated my life in many areas, and the fight to live and survive is yet not over. Although, things look bleak, I must do what I have to do, in order to stay alive. Just because sports have been deleted from my living, there has to be other things in life to do.

I had so many plans for my life concerning sports. Every athletic plan my brain once held is no longer a mental diagram. Never will I walk on the pathway that leads to professional leagues sports again. Never will the ESPN sports casters make comments about my dynamic moves displayed. Never will the NBA cameras catch a glimpse of my leaping ability. I actually messed up my chance to win at least one or two awards in the NBA three-point. There is no way I can play basketball with the physical condition I now have. Since my leg and ankle are suffering from paralysis, to me, sports are now over. From the paralysis my leg now possesses, playing sports is not a desire my heart seeks to be involved in. I believe sports are now over for me; they have become corrupted to my living. The paralysis in my leg, and the weakness in my arms, remind me that sports are long gone. All my athletic plans, I once had, have been washed away by the power of drugs.

One day, two friends of mine, Mike and Darryl were playing catch with a football. They were in the middle of the street tossing the football to one another. They seemed to be having fun. While they were playing catch, I was sitting in the wheelchair watching. As I was in the wheelchair watching them play catch, I began talking within my mind, saying… "Only if I could show these guys how accurate and far I once threw a football.

As I was watching them play catch, I was on the sidelines building up my courage to participate. When I finally motivated my mind to participate, "I yelled out saying, "aye fellows", throw me a pass. I began rolling in the wheelchair as if I was a wide receiver. My friend Darryl threw me a pass. When the ball reached me, it hit me on the forearm, hard, and fell to the ground. Although, I did reach my arms out to catch the ball, I did not close my hands to grasp it. It seemed like the ball traveled through the air too fast, and my brain did not react fast enough to close my hands.

My cerebellum (hand mover and coordinator) did not close my hands together to catch the ball. My hands stayed opened the entire time. The ball was thrown to me on target and perfect. As I now think about it, I am glad the ball did not travel towards my face, or else I would have been in some serious pain. The football probably would have smashed right into my eye. After experiencing this, my heart began to pain. I build up the courage to participate, but it was not a successful challenge.

Even shooting a basketball is hard to do. Not only that, but also, handling one is a task as well. When I first put a basketball into my hands again, it felt good to have it in my possession. Every time I look at a basketball, my sport memories are brought back into my mind. My mental man (my brain) began to rehearse many of the splendid skills I once displayed on the basketball court. As of now, I cannot shoot a basketball, I cannot catch a football, and I am scared to play catch with a baseball because of its small size. I really messed up my life for real this time, and my heart is travailing in pain.

On occasions, people say unto me, "you should participate in wheelchair basketball. Wheelchair basketball is probably a great activity. However, to me, I felt like my sports career was over, and I figured that I should move on to other things in life. I just could not put the love of basketball back into my heart again. It's not that I was afraid to play wheelchair sports, however, if I can't do a juke move and charge to the rim and dunk on Anthony, or Ron, I have no desire to play it. Drugs have forced me to retire from all sports at a very young age. I did not want to retire, but since I was dealing with wickedness and drugs, from their evil power, retirement was granted.

One day I tried shooting a basketball, and it did not even touch the rim. My arms were too weak to toss the ball that high. Not only that, but also, I could not even use one arm to throw the ball that high. Well, I guess I will never be compared to NBA stars again. I already knew basketball was over for me, but when I took that shot, and it did not touch the rim, I was hurt within my heart all over again. Ninety-five percent of the athletic world does not know how it feels to be able to say, "I am one of the greatest athletes in the world", and then losing your talents and skills to drugs.

Another thing that hurts me is this; I messed up the chance of watching young people wear a pair of tennis shoes with the name Brian Irons embedded on them. My tennis shoes would have been just as popular as any other basketball star tennis shoes. People would have been walking around saying, "I got to get me a pair of those new "B. Irons".

Although, my leg has a bit of paralysis in it, however, by the power of God it can be restored back to normal again. Whether God restore it back to normal, or not, it is not a concern to me. I truly believe God just MIGHT allow me to walk through life with a nerve damage ankle. If he does, why should I complain about it? Never will I curse God about it. If this paralysis lives within my leg for the next 60 years, I am content and totally prepared. Although, walking normal again would be great, but I realize, I am the one who messed up my own body, not God. Many people, as well as myself, would love to see God perform a miracle on my leg. I do not pray for leg healing anymore. I only need this pain within me to be healed first.

When I die, and be placed in a coffin, and my leg still has paralysis in it, I see nothing wrong with that. I see nothing wrong with it because, I was not supposed to be here on earth anyway, but glory be to God, he gave me a second chance. I am just so happy to be here in the land of the living, after facing 11 minutes of heart failure. Since I am still human, and not a robotic being, I still have an emotional side, and yet, I still have pains within my heart. A paralyzed limb does not mean that life is over for me.

Although, the power of drugs did beat on me, I learn many of its ways. I also learned that, drugs, wickedness, and evil are all associated. Also, the best thing I learned is, "one bad made decision, or one illegal move, can send a person through what we call, "hell and back".

Many times, as I sat and thought about all the horrible situations drugs created in my life, I can honestly say, "God was doing his best in trying to help me. God, through mercy, was only trying to steer me away from future disaster. Every time a dangerous episode came into my life, it came unexpected. Time after time, as my brain and body was being snatched into dangerous and life-threatening situations, it is all because of the mercies God I made it out alive.

When people are performing works of evil, and a judgment have not been pronounced upon them, it is because of the unfailing "mercies of God". God's mercy is the parallel reason many people have not been punished right now. God's mercy might be powerful, but it will only hold back the Day of Judgment for oh so long.

God allowed me to see many signs over the years. My own vision and mental knowledge have experienced the acquaintance of these signs. My own two eyes have seen everything pertaining to substance abuse, and its controlling power. Whether the experience was my drug usage, or a visual encounter, my life has seen and felt it all. The horrible things my eyes beheld, I would like to say, "that only a man of wisdom and understanding would have comprehended the insights of such events". To mentally understand and comprehend the "signs" of life in any situation, "good wisdom" is needed to discern certain events.

In my life, I did not use "good wisdom". Well, shall I say, I did not use "good judgment". I had wisdom of course, but it was of my own personal kind. My personal wisdom needed to be filled or touched by God. My personal or "Self-wisdom" did not mount up to understand that death is in the lifestyle I chose to live. In high school, I thought about all the fun; never did I think about violence and death. However, good wisdom, which comes from God, is what we all need.

Proverbs 9:10 the fear of the Lord (God) is the beginning of wisdom. When a person fears the Lord (God), a certain type of "wisdom" is automatically utilized. A person's heart and mind become precious to the Lord when fearing him.

Having the fear of the Lord living inside you, is what I would like to call, "good wisdom". This wisdom, which shows a fear of the Lord, will bring great joy into the living of your life. Good wisdom, once you get a hold of it, it will sit at the seat of your thoughts, and on the table of your heart. It will relax within you, and when it is time for it to stand up and prove its power, it will boldly perform. This wisdom sits inside your inner being (brain and heart) waiting for the opportunity to prove its real power. Good Wisdom is a nutrient unto your life. Get a taste of it! Let good wisdom become a meal to your life, brain, and body. Open up your heart and receive it. The organs in your body need to be acquainted with good wisdom.

Many people often confess they fear God. Confessing you fear God means nothing. As I said before, "actions speak louder than words". You do not fear God, if you're not obeying his laws and commands. When a person fears God, that individual is very shaky about doing certain things. When fearing the Lord, you've realized God is the judge, and you do not want him to pronounce judgments upon your life. Having the fear of the Lord in you will cause you to live a lifestyle God is well pleased with. You will fear the events God can allow to enter into your living. Not only what God can allow, but also, what he might send your way. Whether it is a judgment in court, or a judgment through biblical prophecy, you will fear what can truly happen in your life.

In my 10-year (age 14-24) imprisonment with drugs, I have experienced escaping the hands of death many times. Many times, death reached out to grab me, but it did not pull me in. However, for 11 minutes, death had a hand on me, but God's mercy caused death to unloose its hold. Whenever you make unrighteous decision in life, remember, from that decision, invisible wicked hands are waiting for the perfect moment to grab you. Since I did not obey the laws and signs given to me from God, death had its paw on my fleshly body.

I have seen many signs of cautions. While driving in my car, I have seen stickers on car bumpers saying, "Say no to drugs". Driving down the highway, I have seen many billboards displaying the same words (Say No to Drugs). I was walking on the sidewalk one day, and I reached down to pick up a piece of paper. On this piece of paper, were the same words, "Say no to drugs". Those were visual signs telling me what I truly need to do with my life. Sometimes a piece of paper in the middle of the road has a message on it for you. There were so many signs flashing in and out of my life that should have been obvious unto me. Nevertheless, drugs had cursed my mind, therefore my life was locked on nothing but addictions.

Remember, every time you see a sticker, or commercial speaking against drugs, that is a warning to you. You might not take it serious, but if you are on drugs today, it is a serious message. God wants you to escape the death penalty drugs are soon to present into your life.

Here are some of the signs the mercies of God allowed me to see before drugs did this to me. Three cars of mine had been shot at. Two or more windows were blown out by the bullets. If only one car would have been shot, I could probably get away with saying, "I was in the wrong place at the wrong time". However, three cars of mine experienced the same type of conflict. Therefore, those three gun-shooting experiences were signs telling me, "Get out of the drug game". People drove through the neighborhood and shot bullets at me and my friends. I was robbed at gunpoint 3 times. Cops have chased me. I went to the penitentiary for 10 months. I had been fired from a job and I quitted two jobs. I was kicked out of the house because of being associated with dope. I ended up in the hospital overnight one day, because of using heroin, which is a different experience from 11-minute heart stop tragedy. Those experiences and many others were warning signs my life had seen.

Since I did not obey the signs, which God did allow me to see, I caused God to allow my life to experience one of the greatest acts of evil. I gave God no other choice but to let drugs have its own way with my life, brain and body. So here I am, with pain in my heart and body because I did not obey the signs. Since I did not obey the signs, I have to deal with a paralyzed limb, and a heart filled with pain.

At times, I feel so ashamed within my heart because I have to ride around in a wheelchair. Actually, riding around in the wheelchair is not the shameful part. The shame comes when I have to tell people the reason why I am relying on a wheelchair. I must announce to the public, "I use a wheelchair because I was getting high on drugs one day, and the drugs caused injury to my brain.

I wake up every morning and put a brace on my left ankle. The brace keeps my left ankle steady. The brace does help me walk a little better. The brace keeps my ankle stable so that my foot does not hang while walking. I hate I did this to myself. Good lord, I should have obeyed the signs, and then my leg would not be going through this type of sorrow.

If any flight of stairs has no handrails, I either crawl or scoot to get to the top. When a person has problems walking forward, there has to be a problem walking up and down the stairs. I think I am doing a good job at battling this physical weakness my body now has. My legs were very important to me; therefore, I do not like this type of living at all. Nevertheless, I am still content and thankful unto God because I was in much worse physical condition many years ago. Nevertheless, before this tragedy happened, signs were given, and I should have obeyed them. If only I would have stop, drop, and roll out of the drug game, my body would not be struggling with ailments and pain.

One day, at a friend's house, someone offered me a glass of juice. I accepted the offer because I was a little thirsty. My friend went to the refrigerator and poured some juice in a cup. After the juice was poured into the cup, he brought it to me. As soon as my fingertips touched the cup, my cerebellum did not close my hands tight enough to have a tight grip on it. The cup of juice slipped through my hand and spilled all over the furniture.

Sometimes, my friends think they are the reason for the spilling of the juice. Most of the times, it is my fault. Little situations like that hurt my feeling because I have been dealing with issues like that since this dope tragedy occurred. It never fails; I always drop something or knock something over on the table. Sometimes I feel like a little child all over again. But oh well, life still goes on, and so must I.

People look at me crazy when I sometimes use both hands to grasp an offered glass of water. I now put one hand under the glass and snuggle the other hand around it. I do it that way, so I will have a full grip on the glass at once. From all of the incidents I've experienced pertaining to spilling water, using two hands to grasp a cup filled with liquid has become a safety tip. That is one of the new teachings (2 hands to grasp a glass) my brain has learned.

When people do unorthodox things in your presence, sometimes we need to consider having mercy on them, because we just never why people do things a certain way. We never know what a person has experienced in life. Now that I think about it, my brain is still learning and teaching my body how to cope with everyday living. Although, Mount Vernon Rehab Treatment Center taught me how to cope with life from a brain injured point of view, however, the greatest teaching comes from my daily activities. It seems like there is always something new my brain learns.

Although, I use a wheelchair on a daily basis, my legs are impressively receiving satisfying strength. My brain cannot move the ankle up or down, but I can still stand up and walk on it. Although, my leg suffered greatly, I thank God; it is still attached to my hip.

After putting on tennis shoes, tying up the laces was very confusing. I literally forgot how to tie shoes. The memory (procedural) had suffered greatly while my brain was under the attack of the coma. When I first learned how to tie my shoes, the procedural memory is where the taught data had been stored. Being a grown man at this particular time, and not being able to tie my own shoes was another hurt that rested inside my heart. I would relax the strings on the inside of the shoes. I did that for the entire 5 months while being at Mount Vernon Rehab Treatment Center. My brain had to teach my hands how to tie shoes all over again.

One day a friend of mine came to pick me up at my parent's house. I was already dressed and ready to go wherever. When my friend arrived at the house, I began putting my tennis shoes on. Then I began tying them up. I was having trouble doing so. My friend saw I was having trouble. Then my friend kneeled down and tied my shoes for me. Friends need to be caring and true helpers in matters like these. The friend's name that tied my shoes is "Lamar".

Putting my clothes on was a task as well. I could not perform the normal routine of putting on clothes. I once use to be able to stand up and put on pants, but now, I can't. I have to sit or lie down when putting on my pants. When I realize I was not able to stand up and put on pants, my heart became tremendously shattered. I never complained about, nor did I question God. If I have to sit on my bed to put on pants and socks for the rest of my life, I will still thank God for what he has already done.

Speaking of clothing! There always comes a time when my clothes need a washing. A washer and dryer I cannot afford. There is a Laundromat in the area, and I wash and dry my clothes there. I stash my clothes in trash bags and use my wheelchair to U-Haul them to the Laundromat.

The laundry mat is about ¼ mile away. I once was ashamed to use my wheelchair to take my clothes to get them washed. Nevertheless, the shame has been washed away. I must do what I have to do, in order to take care of me.

In the wheelchair, I get from point A to point much B faster. My wheelchair has become my physical means of transportation. I am grateful to be able to use a wheelchair. I definitely need my manual wheelchair, and no living man or woman on earth can tell me anything different. Sorry to sound so blunt about the matter, but I love using my wheelchair, because I use it for more than one reason. Using my wheelchair gives me the power of not having to wait for people to take me places.

It vexes me when people speak against me using a wheelchair. People do not understand why I really use the wheelchair. The only thing they know is that I can at least walk. From that fact, which has become known too many people in St. Louis, sometimes I get in debates with them about my personal condition. Sometimes I get defensive. When people debate with me about my wheelchair usage, I get so deep with them and say, "The day you stop smoking weed or drinking alcohol will be the day I will throw away my wheelchair.

We all have holes in our lives that need patching up into perfection. So people in the world, do not worry about my wheelchair, if I am happy with using it, then let me be. If the truth be told, I am happier in life, than most perfectly physical in shape people are.

My wheelchair definitely comes in handy when going grocery shopping. I rather roll around in the store than walk. Carrying groceries in my arms, and keeping my walking balance at the same time, is hard to do. When I go shopping for food, it is easier to sit groceries in my lap, while rolling through the store. Going grocery shopping is another reason why I use my wheelchair. Just the other day, I went grocery shopping, and put a loaf of bread, a 12 pack of noodles, a bag of chicken, and a gallon of juice on my lap. I am good; I am the best, and I am still a bad man.

The wheelchair has become a motivator to me. I ride in my wheelchair everyday while traveling outdoors. When going somewhere outdoors, and I need to catch public transportation (city bus), my wheelchair goes with me. When the bus arrives, the driver pushes a button from the dashboard, and a ramp slides out electronically. Then I roll the wheelchair onto the ramp, and onto the bus. When I get on the bus, I then roll to the wheelchair parking spot. I love public transportation. My mind has become accustomed to it. Of course, I never wanted to be in a situation such as using a wheelchair, or in a position of being handicap, but as I said before, you just never know what your life will experience, when indulging in drugs.

Sometimes, while rolling through the streets of St. Louis, I lift my hands high toward heaven. I be thanking God for sparing my life. Not only did God spare my life, but also, he gave my brain back enough sense to have a little understanding as well. Many people in the world have a brain but are without realistic common sense. Well, if you have drugs in your brain, you are a person who has no realistic common sense. Although, at times, my heart still pains inside, however, in the wheelchair, my hands will continually be lifted towards heaven.

There is an old saying that goes like this; "everything that tastes or feels good is not good for you". Many things might cause the body to like the pleasure of it, but it might not be good for it. I now find that to be a statement of truth, because drugs felt good to my mind, however, they were not good for my body. Although, the formula of drugs felt good to the mind, my experiences prove drugs are not good for the body.

Many people are like me: crazy, stupid, and ignorant. It takes near death experiences in order for some of us to accept the facts. However, many people who are reading this book have not experienced the events I have. `This word is for you; stop putting dope in your brain and body before your heart stops longer than mine did. My heartbeat paused for 11 minutes, but yours might pause, and stay in that mode forever.

About 3 years after the tragedy occurred, I moved out of my parent's house. It was time for me to go back out there into the world and be on my own again. A grown man needs his own space. I felt within myself, it was time to step out on faith, and not depend upon family.

When I moved out of my parent's residence, and into my own apartment, a housing program provided me with assistance. This housing program is called, "Section 8 Housing". This housing program paid a portion of my rent every month. Indeed, the housing program helped me out a great deal. If it had not been for this housing program, my life, financially, would have been rough. I do not think I can pay full rent anywhere receiving disability payment and survive in days like these. On second thought, I probably can survive anything.

I remember, I wanted to move into this redesigned apartment building. This building had been renovated. No one has ever lived in it since it renovation.

I called the office and spoke to a manager. We scheduled an appointment to meet up, so I could view the building.

This renovated building was located about two miles from where I was living at the time. I rolled in my wheelchair the entire two miles to meet the manager. It took me a little over an hour to get there. Depending on the many hills I had to face, getting there faster could have been done.

The manager was a nice person. She was very sweet. She gave me a tour throughout the entire building. She took me to a few apartments that were handicap ready, or shall I say wheelchair accessible. In each apartment, all the appliances were brand new. The carpet was new. The kitchen cabinets were new. Everything was completely new.

In order for renters, including the owner of the apartment building could get inside of the building, a key is needed. There were 21 apartments inside the building. There were only two entrances leading into the inside. After viewing this place, I fell in love with it. I wanted to rent an apartment here oh so badly.

In order to have one of these apartments, an application must be filled out. I am so glad I learned how to read and write. On the other hand, should I say, "I am so glad my declarative memory held on to reading and writing skills. I am also glad my cerebellum has the strength to write. Not only did I have to fill out an application, but also, I had to give the company 35 dollars. I am so glad my brain still knows how to count.

The $35 had to be given, so that the owner of the building could do a background check. Before I left the building, the manager gave me a time to return. Actually, the next appointment is like a judgment day, because, these people are going to tell me if I've been denied or accepted to be a tenet in the apartment building.

I returned to the apartment building to hear the outcome. Well, they told me I was denied. That was a slap in my face. I had exceeding hopes on moving into this new building. The manager said, "my financial history did appear to be bad, however, the owner overlooked it". The manager said to me, "Your criminal record caused the company to deny you.

Those cocaine charges from years ago had haunted me. When I heard my criminal report was the reason for the denial, my heart pained again. I was hurt because, although, those cases were put on my law's record many years ago, I am still reaping from them. Wow, those drug cases are on my record for the rest of my life. After I had been denied, I rode back home in my wheelchair with a heart beating while in pain.

As I was riding back home in my wheelchair, I repaired my mind and put the sad news behind me. My past is in the past. I cannot change that. Why let bad news bother me? That's minor mental hurt, compared to what I just came out of many years ago. I might not own a set of keys to one of the apartments, but I still have my "TESTIMONY". Therefore, as I was riding home in my wheelchair, I dust myself off, and still believe that things will change for me somehow, someway, and someday.

Yeah, life will go on, and so must I. Monday is going to turn into Tuesday, and Tuesday is going to turn into Wednesday. If you do not get with the program of life, then that is on you. Life will never stop for any reason. A paralyzed limb, a wheelchair, and a criminal record do not mean that life is over for me. For me, it only means I have to be mentally stronger and fight from the heart to gain what I need and want in life. The physical disaster has happened, so I must encourage myself every moment of my life.

The monthly or disability income I am receiving is okay, meaning, it pays the bills, and not too much more. All bills have demands; and they demand payments. Bills want that money that is in your pockets.

Bills do not even have a mouth, but they give out demands.

It is somewhat amazing how I once had strong athletic hands for protecting myself, and now they are weak and feeble because of my usage with drug. My hands are weak and feeble all because of one bad choice, which was to smoke marijuana. Listen to these facts: my hands, which were great in all areas of sports, were the same hands that caused sports to be deleted from my life. My own fingers, which are attached to my hand, had guided marijuana to my mouth to be inhaled. My own hands and fingers were used to put heroin up to my nose to be snorted. I caused my brain to control my hands to reach out and grasp a hold onto every drug product that ever went inside of my anatomy. My hands, which could have made me rich by playing pro league sports, were the same hands that caused me to live on a monthly payment plan (disability). All because of my own disobedient hands, disability checks have become a source of income. Now I must patiently wait for a check to be mailed to me every 30 days (once a month). That has been hurting me for a very long time.

The amount of money I receive is about $600 dollars per month. In today's world, 600 dollars a month is petty, especially when it is received once a month. I have never had money in the middle of the month, unless given to me from a family member or a friend. Other than that, I was without money for more than 20 days out of the month. After paying bills, I was left with a small amount of cash.

Hey, **Brian K.**, you are doing very well in life, and don't let anybody tell you different. Most people do not know the strength of your heart. If the truth be told, you are mentally stronger than many hard working financially stabled people.

I remember when I purchased a computer to type my writings on. The computer cost $399. $399 was way out of my budget range. But I bought the computer somehow anyway. When I bought this computer, I did not pay one bill in the house. I took a chance on purchasing this computer, and hoping my light or gas would not be turned off.

Of course, I had to get my haircut; therefore, another bill was added to my check. I had to take care of my beautiful waves. I try to get my haircut at least 2 to 3 times a month. Blessedly, I came across a few awesome barbers, who cut my hair, and allowed me to pay them on the first of each month. That hurt my pockets at times too. I had to give those men their money. Even right now today, I am still paying barbers on the 1st of each month. I have been doing this for more than 13 years.

I would like to congratulate myself because I do not owe one barber a dime. The only payments I still owe to this very day are housing bills.

I wrote this book to encourage millions of people, one way or another. My writing will encourage people for the next three decades, or perhaps centuries. If the earth stays intact for the next 3 centuries, I might not be here, but my books will. In a later chapter, I am going to tell you how I know so.

One day, I went to a department store and asked the manager about a certain job position. I felt I could perform at this position very good. This job did not require physical ability to be a necessity. Hand speed and office organization is not an issue at this position. Being judged by a staff, this position does not need such. The only thing that can hinder me from being hired is if the company is not hiring. This position is truly a very easy job. I was looking forward to working at this position. At this job, I was hoping to work as a greeter or porter.

The porter or greeter's job is to welcome customers as they enter the department store. Smiling and looking happy while greeting customers is a part of the deal too. Presenting customers with pleasant words is the porter's assignment. On the other hand, if I am hired, I can direct customers to his or her desired area in the store. This job can be done while sitting in my wheelchair. If a customer was searching for a product, I can tour the person there while riding in my wheelchair.

I went to the manager of the store, and asked, "Could I fill out an application to work as a "porter or greeter". The manager told me the position is not an option anymore. He said, "No one works as a greeter anymore". I thought the company had recently ended that position, because just the other day, in the same store, a greeter greeted me.

A couple of days later, in my wheelchair, I went to that same department store to buy some soap and shampoo. Of course, it was the beginning of the month because I had money in my pockets. As I rolled into the department store, the "porter" of the store greeted me. After I had been greeted, I became angry within myself. I felt like the manager of store lied. He told me the porter job is not an office anymore; yet, someone greeted me as I was entering. Within me, I felt like the manager showed partiality towards my wheelchair situation. Nevertheless, if he did lie, oh well, life is going to venture on, and so must I.

I do not care how crushed or hurt my heart becomes; my heart is strong, and I am relying on it to not give up and become defeated. I am not going back to the streets and sale cocaine again. I will find a job; I know I will. There has to be something I can do to bring myself out of this financial poverty. My financial situation is truly struggling level, and I desire not to live this way any longer.

Years ago, this married woman shared her testimony with the people in the audience. In her testimony, she said, "she makes over $60,000 a year". With $60,000 a year, I can do a lot with that. A person making over $60,000 a year, I was thinking she should not have one complaint.

This woman is very pretty, and from the way she dresses, and the car she possesses, I can see that the $60,000 is taken very good care of her. After she shared her testimony, I became crushed within my heart. In one year, she receives $60,000. In a total of ten years, I receive a little above $60,000. Hearing testimonies such as hers encourages me to want more money in my life. Whether people acknowledge the fact that money is needed or not, I realize that without it, living on earth will be full of pain.

Although, I struggled in finances, I was still happy in life. I realize money will never insert true happiness into a person's life. As you have just read, that, I really didn't have much money, but I was still happy. Besides, I had a vision, and that was to publish a book, and have it displayed in bookstores.

Now you know why I published this book. I had two choices to make: either publish this book now, or struggle financially another 18 or more years. I published this book hoping for a financial miracle. I did the best I could in writing and editing this book. If I were able to afford online writing classes, I am sure; a better job of writing could have been done. I am still proud of this writing accomplishment. For the past 18 years, God has been good to me, but my finances have not.

Chapter 12

OPENING DOORS AND GOD'S WORD (BIBLE) CONCERNING SIN

Before approaching any door, a decision must be made before entering therein. You must realize, if there is a way in, there is a way out. If you got yourself in it, then you must get yourself out of it.

When you open a door, you have done so intentionally. No door opens on its own. Automatically, every door is tagged with numerous of tests. Remember this; your life is based upon the doors you open. Whether good or bad, you can expect life's experiences to be based on your entrance.

In my life, after opening the door of drugs, <u>I Did Not Know</u> I was about to walk into a lifestyle full of stupidity, ignorance, and destruction. In addition, I also entered into the messy ways of wickedness. As a mouse walks onto a trap filled with cheese bait, in the same sense, when I opened the door of drugs, I walked into a living filled with prophetic judgments.

If you walk through a door where wickedness is, you have just taken your body into a place possessed by demons. Wherever demons are, they are there because of performances of wickedness. Not only that, but also, you have walked through a door where the activity of breaking the laws is. The longer you stay inside a place where wickedness is, the greater and stronger demons become. Demons will become familiar with what you like to do in life. Demons will take control of your mind, and soon make you powerless to close that door.

Demons do not build strength in time, only people do. People exercise and lift weights to get stronger. But demons, their strength is built through people's daily acts of wickedness. When I kept smoking marijuana, demons were getting stronger and stronger. From the building strength of demons, destruction I saw ten years later.

Through the power and strength from demons, the wickedness in my life had gotten stronger. When I opened the door of wickedness, I was trapped inside for ten years. I had nowhere to run, and nowhere to hide. When I opened up the door of drugs, I Did Not Know I opened a door where demons were located.

Only demons lead people to experiencing disastrous and horrifying events. A demon is one that has the ongoing desire to do evil. When a demon is inside of a man, an evil task will continually be performed. Wherever evil is in operation, surely, demons are present as well.

Demons do not travel in one's and ten's as people think they do. Demons operate in packs of hundreds and even thousands. Yeah, that many demons will enter into your life and mind, after opening the door of evil. Just as lent sticks to your clothes, however, after opening the door of evil, demons will stick to your life.

Why do you think it was so hard for me to leave drugs alone? As my drug addiction level increased, more demons were added unto it. Drug addictions and demons go hand and hand. I advise you to know what you are getting yourself into, before opening any door in life.

Whether your door be a job, a relationship, or whatever, you need to know what lies ahead. Before two people get married, the door of relationship opens first. As I said earlier, know what you are getting yourself into, before opening and entering through any door.

A drug's addiction is actually the demon itself. From the addiction, it became drastically hard for me to turn around and walk back out that door. The reason why the door of drugs became exceedingly hard to close is because; dozens of demons became attached to my brain's organs, and I Did Not Know it.

Demons through drug's addiction actually use my brain as a home. Demons lived inside of my head. They got comfortable; they relaxed. Every time I kept putting drugs in my brain, it gave demons the power to live.

Every door (situation) that appears in life needs to be inspected. I am not talking about the doors at your local mall; I am talking about the "doors of life". Before walking through any door of life, be weary of what's inside. Some entrances have invisible locks inside waiting to clamp on your life. You will be in a position where there is nowhere to run and nowhere to hide. You'll become trapped inside, and it will become too dark for you to find an outlet. Once you become trapped inside, demons will beat you to death.

I met a young man who was 21 years old at the time. I met this young man at Mount Vernon Rehab Treatment Center. His injury was so serious, that Mount Vernon Rehab Center was the place for admittance. Remember, no one goes to Mount Vernon Rehab Center with minor bruises or injuries. Although, my heart experienced 11 minutes of stoppage, and another person experienced bullet wounds to the body, however, this 21-year-old fellow's situation was one of a kind.

This 21-year-old young man was in a street gang. The 21-year-old and his other gang members labeled themselves "bloods". All "street gangs" are promoted by demons.

This gang (the bloods) made a decision to go and check out a party. He and his gang associated friends decided to pull the vehicle over and park. Then, the bloods got out of the car and started walking toward the party. As soon as they approached the door, they quickly knocked on the door. They were probably anxious to see if the party was packed.

Maybe the loud music or the crowds of people drew the bloods attention. On the other hand, maybe people were going in and out of the door, which was probably another reason why the bloods pulled over.

As my friend and his gang partners entered through the door of this party, they had no clue the party was filled with a bunch of crips. Since that is so, the party is filled with a bunch of men who are enemies to the bloods. In other words, the 21-year-old man, and his friends (the bloods) opened a door and walked into a house filled with their enemies (the crips).

Nevertheless, my 21-year-old friend walked through a door, not knowing what was on the other side. Soon and very soon, the bloods are about to find out what type of door they just knocked on. When my 21-year-old friend and his group entered through the door, the "crips" immediately recognized them.

The crips is a gang that wears dark colors, preferably blue. However, the bloods wear red. I suppose my friend and his partners were all wearing bright red colors. When the bloods entered through the door, the "crips" rushed them. The crips physically mishandled the bloods badly. The bloods were outnumbered; therefore, the bloods were physically bashed and violently manipulated by the crips association.

The bloods walked into a party, which apparently was the wrong party. Nevertheless, the gang of bloods came dreadfully close to meeting the character called, "death". When they entered into this door, I am sure they did not know that the faces of death and demons would be seen.

I am sure the bloods and crips does some sort of drugs. All gang members use some sort of drugs. Not too many gangs have parties without drug usage in action. Therefore, the party was filled with wickedness, evil, and demons, because of the presence of drugs. The "crips" are filled with demons, and the "bloods" are filled with demons. When the two gangs fought against one another, it was a battle between demons and demons.

When you open up the door of drugs, and walk through it, a brutal day of beating is soon to happen in your life. Some door openers of drugs will be beaten on the first day of entry, just as the bloods were. On the other hand, some will be beaten in a ten-year span, just as I was. A gang of humans has never beaten on me, however, a few men did surround me a couple of times, but I manage to flee and escape out of their presence. However, another gang did beat up on me, which was marijuana, cocaine, codeine pills, and heroin. I opened the door of drugs one day, and they beat me badly on July 26.

People of the world, never think that one drug by itself cannot kill you. Anything that awakens demons can also awaken death. Demons are inside of all street drugs, and I have never in my life, known a demon to be a good servant. That is why drugs are not good for the brain. Once drugs intoxicants are put in the brain, the only activities done are events persuaded by demons. I advise you to close the door of drugs and wickedness, which will prevent demons from taking control of your life.

Just as movies are advertised on your TV screen saying, "Coming soon at a local theatre near you". It is the same order drugs will present unto you. Once people put dope in their brains, the beating from drugs is coming soon within your local brain that sits inside of you. The only difference between the bloods being beaten, and your brain being beating, is the fact that you are beating your own life when you put drug intoxicants inside your brain. From the intoxicants of drugs, a demonic force then becomes active, and it will use your life for its own purpose and pleasure.

Being disappointed will be an ongoing task when a brain has been exposed to the pleasure of drugs. After I opened the door of drugs, my life became mentally frustrated and very much disappointed. Horrible experiences were continually coming into my life. Once I opened the door of drugs, it did not take long for the windows of crime, court appearance, and violent activities to become a part of my living. When I first entered through the door of drugs, I was actually walking into "The House of Horrors" and <u>I Did Not Know</u> it. Not only is it called, "The

House of Horrors", but also, it's the "House for Planned Destruction".

After experiencing so many tragedies, the thought of attending church popped into my mind. Now, my cerebrum has thoughts of opening a different door. When the thought of attending church popped up in my cerebrum, I thought about this one church. This same church prayed for me, when I became ill at my friend's apartment.

As I came rolling to the front door of this church, the assistant pastor and two of the associate ministers, picked me up and rolled me in.

While sitting in the wheelchair, I was taken to the front area of the church. The people in the church were now able to see the miracle God had performed. I'm the miracle, and I am the show of the hour. The entire church was now able to see what drugs had done unto me. There I was, sitting in the front row of the church, bruised up in heart, and beaten in the physical from the bashing of drugs.

As I was sitting in front of the church, I broke down "crying". Oh, although, I am a grown man, and was very tough on the streets, I am not ashamed to cry in front of people. Besides, when the power of God hits anyone, who is in sorrow, he or she will cry in front of anyone.

At this particular time, my tears were of great sorrow. This was my first experience of feeling the presence of God in a church. Although, I was a man, and very tough on the streets, when I attended church service, I became a big baby under the power of God. I cried because every drug scene my life had witnessed swiftly flashed through my mind. Incident after incident, robbery after robbery, drug use after drug use, and finally, my sports career is now over. I cried, I cried, I cried!

Not only was I opening the church doors, but also, I was opening a bible on a continual basis, or as much as I should. In my life, my thoughts never did conceive the mental pleasure of reading a book, especially during school. I do not remember ever reading an entire book in my life. Reading was not one of my desires. I could not seem to prepare my mind for the mental session of reading. Reading a book filled with a bunch of words, I just could not do it. There was no power in the world that could excite or motivate me to read a book. However, since I began attending church, reading the bible became one of my daily chores. Now a day, I really enjoy reading other author's stories, and most definitely, I enjoy reading the bible. I wish I had the mind to read years and years ago.

While I was attending church and reading the bible, I learned that, being the physical man I am, I had not the potential strength to stop the persuasive force of drug usage. Neither my physical status, nor my mental power mounted up in defeating the warring temptation of drugs. Although, I did have great mental awareness to protect myself from physical danger, however, when it came to protecting my inner body, I was dumb and weak in that area of life. I did not have Godly power to protect my inner man (brain) from the enticement of drugs.

You need to read your bible too, to learn the power it has. If you go and grab a hold onto your bible, if it has dust on it, that means, many months passed by, and you have not been reading about the power God.

People in the world will never have the full strength to cease their bodies from performing actions that feel so remarkably good. A person's body is fascinated by good feelings, which the brain's limbic system plays a high role in. The limbic system interacts with the body to give it the treatment of pleasure. Your brain will strive to get that good feeling and sensation as much as it possible can. When the brain becomes fascinated by the sensation of pleasure, the mind becomes trained and feign for that same feeling. Once you put drugs in your brain, the body then becomes a prisoner to the pleasures of that operating chemical. Now that your brain and body have become addicted, the mental power to sustain from drug affiliations has been cast away. The hidden operation of drugs is to imprison the brain with its pleasures, and in due time, they weaken all users.

I read a scripture in the bible that <u>I Did Not Know</u> nothing about, until I started reading it. The biblical book's name is called, "Romans". In the book of Romans, chapter 5, verse 6 is a scripture that I feel the need to share with you. This scripture enlightened my mind concerning the strength every man and woman possesses on earth. The scripture reads as this, *Romans 5:6 "for when we were yet without strength, in due time, Christ (Jesus) die for the ungodly.*

Allow me to enlighten your mind about that scripture. It says *"for when we were yet without strength, in due time, Christ (Jesus) died for the ungodly.* People, who do not accept God's blessed plan for their lives, are called the ungodly. God's mercy tries pulling the ungodly in unto Him, but they keep denying his call.

People are called ungodly because their minds constantly concentrate on wickedness, inventing evil things (drugs), and searching for ways to do ungodly activities. We all were once led to do many acts of evil. None of us had the strength of God dwelling in us at certain points in our lives. We all have knowingly lied before. We've all done something deceitful and sneaky before. We all were without strength. You may not have done the ungodly deeds I've done; however, I am sure you've done something evil before. Whether it was a small lie, or you stole 50 cents, you did something unrighteous before.

On my very first experience of using an illegal product, which was marijuana, I Did Not Know that something on the inside persuaded me to use chemical-controlled substances. You mean to tell me there is something on the inside of me, and I Did Not Know it. That is quite naturally weird or mentally scary to have something on the inside of you, and not even knowing what it is. It makes me seriously think, and mentally wonder, how it actually got inside of me. How long has it been inside of me? Who or what it is that's in me? From what I read in the bible, it was something inside of me that led and empowered me to try drugs, and definitely caused me to break the laws of God. After breaking the laws of God, that, which was on the inside of me, led me to harm my own brain and body. Nevertheless, when I was living the street life, I continued to do drugs on a daily basis, because of an inner being motivated me. It was a hidden character living inside of my brain and body, and I Did Not Know it.

Here is the scripture that speaks about the hidden character;

Romans 7:19- for the good that I would, I do not: but the evil, which I would not, now that I do.

Romans 7:20- now if I do that, I would not, it is no more I that do it but sin that dwelleth in me.

Many people have no idea what that scripture is saying. You need to read the word of God and learn the messages it speaks.

Throughout my years of living on the earth, <u>I Did Not Know</u> what sin fully meant, neither did I know that it was dwelling in my body. <u>I Did Not Know</u> sin was the main reason and purpose why my life went through "so much disaster". Finally, yet importantly, <u>I Did Not Know</u> "sin" is the ultimate reason why my body almost ended up a dead man's casket. Although, drugs were the substances that messed my life up, however, sin, which was dwelling in me, was the head leader of it all.

Allow me to explain and provide you with an example of that scripture mean. Consciously, you already know wrong from right. God provided within the brain a sensor so it can automatically discern right from wrong. However, <u>*Romans 7: 19-20*</u> is saying; we know it is wrong to indulge in certain activities, but sin is the character that led us to commit the act anyway. We know it is wrong to indulge in drugs, but from the power of sin, we snorted and inhaled dope anyway. We know it is against the law to have drugs in our possession, but sin enabled us to handle drugs anyway. Men know it is wrong to have sex with a woman without her approval, but sin empowered him to rape her. Sin is the controlling power that has led us to do all activities of evil.

If sin is not living inside of the people, then, going to court to be judged will never be an experience. Sin is the controlling power that has caused a world of people to transgress all the "Ten Commandments".

When human beings first put God's blessed plan into their lives, and make church their place of fellowship, instead of the nightclubs, many hidden facts about sin and drugs will be revealed. He (God) desires to teach and reveal unto us every "good" and "bad" outcome in our lives. God is the truth revealer to all humankind. God is able to teach and reveal unto you great facts. Since God is a teacher, then willingly you should become one of his full-time students. Whether you do good deeds in life or bad deeds, God's word (bible) will teach you from both perspectives.

Results from committing sins are actually occurring in people's lives right now today. Everyone is ignoring the signs and warnings being displayed. I know I'm not the only person in the world God has given warnings too. If I were the only person in the world who God has sent warnings too, I would be the only person whom God loves. However, I am not the only person who God loves. God loves us all, whether clean or dirty, righteous or unrighteous. Even while people are committing sin, God still shows his love. Nevertheless, God desires to get the most out of our lives, then what sin is getting. Sorry to say, but sin is doing more influencing in the world, than what we are allowing God to do. It's not that sin is more powerful than God; it's just that, people are filled with the strength of evil, rather than the muscles of righteousness. It's very easy to do what's wrong, but it's a battle trying to do what's right.

When people were shooting bullets at me, sin and Satan was in control of their actions. Whenever sin leads and empowers a person to do anything, it is something against the commands of God. Satan is the entity that leads humankind to participate in evil. Yeah, Satan is the demon in this world. Therefore, when I was in that gangway, plotting to commit a murder, sin and Satan was operating in my mind, encouraging me to commit the act. Satan and his demons cause us to sin, and when we commit sin, Satan gets the glory.

Although more than half of the people in the world is not spiritually inclined to claim being in a true relationship with God, more than half of the world knows why Jesus was murdered. More than half of the world has acknowledged a biblical fact that Jesus died on a cross for our sin. Many of us have never read the story of Jesus, but we still know a little something about it.

We have heard that Jesus was beaten, nailed to the cross, and killed on the account of our sins. Human hands beat upon Jesus, until He died. While Jesus was lying on the cross, the people hammered long nails though his hands. However, those things were done, because Jesus agreed to die for the sin of the world. Not only did Jesus agree to do this, but his father made it his son's will.

People who look and act just like you and me, actually laid hands on Jesus and brutally killed him. A "gang" of humans gathered up in numbers, surrounded, charged, beat, and killed Jesus. Just as a gang of members charged and beat up my friend, who was in a gang called, "The Bloods", the same scenario applies with Jesus.

Jesus did not die from an old age ordeal. Jesus was crucified and murdered by the hands of people in the sight of men and God. The people who forcefully laid their evil hands-on Jesus were led to do so by the strength of sin. As I said before, anytime an individual or a group of people commit a murder (or an assault); it is sin, and Satan, involved in the process. Even before the murdering of Jesus took place, God saw how it was all going to transpire. God led Jesus to face death for the sins of the world. Nevertheless, God led Jesus to face death, and sin led **Brian Keith** to face death. Do you see the difference yet? If not, let me break some more stuff down unto you.

There is more to realize and understand, than just to know Jesus died for the sins of the world. Actually, from my spiritual understanding, God has given me another revelation why Jesus came to earth to die on the account of all sins committed. The other reason why Jesus came on earth to die is that, while the raging and violent act of killing the body of Jesus took place, his bruised and damaged body is an example of what sin will do unto our bodies. When we look at the cross of Jesus, we see a man bruised, beat up, and whose physical appearance looks like a worth of nothing. That is what sin did unto me, it bruised me, and it beat me, and made me look like a piece of nothing. Although, the death of Jesus means everything to the world, however, when **Brian Keith** face death, it meant nothing but a body's waste. Jesus faced death by the will of God, and **Brian Keith** faced death by the force of sin and Satan.

When sin is operating through our bodies, it will empower us to become murderers to our own lives. Just as sin led the people to harm the body of Jesus, sin led me to harm my own body. With my own personal hands, and with the help of sin, a murder I performed on myself. Drugs and sin, when they operate in a person's life, they become a team. Yes, sin, Satan, and drugs are a team. They will always win; you are not clever enough or strong enough to conquer sin and drug tactics alone. It is time for you to accept the blessed plan of God for your life, rather than being led by sin, which in return will bring death in your life. Yeah, sin's job is to kill all those who allow it to work through their bodies.

Roman 6:23 says; for the wages of "sin" is death. In other words, when sin is operating in a person's body, his or her payment, or wages will be death. If you continue operating in sin, you will always receive a salary. Committing sin is a job; every time you break the law, God looks at that as a job of evil performed. Therefore, a payment from sin's results is to be expected. Every time a person commits sin, his or her body is being toured to the graveyard (death). If sin is controlling your body, as drugs physically controlled mine, you are heading towards unexpected danger, in which death will be the outcome (your wages).

Even while being infants, we've all committed sin. *Psalms 58; 3 the wicked are estranged from the womb: they go astray as soon as they be born, speaking lies.* This scripture speaks about being born and speaking lies. Infants, toddlers, babies, all speak lies after being released from the womb.

I am not going to talk about being born on day one; I am going to take it 3 years later. I am about to talk about committing a sin even at the age of 3 years old.

When a 3-year-old baby has shattered a glass lamp, or has broken an object of value, that little infant will look the parent square in the eye, and then lie about it. When the 3-year-old child lies about breaking the glass, the infant has just committed sin. The sin the baby is born in ignites the infant's brain, to cause him or her to lie. The

3-year-old child knows nothing about lying; yet, an act of dishonesty has been performed. Now I know why the bible says, "*The wicked are estranged from the womb*", because infants are empowered to lie, even at 3 years after birth.

The parent is not dealing with the fact that the baby has cleverly lied from the mouth; the parent is dealing with the sin born the baby is born in. That same child can break something of value the next day and will lie about it again.

That is what sin empowers grown folks to do; we do the same ungodly acts repeatedly for years. If sin causes us to go astray from God, and we perform lies at the age of 3, then the ruler or master of evil is born with us. Nevertheless, for most of us, God's mercy operates in our lives long enough until a decision, which is to seek freedom from sin can be made.

Let's say a 3-year-old baby, which the bible says is born in sin, has died or been killed. Although, the infant died in sin, heaven is still his or her home. The child never reached a mature age. At the age of 3, an infant does not have the mental ability to make their own choices. They must be taught on a regular basis. The child is still learning what the word "no" means. However, my overgrown self-lived to see the age of 24, therefore, I was old enough to make my own decisions in life. But, I never sought the path leading to freedom. Therefore, after my heart stopped beating for 11 minutes, the "gates of hell" opened up to receive me, along with my sins.

If God's mercy had not shown up when it did, a picture of my face would be on an obituary sheet being passed around at a funeral session. My obituary should have said, "**Brian Keith** died during the night from drug usage". Actually, the obituary should say this; sin, wickedness, and drugs killed **Brian Keith** on July 26. It is the truth isn't it? All because of my life being controlled by sin and drugs, a funeral was about to be arranged. If God's mercy had not done one more work for me, then on July 27, my family would have been seeking a funeral home to give last remarks about me.

The wicked life I was living almost sent me to hell. The bible states, in *Psalms 9:17-the wicked should be turned into hell, and all the nations that forget God.*

I thought the penitentiary was rough. My Lord, my Lord, I do not want to go to "hell". Hell is a place that is worse than any number of penitentiaries put together. At least, in the penitentiary you can run, and protect yourself. However, in hell, you cannot do anything but sit and be tortured forever. Wickedness almost brought my life down to the grave of hell. Anything that takes you down, or brings you down, there is no other place to go, but to the lowest of the lowest. The wicked one, which is the devil, if you are hired by him, he then has prime rights to take your life downward. Hell is the place where the wicked one lives. If you are working with him, in the end, death and hell will be your reward (payment).

God is so serious about wickedness, that he once destroyed the whole earth because of it.

Just the other day, I overheard a young woman say, "he going to hell". People see all the wrong other people do but are blinded to their own actions. Every time we see someone doing wrong, we say, "He's going to hell". Well, are you breaking the laws? Is your life an evil mess? Is wickedness living inside of you? Are you lying to get money? Are you cheating on your spouse? Did God's word tell you not to do it; but you did it anyway. If so, what makes you think it's not possible for you to be sent to hell, too? You folks need to stop it! We love examining and speaking "hell" into people's lives, but won't check up on our own selves. If you take a quick look at your life today, you should see you have no space to talk about anyone. One of the world's greatest pop star sang a song many years ago, but it got pass all of us—— "Man in the Mirror"! Before you talk about the next man, look within yourself, and tell me what you see. If you do not see a person in need of forgiveness, go to the altar, and it will tell you how wicked you really are. Do you see a perfect person, or a person who needs spinning on the Potter's Wheel? (God's circle of forgiveness)

People in the world always say, "God knows my heart". Well, of course, that is true, but if you're not seeking to live in righteousness as the bible speaks, then God knowing your heart means nothing. Once you begin walking upright with God, that's what moves him. For decades, people have been walking on the earth confessing, "God knows my heart". If your life has never came to a point where God has forgiven your sins, and you die in them, then hell will be your home, and God still knows your heart. How can you say a person is going to hell, while your living is fully filled with all unrighteousness? People in the world are truly off course, but they know it not. Everyone thinks he or she is so right, and then proclaims the bible to be a book of false advertisements. Anything pronouncing statements against our doings, we immediately proclaim our ways or reasoning.

The bible has a scripture in the Old Testament that I would like to share with you. *<u>Ecclesiastics 11: 9 Rejoice, O young man, in thy youth; and allow thy heart to cheer thee in the days of thy youth, and walk in the ways of thine heart, and in the sight of thine eyes: but know thou, that for all these things God will bring thee into judgment.</u>*

This is what the scripture above is saying; God is saying this; young man, young woman, go ahead and do whatever your heart desires. Whatever your heart desires, withhold nothing from it. Whatever your eyes behold, go after it and get it. Go ahead and celebrate your earthly accomplishment. Do whatever you want to do. God gives you the right a away to use drugs and commit sin if you want to. I give you the right to choose your own road in life to walk on. I, the Lord God will not step into your life and stop you. If you want to drink alcohol, and intake drugs, then go right ahead, and while you are doing it, salute yourself. You do not have to follow my blessed plan if you do not want to. You are a man, you are a woman, and you have been given full rights to make your own decisions in life. *But know thou* this, I (God) do want you to know I am going to judge you for all actions done. If you want to live a dangerous life, that is your business, but my prophetic words are going to perform. Go ahead and do whatever your heart desires, *but know thou this*; my judgments have desires too.

In this story, you have read how I rejoiced, celebrated, partied, and had ongoing pleasure with drugs. My heart was glad in the days when I was able to buy cars, and spend loads of money. Buying clothes at will made my heart cheerful. Whatever my heart desired to have, I sold drugs, earned enough money, and then buy whatever I wanted. In my youthful years, I did everything without the mental persuasion of "good wisdom". In my heart, it was all about the cash, sex (with women only), and having materials. Whatever my eyes perceived, and whatever they lusted after, I did not withhold anything from them. If my mind creatively thought it; if my heart willfully desired it; once my eyes beheld it, I had to have it in my possession. I was not thinking about judgments; I was only thinking about being cheerful (or satisfied) in the days of my youth.

As a bottle is filled with soda, my heart and mind was filled with the pleasures of wickedness and evil. Just as soda is drank by a person, my inner man drank up the fluids of sin. As the blackness of tar covers the roof of any housetop, sin and evil covered the inner parts of my soul. As the queen bee searches for honey to satisfy its appetite, my brain searched for sinful activities to satisfy lustful desires. As the eagle can see miles ahead of him, God saw my wicked disaster happening 10 years before it hit. By Brian K. Irons

Let me share with you a few categories that sin will persuade you to perform when it stays in your brain and body. These sins are called **"The Works of the Flesh"**. There are 17 works of the flesh, which are empowerments from sin. The 17 works of the flesh, which I am about to mention, are physical performances people do when living in sin. These performances are done because people have decided to do the desires of their own heart. After doing the desires of thine heart, which are the 17 works of the flesh, *know thou that for all these things God will bring thee into judgment.*

Galatians 5: 19 says, now the works of the flesh are manifest, which are these; adultery, fornication, uncleanness, lasciviousness,

5:20 idolatry, witchcraft, hatred, variance, emulations, wrath, strife, seditions, heresies,

5: 21 envying, murders, drunkenness, reveling.

1. – Adultery- When two people are about to be married, a scene called wedding takes place. In a wedding, a bride and a groom are both present. The bride and the groom stands chin up at the altar. Face to face, this couple exchanges words, which are vows of commitment. Not only are words of vowels said, but also those same words become a promise. While the couple is exchanging vows, usually, an authorized minister is present reading the holy script.

As the couple looks one another in the eyes, the licensed minister asks them both questions. The minister asks, do you take this man/woman to be your lawfully wedded spouse? After the minister has asked the question, he is expecting the answer from them both to be "yes, I do". After both parties have said, "I do," the two have just become married. These two have just agreed upon the covenant of holy matrimony. Not only did this couple commit and make vows to one another, but also, a vow has been made unto the Lord and the law.

When two people finally become married, I hope they do not think they have the fullness of God in their lives. Just because being married is a righteous act before God, that does not mean you have been freed from sin. People can be married and still live wicked lives. People can be married, and still live the same lifestyle as I lived.

We all know that, after a marriage has taken place, it is commanded neither party is to have sex with none other, than with the spouse. If one does have sex with someone other than the spouse, adultery has been committed. When a person commits adultery, that individual is sharing his or her inner being with someone else.

God presented the earth with a commandment that demandingly says, "Thou Shalt Not Commit Adultery". If adultery has been committed by anyone, that person has disobeyed the commands of God.

Adultery is committed through deceit and crafty scheming by the man and the woman. When adultery has been performed, it is by the strength of sin that such an act has been committed. Sin is the forceful power that strengthens two people to activate this deed of adultery. Never can a person commit adultery alone. Either adultery is committed with a person, or with idols.

When adultery has been committed, even before the very act, a work of deception was in operation. Although, at the altar of marriage, most ministers do not mention the word "adultery", however, the couple already knows the meaning of the word.

An adulterer (the cheater) will tell ongoing lies to get this evil act in session. Lies will always be told to his her or spouse when adultery is planned to be committed. Married people, who are caught up in the sinful ways of adultery, will lie about where they are going: they lie when they say, I am on my way to work; they lie about going to the gym, and they lie about going to the grocery store. They even lie when they say, they are going outside to take a little walk around the block. Lies, lies, nothing but lies will be told when a spouse is caught up in the evil works of adultery.

Another evil act that happens is when people are caught up in adultery, is not answering their cell phones. Now a day, these cell phones are used as evil gadgets. Every time a married person is with someone, and his or her mate calls the cell phone, that person will not answer the phone. Then, when the cheating mate walks into the house, and his or her spouse asks, "Why didn't you answer your phone baby"? He tells his mate, "The phone did not ring, you know how these cell phones act; one minute they ring, the next they don't". Although, at times, the cell phone might not ring for real, however, these days, you don't know whether to believe your spouse or not. But if you sit back and let God expose the spouse deeds, that darkness will turn into light.

Because of sin being an active living force in the world, from it, many people have become true idiots. I've heard people say, "In the Old Testament Days, King David had two wives". Therefore, we should be able to do the same. The Old Testament is a book written about people who God allowed to do the cheerful things of their heart's desire. Just as God is watching you do ignorance, he watched them do it too. God never intended a man to have two wives. The people in the Old Testament walked in the ways of their own hearts, and God allowed it to continue. Just as you are disobedient by sleeping with a married person, King David was disobedient too. Here is just a little note for your personal understanding; the Old Testament is a book filled with sinful stories, which proves that a New Testament savior is needed.

As the act of adultery is being committed, the limbic system in the brain causes pleasure and sensation to be felt. Soon and very soon, the person's limbic system will become sexually addicted to a person who is not his or her legal spouse. After the addiction kicks in, this person has just lost the control to stop having sex with this married person. Once you hit it the first time, you will be mentally pressured and lured to hit another 99 times. Now you know why adultery is called, "the works of the flesh". People need to stop thinking they can control sin, and adultery! This sin will manifest itself unto your spouse one way or another. Yes, my sinful and drug filled body slept with married women too. God please help me!

2. - Fornication - is having a sexual encounter with someone, that's not your spouse. Single people are the ones who commit fornication. Biblically, if you are having sex, while not married, fornication is the active sin in your life. Single people commit fornication so long, that their conscious does not even operate in guilt anymore. Having sex, while not being married has become so common unto us, we think it is a rightful act to do. In the days of our youth, and even in our older days, we cheerfully commit fornication, and care not about the judgment. After committing fornication, people aren't judged by the law, they are judged by God's prophecies. The law doesn't judge fornicators, but the Word of God will.

When people are caught up in fornication, they are performing an act, as if they are married. Marriage neither took place, nor was vowels spoken into the ears of one another. And yet, sexual activity is in motion. The Holy sacred altar has not been seen in this relationship, but people act as if it has. Having sex while not married is considered a sin in the sight of God. Since more than 85% of the world is committing fornication, condemnation has come upon all those who indulge in such an act. Eventually, it will be revealed that you are having sex (fornicating), while not being married. We've become so ignorant, we think, certain things are happening in our lives by mistakes, when in fact, its condemnation.

When I see young women who are pregnant, I already know, they were caught up in the sin of fornication. In this world, you might bump into one or two teenagers who became pregnant while being married. But not many of them were virgins before the marriage took place. Since fornication is a sin, every time a woman performs this lustful act, and becomes pregnant, that just might be condemnation. Just as I was using drugs, and suddenly became physically exposed to the world concerning my sinful drug habits; teenagers when becoming pregnant, and not married, you all have become sinfully exposed too. As I said before, do not think judgments are only executed in court. Even having sex while not being married, reaping will perform its mark.

Let's say that a woman isn't married, and is now pregnant. As this woman walks around on the earth pregnant, her known friend's approaches and ask, "Are you having a boy or girl"? On the other hand, her friends might ask, "How many months pregnant are you? Nevertheless, the pregnant lady thinks it's pretty, she thinks it is cute, but she does not realize she is about to give birth to a child, because of the performance of fornication. Now I see why a baby is born estranged (in sin) from the womb, because, more than 85% of the people in the world were born from the act of fornication.

People on the earth are having sex with any and everybody, and not even thinking about the judgment. Every time a woman commits fornication, and contracts a disease, she has brought judgment upon herself, and this is vice versa with the men.

Many kids in the world were probably never supposed to be here.

We have been led by the works of the flesh (sin) to have sex with many people that God never intended us to be with. I've had sex with a great number of women; do you think that was God's plan for me?

I shot the seed of sex in many women. I could have gotten more than 30 different women pregnant. These pregnancies would have been by women whom God never intend to be my mate.

These women, when I saw their faces, and viewed how sexy their bodies looked, I went after them. *I walked in the ways of my heart, and in the sight of my eyes.* Therefore, I was driven to these women based upon lustful desires, and that is not the blessed plan of God. If people keep sowing fornication into their bodies, then sicknesses, diseases, and kids will be their judgment and or promotion. We have become so comfortable with fornication that we forget it is a sin, and it is to be punished.

We people are so ignorant. We have taken the quote from the bible, which says, "*be fruitful and multiply*", out of content. Single pregnant women walking around on the earth saying, "*God said be fruitful and multiply*". We take biblical quotes for our own personal satisfaction, because of the lack of spiritual understanding. When God spoke the quote, "*be fruitful and multiply*", he was talking to two people he gave to one another in marriage, Adam and Eve. These days, fornicators are walking on earth thinking that the *"be fruitful and multiply"*, is speaking to them. Sin has our minds so far gone in fornication that we've become mentally confused. The sin of fornication is powerful. Why? Because people are quick to finding a companion, before seeking a relationship with God.

Every sin committed has an ending act of misery. If we would do it the way God intended, many children would not be fatherless. In the beginning, God intended the sex drive to for married couples. But the sin fornication is so strong in the land, that having sex before marriage has become almost automatic. The sin fornication has our minds programmed, and it has gotten out of hand. I mean, honestly, if fornication (having sex before marriage) is a sin, do you really think God want us performing it? Do you really think God it is okay with it?

Then we wonder how the disease Aids came into our land. We go from one relationship to the next, to the next, and to the next. Are you still wondering how aids came into the land? Look at how many people we've had unprotected sex with. Me, myself, when I was in the drug life, I am sure I had sex with a great number of women in 12 months, and didn't wear a condom. It was all about my desires, and nothing else mattered.

I have had sex with so many women, that I can't remember their faces or their names. I am sure, in my wheelchair, I have rolled across the path of more than 30 women who I've had sex with, and did not even remember whom they were.

One day, I saw two women. They both approached me. One girl said, "Hey Light, do you remember my friend right here"? I looked at her friend and said, "Nope". Then she said, Light, that's a shame you don't remember that girl. Then, I said, "Well, I am sorry that I don't remember her, who is she"?

As I was riding in the wheelchair going to my destination, my mind began wondering, "Was that a girl I had sex with back in the days, and don't remember who she is. Throughout the years, I've taken so many women to the hotel from the nightclub, had sex with them, and that was it. I do not remember the names of many women I've had sex with; and that's a nasty shame. It makes me wonder, how many women have seen me, and remember having sex with me, and I said nothing to them because <u>I Did Not Know </u>who they were.

Just because condoms are on the market, does not make it right for you to have sex at will. We are some ignorant folks. The other day, I overheard a woman say, "If God didn't want condoms on the earth, then they would not be here". God's protective way from diseases is for you to stay away from fornication. Man's protective way from diseases is to wear a condom. Which way (man's or God's) do you think is safer and perfect? Wearing a condom is no guarantee you will not catch a disease, or get the woman pregnant. While having sex, the condom can rip and tear. During sex, if the condom does tear, you will continue performing. Then, either a disease will be given, or the woman can become pregnant. While having sex, once people reach a certain level, they don't care if the condom breaks or not. It is all about fulfilling that 8 to 10 second pleasure.

Deadly diseases such as aids were here on earth before us all. In the past, sexual deadly diseases such as Aids, had another name. Now, in the 1900's, the disease has been named Aids. Just as our ancestors passed along sins, they also passed unto us Aids. I don't know the names of the sexual disease during the 1100's, however, if it was deadly, it might as well have been called Aids.

Aids didn't just pop up from out of nowhere. Aids was created from sexual encounters. As the people in the world say, "it takes two to tangle". Well, let me make up a saying; "it takes two or more disease to form a more potent disease".

One day, a man and a woman were having sex. The woman is diagnosed with gonorrhea and syphilis, and the man has a horrible case of hepatitis. While these two diseased filled people were having sex, they both shared one another's inner being fluids. Then suddenly, gonorrhea, syphilis, and hepatitis united and became one. While all three diseases were mingling with one another, Aids was then created. Once a person catches a disease, he or she has just experienced moment of harvesting. You sowed fornication in your life, and aids was your harvest.

Diseases come from germs. Dozens of germs get together to form one name of sickness, such as, "Aids". I am not saying my statement about aids is a scientific fact; however, it just might be true. With all the sin and free sex being performed these days, Aids is not the only deadly disease earned.

Anyway, even while in fornication, people live in the same house, as if they are truly married. The man and woman actually believe the relationship is God given. The bold character of sin has caused people to live in a relationship God hates. If you are living in fornication, you're living in sin; if living in sin, you're living in a work that God hates. Many people are so caught up in fornication that they are going through rough times in their so-called relationship. If fornicators would go to God for truth, there is a great chance you will see you are living with someone who will probably never be your wedded spouse. Living in fornication will cause you to believe every boyfriend or girlfriend just might be God given.

What is a girlfriend? What is a boyfriend? Who made up those titles? Those two words were never supposed to have a definition. Girlfriend and boyfriend was supposed to mean just what it says. In other words, girlfriend is supposed to mean, you have a female who is your actual friend. They were never supposed to be in the nation's translation. It was always supposed to be, "Husband and Wife". The sin of fornication has our minds so messed up, that we claim boyfriends and girlfriends, before proclaiming the way of God.

Now a day, most people think a true mate has been found, but lust was in action from the very start. There is a difference from finding a soul mate, and finding a lust mate. These days, we have sex before we get the chance to know the person. We need to spend time with someone for about a year or two, before concentrating on marriage and having sex. We are so quick to becoming attached to someone, that we think we are going to die next week. As I said before, sin is causing us all to do things our very own way, rather than God's way.

Well, I have slept with many women, and never been married; therefore, I committed fornication too. While I was out there in the world of sin, fornication was practice by me for a number of years. Never did I stand before a holy altar. Never did a minister ask me pre-marital questions, nor were there vow exchanges. During my moments of committing fornication, I have earned two kids. God, please help me?

3. - Uncleanness- is a sin that empowers people to do perverted things. Lesbians, gays, and bestiality (sex with animals); operates from an unclean spirit. Not only does having sex with same agenda, or with animals, operates from an unclean spirit, but just by having sin in your life marks the uncleanness right there.

An unclean sprit was operating in my body while I was on probation. When my probation officer tested me for drugs, and the results came back positive, I was declared "unclean". Many other works of evil operates from an unclean spirit. Now you know why uncleanness is categorized as one of the works of the flesh. A person is declared unclean, because of living in sin. I need some help! I am unclean; God, please help me!

4. - Lasciviousness- is a sin that plays many roles in its practices. The prevailing role lasciviousness plays is when people are plotting to do a work of evil. A person becomes so deceitful, while trying to make an evil work happen. You want it to happen so bad, that you will do anything just to experience the event. Even if your life is on the line, lasciviousness will lead you to go after it anyway. If it takes days, weeks, or even months to get it going, you will stick with the plan, until it happens. If it is a thought of evil, and you are trying to bring the wicked event to pass, then lasciviousness is in action.

Here is a written example of how lasciviousness operates: a person who commits adultery is sneaky, and uses crafty ways to get an event going. When people plot, plan, and arrange to commit adultery, from the plotting of it, lasciviousness is very much active. Since lasciviousness is a sin that gears people to arrange and organize events, the brain's frontal lobes are at work. Lasciviousness operates before any wicked work is performed.

When my friends and I thought of places to smoke dope, the sin of lusciousness caused us to do that. Together we plotted, planned, and arranged to get high. When I plotted to sneak out of the Halfway House, lascivious was in operation. Therefore, the sin of lasciviousness was dwelling in my body because I planned and plotted to do many acts of evil. Now you know why lasciviousness is categorized as one of the works of the flesh. God, please help me!

5. - Idolatry- is active in a person's life when perceiving an object to be his or her source of power or help in life. Idolatry is also practiced when people give their full attention to what is before their eyes. They become fascinated by what the object does for them. Whatever the object maybe, it becomes plastered to their hearts and minds. When a person's living is caught up in idolatry, it is all about the object more than anything else. Sometimes people jeopardize their own life, when cherishing the object. The object becomes a person's daily devotion in life, because the heart has deep reverence and relies on it for support.

Well, drugs were my objects of idolatry. I trusted and relied on drugs to help and do good things for me, rather than God. When you trust in something, your thoughts are positive about it. Hey people, it is not hard to be caught up in idolatry. Even the cars I owned became objects of idolatry. Therefore, my cerebrum (my head thinker), and my brainstem (heart regulator) was plagued with idolatrous ways and its formulas. Idolatry is another sin that was operating in my body and life. Now you know why idolatry is categorized as one of the works of the flesh. Truly, idolatry was manifested in my life. Will somebody help me, because as of now, five "works of the flesh" has been operating in my body? I have been committing idolatry for a very long time and <u>I Did Not Know</u> it. Lord Help me!

6. - Witchcraft- when people believe things can change their living situations, other than God, that is witchcraft. Only God has the power and authority to change a person's living. Many people believe zodiac readings and chemical substances gives them future hope. Zodiac readings or chemical control substances will only sell you pretense visions. Just because a zodiac reading said something that relate to your life today, does not mean it is your prophet.

Let's say a zodiac reading gave you a true-life experience quote on Monday; do you think it is going to do the same next Monday? Well, probably not! People actually believe readings can match them up with relationships. Go read a bible; only it will give precise future living endeavoring events.

Witchcraft takes up numeral accounts in its meanings. However, people who put chemical-controlled substances in their bodies are filled with witchcraft. They have been made to believe dope relieves them from stress or whatever. From the power of drugs, people have been made to believe that drugs are party enhancers. Although, filling your brain with drugs does increase the intensity level, however, a witch, which is your drug of choice, has forced you into believing that.

People's minds have been cursed, and their heart has been cast into a "spell". Who or what gave you the mental power to believe drugs kill's stress, and enhances the movement of a party. I believe a witch apparently did. What led you to believe such a healing will take place from chemical controlled substance? Sin did, well; a witch did. Just as a witch or a psychic will advertise false words unto you, and show you lustful visions of future actions, putting chemicals in the brain has done the same thing unto you and me.

Why wait until Halloween to see a wicked witch. I thought the wicked witch only shows up, dressed up on Halloween". However, since the world is tied up in chemical control substances, then the wicked witch is located in every state on the globe. Every time you put a chemical controlled substance in your hand, you are handling a product that causes "witch tendencies".

2nd Samuel 15:23 says, for rebellion is as the sin of witchcraft. As you have just read in this book, how rebellious I was toward the laws of God. I became rebellious after putting drugs into my brain. Since I was being rebellious, my mind was filled with the works of witchcraft. In other words, when a person is rebellious unto God, the unseen power of a witch is operating from within. My, my, my, I need some serious help in my life. Oh my God, you mean to tell me, that as of now, I have six sins working in my body. Lord have mercy! Please help me? This stuff is ridiculous. All this time, <u>I Did Not Know</u> that witchcraft was operating in me.

7. - Hatred- is when two or more people are involved in drama. When I think of the word "drama", I think of screenplays, TV shows and movies. While dealing in drugs and wickedness, my life appeared to be a movie. Actually, the drama in my life became a movie to God, because the cameras of God's eyes were continually rolling. In God, there is no such thing as take 2. This is real life, and the tape never stops to rewind. Just as I watched drama on the TV screen, God watched drama take place in my life. God watched me performed much hatred on the streets.

Every day of my drug filled living, the film and cameras were rolling. As the cameras of God's eyes were rolling, nothing but actions of hatred was being recorded. My life became a screenplay. Much hatred lived in me because of my enemies. They did not like me, and I could not stand them. Therefore, the sin of hatred was working through me as well. Lord Help me!

8. Variance - is a sin that brings conflict and disagreements between two or more people. Arguments stay active when people are demandingly trying to get their point across. Some arguments take place when people are trying to justify themselves.

When people use their mental energy to prove a point, soon, the situation grows into negativity. Allowing the sin, variance, to live in your body will soon persuade your mind to think from a hatred point of view. After hatred has become active in the brain, physical violence is then brought into play. Having debates and battles all the time is from the work of variance.

As I was living the drug life, many conflicts and disagreements approached me through different people. My life was filled with much conflict; therefore, the sin, variance was plugged into me too. This too was manifested in my life. If you didn't see it, God saw it. Is there anyone who can help me from the sins that are reigning in my life and body?

9. Emulations- means striving to be in control or ahead of someone. A person does his or her very best to be seen as the better person. Well, I was a drug seller; the only thing I knew was to seek and strive to look better than the next man. I fixed my cars up just to be seen. I purchased the finer clothes, just to appear to have more than the next man. Therefore, the sin of emulation was connected to my brain and heart too. Lord have mercy, already, nine sins are living inside of my body, and <u>I Did Not Know</u> it. God please help me!

10. - Wrath- means to have a high level of anger in you that tends to lead to violence, which will soon promote you to cast self-judgment on someone. When a person has wrath in his or her heart towards another human being, usually, physical violence is brought forth next. When violence is brought forth, people are actually recompensing one another *evil for evil*. Yeah, the sin of wrath was definitely in high pursuit within me, which soon led me to plot a murder. We know that all homicides are performed by physical violence, through personal wrath and anger. Yes, I was filled with much anger, violence, and wrath while living the drug life. God Help me?

11. Strife- means, to not agree with someone, and the two become contenders. Two people can be in the same neighborhood, doing the same thing (selling drugs). Then a person tries to run another person off the premises. The person wants to sell his drugs, and make all the money. Therefore, he seeks to run the other drug seller away.

A certain person came into my neighborhood, and tried running me away so he can sell his drugs. He was against me, and I was against him. Strife was going on. Not only was strife in action, but also, quarrelling was in progress too. Therefore, one day, I gathered up my friends to watch my back, just in case his boys would try to jump me. I called the person out to a one-on-one fistfight. Yeah, I dropped him, hit him with my combination punch, and the fight was over.

Always being against one another is a sign of strife. Well, of course, this sin was in my life as well because I was performing much strife in the streets of St. Louis. This sin too, was manifested. I need some true help, for real. Lord God please save me!

12. Seditions - is being rebellious against righteous rules or disobeying righteous statues. When the police found drugs in my possession, afterwards, I continue to handle dope. My life was filled with the sin of seditions. The power of sin (sedition) strengthened me to do so.

Therefore, the sedition sin was wrapped up inside of me as well. Lord have mercy! Please help me!

13. - Heresies- is a denying of a truth that has been revealed. A cousin called me over the phone one day. She was telling me about a vision she had seen. In the vision, she saw me being killed. When my cousin told me the vision, I guess did not believe her. I did not accept the fact that a truth has been told; I kept on hanging with the fellows, and kept on selling and using drugs. No matter what truthful heresies I've heard, sin empowered me to push it all to the aside. However, the greatest sin of heresies is not to believe what the Word of God (the bible) says. Yep, I had this sin in me too. I need some help.

14. Envying- is a work that exposes jealousy and or resentment towards another. When a person has something you do not have, and you become jealous, envy is working from within. People even envy other people because of how they look. Men have this envying problem bad, but women have it grossly. I can raise my hand up, and admit to God, that this envying sin is reigning in my body, too. This is ridiculous, as of now, I have 14 works of the flesh (sin) operating within me, and I Did Not Know it. Lord help me!

15. Murder- to take the life of a person. Although, I never committed an act of murder, I ruined many lives by introducing people to the drug game. Although, I did not commit a murder, however, when my heart stopped beating because of using drugs, God would have judged me as he does a murderer. Actually, in the sight of God, I would have looked like a person who has committed suicide. The person who puts a gun to his head, or slit the wrist, is no different from me. They used a tool to kill themselves, and I used a tool (drugs) to kill myself. Therefore, I believe I am capable of saying; I almost murdered myself.

Another murder I want to talk about concerns women having abortion. Yeah, when women go to hospitals and get abortions, they have actually murdered an infant. A living soul (infant) is actually living inside their stomachs, and an appointment was arranged to kill that baby. Not only did the woman plan to kill the baby, but also, it was done in premeditation. You made plans, and scheduled an appointment to kill this baby, and this was done by lasciviousness. Since planning events are done by the frontal lobes, that part of the brain schedules date for all abortions to take place. Wow, you know what, in the sight of God, if any woman has aborted their baby; she has committed a 2nd degree murder. See, that's what women agree to do, when they conceive a child through acts of fornication. But help and forgiveness is for you too.

16. - Drunkenness - drinking booze or alcohol over the limit. Yes, I had the drunkenness sin in me as well. Hennessey was my flavored drink. Gin and juice was second to Hennessy. Every party given has drinks in it. Anytime a person drinks at a party, 9 times out of ten, when going home, he or she is driving while intoxicated. I used to drink and drive all the time. However, I thank God I never experienced being in a car wreck. Well, I must confess, I did hit a dog, as I was driving down Grand Avenue, near Tower Grove Park. If I had hit a person, even not being drunk, and the police gave me a breath examination test, and if it came back positive for alcohol usage, I still would been handcuff. The law does not care how much you drink. The law only wants to find you guilty, so it can provide you with a penalty. However, the dog did live, but I'm sure the front fender broke the dog's jaw. I had many horrible experiences while being highly intoxicated from alcohol. Lord please help me!

17. - Reveling- when people take intense pleasure in performing actions of evil, it is called, "reveling". Taking situations to a higher level is called reveling. When someone has a fight, and then goes and get a gun, that is taking the situation to another level. Many people start arguments, just to elevate the current situation.

Now I know why sin became my master; Look at all the "works of the flesh" committed by me. When sin cleverly lured me into using drugs, I attained within me, every sin that was just written and mentioned above. From the power act of sin, all 17 works of the flesh captivated my life. Daily, weekly, monthly, and yearly, my life was caught up in the works of the flesh. All 17 works of the flesh became moving events in my life. I smoked one joint (marijuana) and, afterwards, I performed the 17 works of the flesh. <u>I Did Not Know</u> one body could commit so many sins in one day.

It seems like 17 sins could only be committed over a period. But that is not so. In a complete whole day, or in 24 hours, I committed 17 sins. I fornicated one day, and in the same day, I smoked dope, broke the laws, got drunk, had a witch, operated in envy, hatred, seditions, heresies, etc. It is not hard to commit 17 sins in one day.

Now I understand why so many demons were in my life. From all of the sins I've committed, demons were added to my personal being. One sin led me to another sin, and another sin led to another. Yeah, sin literally persuaded my brain to think, and then mobilized my body to perform all 17 works of the flesh.

Every time I hear about a murder, it alerts me to know that someone has just committed one of the works of the flesh. Every time I smell the scent of dope, I already know, someone is allowing sin to dwell in his or her inner being. Every time I hear about a rape, I already know, someone was empowered by sin to perform an unwanted sex act. Every time I hear a person cussing and speaking foul language, I already know, sin is active in that person's life.

God presently has a will, and a plan designed for every human being upon the earth. When people do not live in God's blessed plan, they are living dangerous lives. While people are living contrary to God's blessings: judgments, sentencing, imprisonment, and physical punishments become their life's reward. Always hiding from the law (police) will be a daily activity. Denying God's blessed plan is sort of like running head on with a bull. Your head is no match with the bull. It's not a fair battle. People need to stop bumping heads with God's blessed plan for their lives, because they will lose every time. Going head on with God is a burdensome thing to do.

God has set forth two plans on earth. One plan, if chosen, will provide health and protection for your life. The health and protection plan is designed to lead a person to experience happiness, joy, and peace. The other plan, if chosen, will lead a person to experiencing setbacks, and death. Both plans have a lane, but only one will and can be chosen.

Deuteronomy 30:19 I call heaven and earth to record this day against you, that I have set before your life and death, blessing and cursing: therefore choose life, that both thou (you) and thy seed may live.

This scripture speaks of the two plans God has set upon the earth. While living on earth, one of the plans will be chosen. It says, *"God has set before you, "Life and Death, Cursing and Blessings"* which means, either you will choose life or you will choose death. Either you will choose blessing, or you will choose cursing. No if's, and's or but's about it, one of the two choices will be chosen. Even right now today, while you are reading this book, a choice has already been made. Actually, whatever you are doing today verifies the choice you've made in the past.

If you have chosen the life I was living, your life is now in the "death and cursing" plan. Not only that, but also, you have chosen a living activated by the 17 works of the flesh. Meaning, you just never know what kind of experience you will face next. Not only that, but the judgment of God will continually fall upon you, and death will be in the mix.

On the other hand, if a person chooses *"Life and Blessings"*, he has chosen a plan that leads to all the goodness God has to offer. Choosing the plan *"Life and Blessings"*, your life will be protected from sin's power. Everybody wants blessings to continually rain upon them. People have to choose the plan that is connected to that great shower.

When we work against the power of God, it is the same scenario as your 2-year-old child becoming angry, and then trying to wrestle you down to the ground. How would it look for you and your two-year-old child in a brawl? A two-year-old child does not have physical strength to match up against the parent; in the same sense, you are no match with God. Neither in mental powers nor through physical strength, you're no match with God. No man in the history of all the earth will ever mount up to be a fair contender with God Almighty. If you show me a man who thinks he is stronger, mightier, or smarter than God, you have just shown me a true demonic idiot. I advise you to work with God and not against him. Since God is the one who made you, soon and very soon, it will be revealed unto you, that only God can raise your life out of sin's ditch. Our inner being, which sin has marred and made filthy, it needs to be washed by God. Our lives have been horribly blemished up, due of our sinful deeds done.

In the book of *Isaiah*, chapter 1, verse 16 says, *Wash you, make you clean; put away the evil of your doings from before mine eyes; cease to do evil.*

Isaiah is a prophet who God spoke to in the long past. Isaiah had a relationship with God. God and Isaiah became friends. After God spoke those words to Isaiah, Isaiah's interpretation of what God said is written in the book called *"Isaiah"*. Whatever God said to Isaiah, this is what he wrote after interpreting it; *wash you, make you clean; put away the evil of your doings from before mine eyes.*

Actually, Isaiah is not commanding you to wash and clean your own self. That's a hard job for you to do. Remember, we have sin in our bodies, and it empowers us to fulfill the works of the flesh. The works of sin cannot be cured by humans. Why, because we all have lost the strength to do what is right. We love committing fornication; we love having sex with someone's spouse; we love using drugs; we love fighting, we love causing havoc, yeah, we love performing the 17 Works of the Flesh. Therefore, we will never come to a point or position in our lives where we can cleanse our own selves. If you had the power to clean yourself from evil, then you have the power to clean yourself from sin. Only God has the power to <u>*wash you, and make you clean.*</u> Therefore, Isaiah is saying, "go get God", let him cleanse you, then you'll be able to follow His blessing plan for living.

For many years, I have said to people and to myself, "I need to clean myself up before attending church". I also remember saying, "I need to get my life together, and then start attending church service". Sin is a powerful character; it will make you believe you must get your own life together before attending church service. However, you cannot clean yourself; you do not have the power to clean yourself from sin.

Millions of people believe they need to clean themselves before stepping foot into the church. People, stop fooling yourselves; stop allowing sin to make you believe you can clean yourself. That's a myth! How long, or how many years have you been saying, "I need to get myself together". You have been saying that for years, and the cleansing hasn't been applied yet. Stop being fooled, stop being tricked; I want to let you know, if you are trying to get your own life together, you will never succeed. Sin will cause you to believe you can clean your own self, until it kills you.

Isaiah 1:17 learn to do well; seek judgment. Whether we realize it or not, we have been taught by sin to do much evil in our lives. We have been taught by sin; in return, it has made our bodies feel sick, rather than well. Just as parents lead, and teach their children to do healthy things, well, sin leads, and teaches people to do un-well things.

Why do you think the scripture says, *"Lean to do well"*! It says learn to do well because you must be taught to do well. God is the lesson giver, and he will teach you how to do well. While God has you in class teaching you, he will instruct you on how to do good deeds to your body. When you learn to do "well", by being taught by the written word of God, your life will turn out sweet, prosperous, and healthy. If you allow God to teach you how to do well in life, then your name will turn out to be successfully great. Even while God is teaching you how to live a righteous life, there will still be obstacles. Just because God is teaching you, that does not mean you will not have trials.

Isaiah 1:17 also says, *seek judgment.* When people seek the type of judgment Isaiah is speaking of, they search the scriptures wanting to know how God feels about their current living. Before we do anything or go anywhere, we need to find out what God has to say about it. When the prophet *Isaiah* said, *seek judgment,* he was saying, go to the judge (God), and get his help. Let God convict you, before the law's judgment or biblical prophecies judge you. If you don't go to God for judgment, you might find yourself experiencing the same judgment as Brian Irons experienced. When you ask God to forgive you, you are asking him to help you escape sin's judgment, punishment, and guilt. Go ahead, go boldly to God, get him in your life, and get your conviction over with, and final. If you let God convict you, rather than the law, you will never serve time in jail.

Although, in my living, God's mercy proved to be great and powerful, however, I was still missing something very valuable in life. There has to be something more of a potent protection than just mercy alone. I am not downsizing or underestimating the power of God's mercy, because I've experienced it at its fullest. Mercy is the active reason I am here writing this book; therefore, I will never exalt myself to speak against it. However, mercy alone in one's life is not a fully satisfied life to live. Follow me and I will show you what needs to be added to our lives.

Chapter 13

COME TO JESUS

I finally concluded that I need more of God in my life. If there is such a way to find more drugs, then surely there has to be a way to get more of God. After this dope disaster happened, I realized I was missing something. I realized there is something on earth or in life, I did not have. I was in a world, doing things my heart desired. Nothing could persuade me, other than to realize I needed help with my life. Does God have another power on earth that can be attach to my living?

God has been pulling and pulling on me for a very long time. God, through his mercy was doing his best in steering **Brian Keith** into another direction, which was towards the way of peace. From within, I realized there was something or someone I did not have as a helper. The worker I was missing is none other than "Jesus Christ" himself. Therefore, heavenly God tugged (drew) on me one more time. I inwardly (from the heart), and physically (with the body) went to see the man who God named Jesus.

If God is mercifully "drawing" you in any direction, trust me, God is drawing you to grab a hold onto his son Jesus. If you do not submit to God and accept his drawing, you are wrestling against God's blessings for your life. I have wrestled and fought against the "drawing" of God for many, many years. When you are fighting against the pulling of God, you actually become His contender. Although, I submitted my life to the plan of death and curses, God was still drawing me toward his son, so that peace can be applied to my life.

When you feel low and down, and begin to say within yourself, "I need to go to church"; that is God pulling and drawing on you. Let's say, your life is a living mess. You are on your way to work, and every day is the same, horrible! While driving to work, your conscience character begins to operate. You are actually thinking about going to church, to get rid of the way you've been living. You inwardly feel that you need some serious help. Every day is full of foolishness, anger, and never progression.

Although, after my incident, I began attending church, a time had come, when I began smoking marijuana again. I was going to church, I was hearing God's word, but I did not give my life (brain/spirit) to him. Yep, I was smoking marijuana again. In my mind, I knew I was not going to try any other drugs after what I just went through. However, you just never know how far sin and drugs will lead your life again. Actually, I should not have even done marijuana again. Although, I was going to church, I didn't go to be cleansed (washed). I was going to church because I felt like it was a good thing to do. Although, attending church is a good thing to do, however, only going to show your face means nothing. All the sins I've committed before the coma experience, were still reigning in my body, because they had not been forgiven. Even as I started smoking weed again, God drew (pulled) on me again. God must truly "so love the world".

Many times, experiencing harsh moments, does not deliver us from things that may have caused harm. If the sin remains in a person's body, deliverance from destruction has yet been applied. I know three people right now today who had been shot (guns) because of being in the drug game. They now use wheelchairs, but are still selling and using drugs. Their sins have not been forgiven. Their sins are still active in their lives, because they are still doing the same performances that put them in wheelchairs.

Many people think Jesus is fully in their lives just because they attend church. In this chapter, you will know if Jesus has truly come into your life.

Written below are examples of God drawing me to receive a better way in life. However, I wrestled and kept contending against Almighty God. Example #1: When I had been robbed at gunpoint three different times, and after each gunplay, a thought appeared into my mind saying, "get out of dope game before I get shot and or murdered". Nevertheless, while my mind was under wickedness and witchcraft, I sinfully kept on selling drugs. Example #2: When three cars of mine had been plagued with bullet holes, the thought of leaving the dope game flashed through my mind, but I never took the action to do so. I sinfully kept on selling drugs just to get that wicked money. Example #3- When three drugs cases were placed upon my criminal record report, the thought to leave the drug game floated through my mind, but I still hung in there, and kept on selling drugs.

I often experienced being in numerous drive-by gun shootings. After the shootings took place, of course, I was glad a bullet did not hit me. I never followed my conscience God was dealing with. Those were actual moments I wrestled with the drawings from God. After those 10 to 12, and a dozen other conscience-drawing performances, if I would have had enough sense to stop, drop, and roll out of the drug game, my body would have been preserved and protected, rather than suffering from a serious evil final drug effect. Nevertheless, after all of the bitterness came pouring into my life, I realized it was time for me to try something new. As God pulled on me one more time, I finally allowed it to operate, and went to his son Jesus.

I remember at one point, after being cleansed and washed from sin and drugs, I began attending church seeking and asking God to pour His spirit upon me. I attended church faithfully for 8 months. I wanted to be baptized with the Holy Ghost (Spirit of God).

This particular day, the church praise service was filled with the power and presence of God. The church has always been filled with the presence and power of God, but this day was very special for me. This day was amazing. The music in the church was playing. I was up doing my little praise dance for the Lord. I am always thanking God in the praise dance, and I thank him in my testimony, too.

As I was giving God praise in the dance, I was holding on to my walker for balancing. The two ministers, both grab me and put my arms around their shoulders, and we three kept on dancing for the Lord. As I was crying, drooling, and dancing for the Lord, I begin speaking in tongues, which is a language only given from God. Now that I've received the Holy Ghost (Spirit of God), Gods son Jesus has come into my life, brain, and body. When anyone has allowed the spirit of God to enter into his being, he has just received the Son of God (Jesus).

When people attend church desiring God to baptize them with the Holy Ghost (His spirit), timing varies. It took me 8 months to receive it, while it might take you only 5 days. God knows your heart; he knows when you are truthfully ready to receive a better way of living.

Jesus is the individual, whose job is to help and receive openly every person that the man above (God) sends unto him. The moment I received Jesus in my life, is the moment all my sins were forgiven. Also, when I received Jesus in my life, I became a partner with God. Everything you and I need has been miraculously placed inside of one man's body, and that body belongs to Jesus Christ. Whether we need healing in our bodies, or need relief from mental stress, and most importantly, a need of forgiveness of sin, Jesus is the true source provided to make it happen. Healing is plugged up into the body of Jesus, and every human being must be willing to go after it and get it. Put your hands on His body today!

When people go to Jesus, God has evidently touched his or her conscience and persuaded that individual to march towards that way.

When you finally accept the drawing from God, by going to Jesus, Jesus is standing with open arms ready to receive you.

In the New Testament, *John 6:37 Jesus says, all that the father giveth me, shall come unto me; and him that cometh to me I will in no wise cast him out.* From all of the years of performing works of wickedness, no matter what sins I have presumptuously done in life, or what laws I've broken, Jesus cannot cast me away. No matter how filthy my life and body was, Jesus cannot rebuke me. God sent me to his son Jesus, so that he could help me with my life, and give me the power to make wiser choices. Although, I've been baptized with the spirit of God, sin is still in the world, and I must be careful.

When I went to Jesus, he did accept me, and pulled me in unto him. As I ran unto Jesus, I went unto him in all my filth, shame, and sin, and he did not reject me, nor did he cast me away. When I went to face Jesus, I was filled with all 17 sins, that *Galatians 5:19-21* spoke about. Jesus performed the task his father gave him the power to do, and that is to clean me up from my sinful past. When the prophet Isaiah said, *wash you make you clean,* he was saying, accept the drawing from God by running to Jesus. I thank God he made and created Jesus mental (inner body, the spirit) to act differently from all people, who are upon the earth. Now you know, the only way to be cleansed from sin is through the power God gave his son Jesus. As I said before, you do not have the power to clean or wash yourself. If you want to be cleansed, go get Jesus right now, so he can *wash you, make you clean.*

Matthew 11:28-Jesus said, come unto me, all ye that labor and are heavy laden, and I will give you rest. Well, now that I went to Jesus, and gave him my brain, I am not working in hard labor, which sin and drugs hired me to do. I am not under the power or labor of drugs anymore. Every time I broke the laws of God, it was because I was empowered by sin and drugs to do such labor. The longer my life was under the power and labor of sin and drugs, the heavier the load became. For ten years, I was working in heavy labor under the power of sin and drugs. When I came to Jesus, it was still lightweight for him to remove. When your brain and body is weighed down with the pounds of sin, take it to Jesus because nothing is too heavy for him to lift out of your life. Sin might have caused your life to be low (heavy), but Jesus has the power to lift your life to the highest cloud. *COME UNTO ME!*

My life is no longer under the command of a pager. I no longer meet drug customers. I now presently have rest in my life and body because of finally accepting the *"Life and Blessing"* plan of God. In fact, I do not own a single pager. In my past, it did not matter what time of the day or night it was, once the pager sounded, I physically scurried to the destination to get that sinful money. Every time I tried to get rest, my pager beeped. Then, immediately, I drove my car to meet a customer to sell cocaine. Now that God has led me to his son Jesus, those actions are no longer activities in my life. If anyone wants true rest in his or her life, Jesus will supply him or her with it. The wonderful love about Jesus inviting people to come unto him is the fact that he knows everything you have done. As you have just read in my story, I almost did not make it to accept the invitation of Christ.

The bible is not saying come to the church just as you go to the nightclubs. The bible is spiritual, and we take many of its quotes physical tense. When the bible says, *come unto me*, or *come as you are*, it is saying, no matter what sins you have committed in life, *"Come unto me"* even while in them. In other words, if your body is now filled with all 17 works of the flesh (sins), that's okay, come to Jesus as you are. Don't worry about what you've done in the past. Every sin you have committed under the sun and under the moon, *"come to me as you are"*. The scripture is not talking about your clothing. This scripture is speaking about going to Jesus, and realizing you need a forgiveness of sins.

That's what the scripture means, for Jesus to accept us as we are, yes, he accepted me as I am. People in the world take the quote, *"come to me as you are"* the wrong way. Women go to church wearing skirts high above the thighs, and every centimeter of breast is showing, and then say, "God said *come as you are*". Men go to church, wearing all kinds of stuff, and then say, "God said *come as you are*". The world of people has messed up minds. We actually do what we want to do, and then try giving God the glory somehow.

I saw a pretty woman the other day. She is one of the prettiest women you ever did see. She was wearing a pair of short shorts that were ridiculously short. So I asked her, "How do you think God feels about you wearing shorts like that"? She said, "God doesn't care what I wear, he loves me". She also said, that's why God put clothes on the earth, to be worn.

You people think every piece of clothing is okay by God to wear. When sin is in your life, you will think any and everything is okay to be worn, even while attending church. Certain clothes we wear, we wear them for self-satisfaction, and not for God's satisfaction. Remember this, every item made by a person on earth, is not heavenly thought of. This book you are now reading is heavenly agreeable, because it has been clothed with the righteousness of God. But some of the clothing many women wear in today's world, makes them look like Adam and Eve in the Garden.

Another scripture I want to share with you, can be read in the gospel of John. *John 3:16 for God so loved the world, that he gave his only begotten Son, that whosoever believeth in him should not perish but have everlasting life.* Eternal life is a living that never ends. This type of living, eternity is not giving freely as mercy is. Eternal life has no market price. It is granted to all those who accept Jesus as their Lord and Savior. Since eternal life comes through believing in Jesus, you have to go to get Jesus in order to inherit that heavenly dwelling. However, in my sinful drug dealing years, when my heart stopped for 11 minutes, do you honestly think I would have lived in eternity with Jesus? You can believe in Jesus, but in order to inherit eternal life with him, a certain work must be done. Not only that, but also, a certain path must be walked on, which leads to righteousness.

Now that I have Jesus in my life, the existence of God's grace has been given to me as well. The bible says, *John 1: 17, for the law was given by Moses, but grace and truth came by Jesus.*

God gave the law to Moses to warn the people; however, grace and truth was given to Jesus to give to people who get a hold of him. Now that I have Jesus in my life, I now attain both "Grace and Mercy" at the same time. When you get a hold to Jesus, your living is now active in grace.

Every person in the Old Testament who grace became acquainted with, God saw that the person wanted to be used by for His righteousness. Most of the Old Testament prophets said, "I have found grace in the eyes of the Lord". They hearkened to the voice of the Lord, and became God's friend. God saw that they wanted to be on his side, and he used them as witnesses of his righteousness. While the Spirit of God was using these prophets to do a certain work, they were giving the ability to claim grace. Grace can also mean, God found favor in you.

John 14:6-Jesus said, I am the way, the truth, and the life: no man cometh unto the father (God) but by me. When humankind does not read the bible, to build a relationship with it, it becomes a book of mysteries. People believe they are going to heaven by their own righteousness. People believe they are going to heaven just because they haven't committed a murder or have cheated on someone. They have no heavenly understanding of what certain scriptures mean. They do not understand, nor believe, that God has preserved a system that leads directly to heaven. God is in paradise (heaven), and Jesus plainly said, *"No man can come unto the father but by me".*

The only way to get to the father, who is in paradise, is to be escorted there by Jesus Christ. When a person first walks into a church, usually, an usher escorts the individual to a seat. In the same sense, Jesus is the one who ushers you into heaven. In other words, if anyone desires to see God, Jesus claims to have the directions and plans to make this possible. If you do not have God's beloveth son in your life, then it is impossible for you to meet God. That is why God directs everyone to Jesus, so that his beloved son can clean us from sin's filth, and then show us a way to contact God.

I have another scripture for you to read. *John 14:2-in my Father's house are many mansions: if it were not so, I would have told you. I go to prepare a place for you.* Do you think Jesus went boldly to his Father's house, which is in heaven, to prepare a mansion for me to live in? Again, when I died in all of those sins (17 works of the flesh), do you think Jesus took time preparing a mansion for me in heaven? If you do not have Jesus in your life, brain, and body, Jesus has no righteous reason to go to his father's house (heaven) to prepare a mansion for you or me. Whatever lifestyle you are living today, it is preparing a place for you to live in throughout eternity. Whether it is heaven or hell, a place is being prepared for you to live in throughout eternity.

Read these examples of my life's preparation: I went to bed one night, woke up the next morning, took a shower, brushed my teeth, put my clothes on, went to work, and bam, being associated with drugs caused me to get fired. I went to bed another night, woke up the next morning; took a shower, put my clothes on, dash to school, and bam, being associated with drugs caused me to quit attending college. I went to bed one night, woke up the next morning, took a shower, put my clothes on, and bam, I quit two jobs. I went to bed one night, woke up the next morning, put my clothes on, and bam, I am on the run from the law (probation officer). I went to bed one night, woke up the morning, took a shower, put my clothes on, went outside to sell some dope, and bam, I got robbed. I went to bed one night, woke up the next morning, took a shower, put my clothes on, and bam I am on my way to the penitentiary. I went to bed one night, woke up in the morning, took a shower, put my clothes on, and bam, I came so close to committing a murder. I went to bed one night, woke up in the morning, took a shower, put my clothes on, and went to get high, and bam, I went into a coma.

Drugs created and prepared all those unexpected scenes to occur in my life. When drugs prepare situations in people's lives, people never know what to expect. Drugs want to prepare an opportunity to kill you! I know you do not want death to be your manifestation of a drug penalty, Do you? Do not give drugs the opportunity to prepare scenes for your life! Now that I have Jesus in my life, he is preparing a mansion for me to live in, which is being built in heaven. Either a person will be escorted to heaven, or commanded by Jesus to take part in hell. The choice is yours!

I read an article in the New Testament, which spoke about a certain rich man and a certain beggar. I am going to give you an easy illustration, so that you can understand the story punch line. As God gives me the ability to teach on this article, the reader should learn much from it. This biblical article will show you how people act when they are in earthly high position, and have the world goods.

Luke 16:19 there was a certain rich man, which was clothed in purple and fine linen, and fared sumptuously every day.

This rich man lived spectacular every single day. Often times, the color purple is somewhere visible in his fine linen. Not only that, but the rich man rejoiced every day. Rich man feels good about the way things are going in his life.

In the New Testament days, and even before then, wearing purple is a sign of royalty. The color purple symbolizes a high praise upon the person's living. It shows that the person has high rankings in certain areas of life. Meaning, the person who wears purple can do what others in the world can't do. Also, in the New Testament days (even so today), royalty means, to have power and authority.

Luke 16:20 and there was a certain beggar named Lazarus, which laid at his gate, full of sores.

While Lazarus was lying at the rich man's gate, his entire body was covered with sores. The bible says the beggar's body was "full" of sores, which means, his body was probably covered with them from head to toe.

I can only imagine how the beggar's skin looked. So many sores were on his body, it probably looked as if was embedded with something contagious. Looking at a body full of sores is probably a nasty sight.

Just the other day, I saw a woman whose skin was full of black bumps. I wondered, "What happened to her"? Why are those bumps on her entire body? Those bumps were not a pretty sight to see. Therefore, I can only imagine how the beggar's skin looked, as it was full of sores. Since his body is full of sores, I bet some of them have open scabs.

Why is the beggar laid out at the rich man's gate? The beggar knows the rich man has something he needs. Even if the beggar did not see it with the naked eye, he knew the rich man had it in his ownership. Let's find out why Lazarus laid at the rich man's gate, and what he begged for.

Luke 16:21 And Lazarus was desiring to be fed with the crumbs, which fell from the rich man's table: moreover, the dogs came and licked his sores.

Now we know what Lazarus wanted. Lazarus didn't beg for the rich man's money, or for materials. Lazarus begged for food, which is a substance that will keep him alive. Lazarus was probably a poor man, and was hungry for the most part. The beggar's limbic system (brain) was yearning to be fed food, to stop its hunger.

Anytime a grown man lays on the ground, hoping it will get him what he want, he is asking for someone to have mercy upon him, Anytime a person does such a thing, that individual has come to his or her last resort of trying to get help. Lazarus probably did all he could to get the rich man's attention. Lazarus did what was most embarrassing, and that was to lay stretched out at the rich man's gate, and beg for crumbs.

When people are going through rough times in life, and are at the point of hunger, they let loose their pride. They put their pride on hold, and do most embarrassing things, just to survive.

Lazarus was hoping the rich man would have compassion and sympathy upon him. Lazarus didn't desire much. Lazarus didn't even want a whole meal; he would have been satisfied with just the crumbs (a small portion), which fell from the rich man's table. The crumbs are probably portions of food the rich man throws away. Better yet, Lazarus probably would have eaten from the rich man's plate. There is no telling, how much food, after becoming full, the rich man let to go to waste.

I do not know the length of time Lazarus begged the rich man for crumbs, but later in life, both Lazarus and the rich man died.

I must tell you folks something before proceeding farther in the story. Some of you folks are mentally slower than a man who has suffered a brain injury. Anytime a woman or man, ask for your left over's; it is possible that he has no food at home. That's not always the case (having no food at home), but most of the times it is. We are so quick at quoting scriptures, many is quick to let the scriptures live through their giving. Let me leave that alone, but I am going to pick it back up in one of my upcoming books, and you had better believe that.

When a person has sympathy or pity on someone, a work of compassion is in action. However, the rich man did not show any compassion toward the beggar. I am sure the beggar laid at the rich man's gate on several occasions. It was obvious Lazarus, the beggar, wanted food for the belly. It was not a hidden act, nor was it a mystery. It was openly revealed unto the rich man that Lazarus desired a meal to serve his body. The rich man knew Lazarus was hungry. Lazarus did not only give the rich man eye service, but also, he opened his mouth and spoke. The scripture said, "Lazarus begged", which means, he cried out.

In this beggar's story, it goes on to say; *moreover, the dogs came and licked his sores.* In other words, the dogs came and catered to one of the beggar's need. The dogs licked the beggar's sores. Yeah, the dogs moved with compassion upon the beggar.

Not only does the beggar need food, but he needs love, too. The dogs supplied the beggar with medical attention, but the rich man did not provide the beggar with any. Food heals the body from hunger. Once a hungry individual eats a meal, the inner being becomes healed. Upon the beggar, the dogs moved with compassion, but the rich man didn't move with any. The dogs freely approached the beggar, but the rich man kept his distance.

Luke 16:22 and it came to pass, that the beggar died, and was carried by the angels into Abraham's bosom: the rich man also died, and was buried.

The rich man died and so did the beggar. Whether rich or poor, every man is appointed to die one day. Death is an act no man can dodge. People have died on the football field. People have died in cars. People have died while at work. Even healthy people at the gym have collapsed dead. Many people have died unexpectedly.

After the rich man died, I guaranteed you his friends and relatives posted R.I.P. on his graveyard site. Engraving the words R.I.P. on the dead has become a common thing. People fail to realize that everybody is not resting in peace. People might die quietly, but many will lifted their eyes on the side of terror. You are now about to read, as well as envision, if the rich man is resting in peace.

Luke 16:22 says, the beggar died, and was carried by the angels into Abraham's bosom. The beggar died, and the angels carried him into Abraham's bosom. The angels took this beggar to a place where Abraham now lives.

The rich man also died, and was buried. The rich man died, and was buried. The rich man didn't go to the place where the beggar went.

Luke 16:23 and in hell he (the rich man) lift up his eyes, being in torments, and seeth Abraham afar off, and Lazarus in his bosom.

The rich man was sent to hell. Showing love to people is so serious to God, that a man went to hell, because of not showing it. People can do all the prophesying, all the speaking in tongues, but if love is not in action, it has no profit.

The rich man is in hell, because God turned him towards that way. Maybe the rich man was once living righteous, and later in life, his heart became attached to selfishness. I believe the rich man treated the beggar horribly wrong, for a very long time. This rich man was probably proud and arrogant, and probably turned up his nose at the beggar. Or perhaps, did the rich man tease the beggar as he ate numerous of meals in the beggars face.

There once was a time, when the beggar respected, and looked up at the rich man, but now, the rich man is in hell looking up at the beggar. From hell, the rich man is now looking at the person he showed no compassion too. As of now, since the rich man is in hell watching activity take place, his occipital lobes are yet active. Yep, in hell, the brain still performs sight. God rewarded the rich man with an eternal brain torturing home…hell. People need to be careful of how they treat others, because God is going to recompense them an eternal reward.

Luke 16:24 And he (the rich man) cried and said, Father Abraham, have mercy on me, and send Lazarus (the beggar), that he may dip the tip of his finger in water, and cool my tongue; for I am tormented in this flame.

Oh wow, the rich man is in hell crying out for mercy to be shown unto him. The rich man is actually in hell, crying to Abraham that he might send Lazarus (the beggar) to bless him. The rich man is now begging that Lazarus be sent to him, so he can be supplied with a little water.

The rich man now realizes he should have shown compassion and love to this beggar. Although, the rich man's story speaks about him and the beggar, I guaranteed you; the rich man probably looked down on many other people who had realistic needs.

Anytime a person is sent to hell, it is evidence that Jesus and the love of God was not active in the person's heart. But do you know what; I believed the rich man was once a child of God's righteousness. The rich man called Abraham, father, which signifies he was of the seed of Abraham. Anyone who is of the seed of Abraham is a child of God. Therefore, if the church folks, who are the seed of Abraham aren't careful, hell can become their home too. The entire bible is written with true series of torturing stories that can become our personal report, if we show not the love of God abroad. Since this rich man is in hell, as the bible quotes, then you people who have the world's goods need to be careful when turning down people who has realistic needs.

Not only will a person know he or she is in hell, but also, they can talk while in there. Yeah, the rich man had conversation with Abraham, which means, he spoke from the place of torment. The lobes that deal with speech are the frontal lobes. Therefore, these lobes are still active even in hell.

Even a person's emotional side is performed in hell, because the rich man desired mercy to be shown unto him. In hell, the rich man was feeling regretful. His consciousness operated a little too late. Once a person is sent to hell, that individual can never go to Jesus and ask for forgiveness.

Hey, people who are in the world today, we all need to have mercy on those who have realistic needs. Realistic needs are things needed to survive on earth.

Showing mercy unto the needy, or to those who have real needs, is imitating the love of God. God performed mercy on you; therefore, it is necessary for you to have mercy on someone else. Show some care; stop being stubborn with substances that has dead president's faces printed on it (money). Show some compassion, because you just never know, how and when your life will suddenly make a turnabout.

Luke 16:25 But Abraham said, Son, remember that thou in thy lifetime receivedst thy good things, and likewise Lazarus evil things: but now he is comforted, and thou art tormented.

Abraham told the rich man why he is in the place of torment. No man will be sent to hell not knowing why he is there. God is going to tell every person in hell, why he is sent there.

Abraham said to the rich man, *son, remember that thou in thy lifetime receivedst thy good things, and likewise Lazarus evil things: but now he is comforted, and thou are tormented.* In other words, Abraham is telling the rich man; you had enough in your life to help the beggar, but you didn't. You knew the beggar was reaching out for food, but you turned away your hand.

Abraham spoke to the rich man who is in hell, and from hell, the rich man heard his voice. Every word Abraham spoke to the rich man, he heard them all. That is a prime example that a person can hear while in hell. Not only can voices be heard in hell, but weeping and gnashing of teeth noises will be heard too. Weeping and gnashing of teeth is probably a noise that will be heard as people mourn and cry for freedom. Weeping and gnashing of teeth takes up many definitions in its meaning. Nevertheless, once a person is sent to hell, it's over, there is no coming back to earth for another chance.

As this rich man is in hell having conversation with Abraham, he asked, could Lazarus be given the power to do a work for him. The rich man stated, *he has five brothers*, and he asked Abraham if Lazarus could be sent to his father's house to testify to them, lest they be sent to hell too.

Maybe the rich man brothers have the same attitude he had. The rich man knows how his brother's attitudes are. He grew up with them. The rich man knows, if his brothers keep living the way they are living (not having the desire to help the needy and the poor) that hell will become their eternal home too.

A financial inheritance could have been left behind for the family, which caused them all to be rich. The rich man's five brothers are probably treating people who have needs like trash.

When the rich man was alive, he didn't show any mercy. And, probably, neither are his brothers. Really, think about it! Why does the rich man want to come back to earth to tell his brothers about hell? If his brothers are living godly and compassionate lives, then there is no reason for him to come back to earth to warn them.

Since this rich man wanted Lazarus to come back and speak warnings to his brothers, he was still able to remember earthly events. Yeah, his declarative memory is still in operation, even while being in hell. The declarative memory memorizes facts, and information. As I said before, the memory of a computer can lose its data, but the human brain lives and remembers it forever. Do not let your brain be sent to the place of torment (hell). Go get Jesus today!

The rich man's story is a true living example of this scripture written below.

Mathew 16:26-for what is a man profited, if he shall gain the whole world, and lose his own soul? Or what shall a man give in exchange for his soul?

Yep, this rich man gained the whole world, but lost his own soul.

He profited with money, but when it came to spiritual or godly principles, he lacked it. He was filled with the motivation of pride. That is what rich people do; they gain the whole world, and lose their own soul, all because of not showing compassion to a person who has a need.

Het, rich man, I am not saying, that every person you come in contact with, you must help. But, consider the options, and know what the help is for. Have a solid reason why you turned someone down.

Chapter 14

GOD MAKING YOUR NAME GREAT THROUGH A RELATIONSHIP

Most people only know God and Jesus by their names. If you ask a person, "Who is God"; they will say, "He created the heavens and the earth". If you ask who Jesus is, they will say, "He is the man who died on the cross for our sins. Those questions are answered with ease.

People believe, when they speak or mention God or Jesus in their conversation, that they know them both. Bringing up the name God or Jesus in our everyday conversation does not mean we know them. We grew up from childhood hearing those names. Therefore, our minds have been programmed to believe we know all about those names. Yet, we really do not know the depth of why those names exist.

Many of you have never met Brain Irons, until reading this book. While reading this book, you have learned many personal facts about me. You learned that Brian Irons was one ignorant individual. You learned that Brian Irons could have become a pro athlete. However, reading a story about me gave you the ability to know me. Well, now it is time to crack open a bible, and learn facts about God and Jesus.

Throughout the years, we all have heard the things the bible speaks against. The reason why many people will not pick up, or read the bible, is because it speaks against un-married relationships (no sex before marriage). That is one of the main reasons why people do not read the bible, and build a relationship with it. Once a person hears that the bible speaks against having sex before marriage, immediately, the declare, "Man wrote that book".

The people are always against or in denial when the topic is against the *works of the flesh*. When the bible speaks against having sex before marriage, it is only saying so for your healthy good. However, people take biblical rebuke so negative, that they just impressively get defensive.

If sex (fornication) before marriage would not be such a practice among the people, diseases would not be a high rated killer. Now a days, people get into relationship and will not consider marrying before participating in sex. Ever since all the fornication has plagued the land, multiple diseases have come forth.

We learn everything from books. A book is all we have in this world to learn about God. When you learned how to do math, you were taught it from a book. When you learned about science, you were taught it from a book. When you learned about world history, you were taught about it from a book. The same thing applies when seeking to learn about God and Jesus. You will learn about those two names in a book called, "The Holy Bible". Read it; build a relationship with God, because you really need too.

One of the people who had a relationship with God is Abraham. Although, Abraham had a relationship with God, he performed a few ungodly deeds. Abraham did a few bad deeds in his life, and so did **Brian Irons.** One of the greatest historical facts about Abraham is the fact that he heard the voice of God. Even though Abraham did some disobedient deeds while growing up, those deeds have been forgiven. The reason why I know Abraham deeds were forgiven is because; he now lives in the high place called, "Heaven". Oh yes, he does lives in heaven. Remember, from heaven, Abraham had a conversation with a rich man, *who lifted his eyes in hell.*

However, with me, there is no way I was hearing the voice of God, because drugs completely filled my hearing center. If I thought to do what was right, sin and drugs told me to do what was wrong.

When you are in a relationship with someone, not only will you learn about the person, but also you will learn his or her voice. The bible is a book written about the many instances of the voice of God. Therefore, if you are not reading the bible, you are not hearing the "Voice of God". If you are not hearing God's voice, then you will never come to the realization of knowing who God really is. God talks, he speaks, but if you do not give an ear to hear what he has to say, you will never receive correction. If you do not read the bible, then you will never know how God speaks.

When two people are in a relationship, they learn one another's voice so well, that they can distinguish one another's voice among a group of talkers. If I was married, which means being in a relationship, and my wife walked up behind me and called out my name, I would immediately know it's her voice. This is because, during our relationship, I have learned the sounds of her voice. As it is mentioned in the bible, that Abraham did learn and did hear the voice of God.

There's a recorded scene in the bible concerning the voice of God, which Abraham evidently heard. From heaven, God spoke to Abraham.

Genesis 12:1 now the Lord said unto Abram (Abraham), get thee out of thy country, and from thy kindred, and from thy father's house, unto a land I will show thee.

After Abraham heard the voice and command from God, he left his country, left his kindred, and left his father's house. God commanded Abraham to go depart from his native people, and he did just that. Abraham had a relationship with God; therefore, he was able to hear God's voice.

If you never hear the voice of God, how can you obey it? Although, you have two ears attached to your head, it does not mean one of them is hearing God's voice. There are many voices in the world, but there is only one voice of God. Whatever you are doing right now signifies the voice you have heard. Also whatever you are doing right now signifies the voice you are obeying. Which voice are you hearing? Listen people, God's voice is in the bible, and I advise you to read it, and give heed to what he has to say.

There is not one living man on the earth whom God does not have a task for. God created the world, which is a place that needs serious work done. Not only does Abraham have a job from God, but also, the people of the earth does too. I do not know the task God has for you, and you do not know the job God has for me. Everyone must go to God through Jesus to find out what it is God wants him to do. Read this next scripture, which is a continuation of what God said to Abraham, after he was commanded to leave his country, his kindred, and his father's house.

Genesis 12:2 and I will make thee (Abraham) a great nation and I will bless thee, and make thy name great, and thou shall be a blessing.

This scripture speaks about God making the name of "Abraham" great. This scripture *(Genesis 12:2),* also speaks about God blessing Abraham. Abraham must obey God's voice, in order for his name to be made great, and to receive God's blessing. In the bible, there is a biblical story about Abraham's seed (name and descendant) becoming great. Abraham name became great through his seed (children). However, I am not going to explain all of that. However, I will supply you with an example to let you know how Abraham name did became great.

When I was attending middle school, my music class sang a song, which mentioned the name of "Abraham". This song had a written verse it, which said, "Father Abraham had many sons". When my class was singing the song about Abraham, that marks the "greatness" right there. The entire class probably did not know who this Abraham was, but we were singing a song concerning his name. Although, I was singing the song with the class, <u>I Did Not Know</u> him at all. Abraham name is so great upon the earth that many people have not read about his living, but they've heard of his name.

Abraham was giving the power to know God. Many people in the world actually think they have a relationship with God, when in fact they do not. It takes being in a relationship with someone in order to know that person.

Also, it takes power to believe every written word and fact in the bible. When people receive new homes to live in, and being able to afford expensive cars, or earning a big promotion from their employer, they believe it is because of being in a relationship with God. Please, I can name a great number of people who know not the Lord, and they get great promotions on the job yearly. We actually believe, knowing God is based upon financial promotions, and the gathering of materials. Purchasing the biggest house, or earning the biggest annual check, does not mean a person is in a relationship with God. As the scripture has said in an earlier chapter of this book, *what profit a man to gain the whole world and lose his soul?*

You can have everything you could possible want in this life, and still have not have God. As the scripture has just said, *"you can lose your own soul".* The rich man did not have God at the time death pulled him in. He was driven to hell, and lost his soul to the earth beneath. When walking with Jesus, which means being in a relationship with God, your soul will never be lost. Got get forgiveness before your end come.

Not only does God desire to make the name Abraham great, but also, God's thoughts are overflowing in making our names great too. God desires to make every earthly being name great for the purpose of his own glory. Once we become connected to God, and begin to hear his voice, the "great name" process is in the making. There is a plan a person must accept, just to claim knowing God. Then you will be guided in the right direction, while God is making your name great. As I said in an earlier chapter, you have to first get a hold onto Jesus.

God will never prepare a way for making your name great, if you do not participate. You have to be a participant, and receive plans from

God. Once God begins to make your name great, the plan will be great, too. If you do not participate in the "greatness", you will never learn the plans, which is supposed to make your name great. Once your name has been made great, you have prospered by God's righteousness. Nevertheless, you must obey God's rules in order to inherit the "great name blessing".

God is the one who makes people's names great, not the individual. When God prepares to make your name great, he will show you how to go about it, piece by piece. Just as a movie is developed scene-by-scene, well, when allowing God to make your name great, it will be done seen scene by scene, too. God can only begin making your name "great", after submitting to his divine plan. The suggestion I have for you; give your life and body to God so he can make your life and name shine like the brightness of the sun during the day, and the twinkling of a star by night.

Just as God made the moon to give great light on the earth nightly, however, if you allow God to make your name great, your name will shine greatly, day and night. By God, your name will touch basis with heavens solar power.

People always go out and make their own names great for worldly publicity. When people decide to make their own names great, it is the individual doing the making, rather than God. As I now think about the lifestyle I was living, I was making my own name great. In fact, I did make my name "great". My name was known in many areas of St. Louis, Missouri for playing sports. Although, sports are okay to be known or great in, however, if I had become that great professional athlete, I probably would not have God in my life. If I would have signed a multi-million-dollar contract to play pro sports, that does not mean God is truly in my life. If the truth were told, God wants to be in a person's life (brain), before becoming a millionaire.

People study hard to earn college degrees, but never work in earnest to learn about God. For years, people work hard to earn financial promotions, before seeking to have a relationship with God. People work overtime hours on the jobsite, just to buy bigger houses, but do not work overtime getting to know God. Many athletes (as well as myself) train daily to get better in sports, but never exercise the mind to build a relationship with God. People shop for the best cars to ride around in, but never seek to put God in the vehicle with them.

True seekers of God, and people who have a relationship with him, will read the bible regularly. The bible is a spiritual strength builder. It is a person's peace creator. When you read it, it will become living words unto you. My next book, which shall be released soon is called, "*Thou Shalt Not Have Any Other Gods Besides Me*". This book will teach you that the words in the bible are also in the earth's atmosphere. In the movie Poltergeist, when the little girl stretched forth her arms, and placed her hands on the TV screen, she then said, "They're herrrrrre". Well, guess what, the words in the bible are herrrrre on earth as well. You will have a relationship with the word or God one way or another.

When God says he is going to do something, such as make a person's name great, he does not need any help or human assistance to carrying out the plan. Actually, God does need you, because you are the vessel to be used. When God gives you a task to perform, he already sees its beginning and its ending. Let's not forget the middle, because that is the central point when God is making your name great. God's title and power is God; therefore, he is sovereign at whatever he does. The only work you or I have to do is to be available to hear him when he speaks. Just as drugs and Satan spoke to my mind through the basketball team, and my name became wickedly great throughout the years, however, God wants to speak to my brain and make my name righteously great in due time.

As I now live in the blessed plan of God, he has given me a job. The job God has inspired (hired) me to perform is to be a writer. Probably, until the day I die, my job is to write books. My next four books will be written about dope. All of my book will mentioned the works of drugs. This job ((writer) that I now have, is far distant from the job of selling drugs. This job will not bring any harm to my mental or physical being. Nor will it empower me to break the laws.

If your name is written in the Lambs Book of Life, that's the greatest way to have your name in the "Great Name Spot". Well, you can add **Brian Irons** to the "great name" list too. God charged me to write this book, and I obeyed the command. Now my name is in the making of becoming great. Yeah, the name **Brian Irons** will be known for the book, which is titled, <u>I Did Not Know</u>.

When God makes your name great, whatever your business is, often times you will mention His name. You've understood that, you did not experience certain accomplishments without God. I truly realize without God, my book would not be displayed on the earth. Not only that, but my name would not have the opportunity of becoming great. When God makes your name great, your business name becomes great too. God is the "great" name maker, and he always performs in "Greatness".

Proverbs 13:22- a good man leaves an inheritance for his children. From the mental (spiritual) guidance and preparation from God, I will pass this story to my children, so they can pass it to their children. I will teach my children how to run a book business, as God provides me with the knowledge and understanding to do so. This book will go from my possession to my kid's possession. This book will stay in the family. God is not going to allow this true story to fade away as grass does. I believe God is going to make sure this book stay available to America forever or at least until Jesus comes and take away earth. Just like every generation, another family member revises the movie "Roots", and keeps its historical facts and scenes on the TV screen; my books will stay here and travel from generation to generation. Thank you Lord, for allowing me to leave an inheritance for my children.

Hey people, do not perceive the wrong understanding from this chapter. Even if your name has become great before God fully being in your life, it is never too late to go and get him. You only have to go to Jesus, receive forgiveness, and Jesus will intercede with you and your business. However, if you've built an empire from selling drugs, God is not going to promote that. You will have to start all over again. For some of you, that will be hard to do. However, if you do have to start all over, it will be worth the movement.

Chapter 15

JUST A FEW PERSONAL WORDS TO SHARE

Hey, you men in the industry of rap music; there is not one rapper or musician who differs in the mental. You people are no different from me. We all have the same brain mechanism, and drugs will do you all the same way they did me. Stop putting the violence enhancer (drugs) into your brains, so that the percentage rate of violence in the rapping community will decline. If the violence enhancer had not been in many rap listeners and rappers brains, there is a great chance many well-known musicians will be alive unto this very day. Please, do yourself a favor, by getting a hold onto God's son Jesus. Remember this, if drugs are in your rapping business, then violence will soon show its face. There is so much hostility in the rapping business it's pathetic. One more thing I must say to all musicians; how can you call women horrible names in your music, and then thank God for the CD's success Just a few personal words to share!

Professional athletes and Celebrities from all across the world; this is a great story for your child or siblings. I suppose, if you have kids who are in the 8th grade or higher, a copy of this book should be purchased for them. Also, pro-athletes, buy copies of this miraculous book, and pass it on to your teammate. Cause a link of my book to be extended throughout the world of professional athletes and celebrities. Yes, you all (celebrities) need to read this book too. Every so often, I read a celebrity story in the newspaper concerning drugs and alcohol. I have seen many celebrities be charged for driving while under the influence of a chemical. I have seen many celebrities catch drug cases. Although, most celebrities are financially secured, however, sin and drugs will not hesitate to mess up their lives. Money has no power over sin. Therefore, pass this story to the next. Just a few personal words to share!

And the Spirit of God moved upon the face of the waters. By the Spirit of God, John the Baptist moved and prepared the way for Jesus. By the Spirit of God, Jonathan moved and shielded King David. By the Spirit of God, Apollos moved and watered Paul's ministry. Therefore, someone has to move by the spirit of God, and water this ministry. The world needs this story now. Just a few personal words to share!

I am so glad, Mephibosheth (a handicap man) sits at the king's table forever (smile). People might show partiality towards people with dishabilles, but the king never does. Just a few personal words to share!

Lord have mercy, the people of God really need to pull together. Do we actually realize how many Christians are dying and not experiencing all the promises of God? Since I have claimed God's glory, I have fallen short many times. But, I refuse to keep falling, and never experience God's blessing promises. If I live to see another 40 years, I am not going to use those years trying to get too the promise, I am going to start walking in the promises. Too many years have passed, and we are still not walking in all God's promises. Jesus did not bleed on the cross for himself. He was bruised on the cross for us. Therefore, you need to bless someone. I encourage you all to touch God's promises right now. In the Old Testament, only a couple of people entered into the Promise Land. In the New Testament days, people have the ability to make it happen. If we live as the Corinthian epistles teach, we all shall see God's promises unfold. Just a few personal words to share!

2nd Chronicles 14:7- If my people, which are called by my name, shall humble themselves, and pray, and seek my face, and turn from their wicked ways; then will I hear from heaven, and will forgive their sin, and will heal their land. What a powerful scripture! Obey it and watch what happens. It will not work if you only pray. You must get into the communities and be a witness. Let every church create its own outreach ministry!

I am one strong African American!

www.ingramcontent.com/pod-product-compliance
Lightning Source LLC
LaVergne TN
LVHW041123140625
813764LV00001B/35